SELF-MADE

PJ MURRAY

COPYRIGHT

Self-Made is dedicated to my dearly beloved mother Hassie Jestina Murray, my daughter Chineka Simmonds and her mother Georgina Simmonds, who have now sadly passed on to rest with our Creator. All far too soon.

I also dedicate this biography to my family: my sons Darius and Dillon, daughter Jada, their mother Donna and to my brother Aaron and sisters Chrissie, Edith and Elizabeth along with their families. A final dedication to my friends, colleagues and foes. In some shape or form you have all had an impact on my life and for that reason I sincerely thank you.

I feel truly honoured and blessed to be in this privileged position to share my life's journey with you all and the world at large.

I trust this biography will in some way enlighten you.

Please enjoy!

PROLOGUE

Having achieved most of my personal and professional goals as a serial entrepreneur, not long after my 50th birthday in April 2016 I decided to realise a lifelong ambition and write my memoir.

The result is this thrilling rags-to-riches story, which chronicles my underprivileged childhood growing up in Harlesden, northwest London; my conviction for possession of a firearm when I was 11 years old; and the decade-long cycle of criminality and incarceration that followed.

In the first half of the book I reveal how I matured into a self-made millionaire and leading sales professional at the age of 25, despite being a 14-year-old father and juvenile gangster who received just 10 weeks of secondary school education.

As I recall events from the racially charged 1970s, consumer-driven '80s, and multicultural '90s, you'll become a passenger on my rollercoaster ride from poverty to prosperity via the engine room of Britain's economy: micro and small businesses.

You'll read how I rubbed shoulders with yuppies, aristocrats, and African statesman, but after 14 years as a law-abiding citizen returned to prison when my fortunes changed at the turn of the century.

In the 18 months following my release in January 2000, my mental capacity was stretched to the limit after my daughter committed suicide and I became homeless, exposed to Jamaican black magic, and named as a chief suspect in a Metropolitan Police murder investigation.

It is only my faith that kept me sane during this period, and in April 2001 I regained my strength, drive and business acumen to set up a company that generated £1.4 million within a year.

The second half of the book details my ventures in West Africa and the Far East and the formation of my most successful enterprise to date, business rescue firm Legal & Recoveries. Simultaneously, it covers topics such as divorce, depression, my fear of mental illness and how I'm plagued by the deaths of my first child and her mother.

This brutally honest narrative offers useful personal development advice and fascinating insights into my life as a street-smart business operator who's lost and gained fortunes and played an integral role in the development of two pioneering media projects in the UK (including Europe's biggest publication for women of colour, *Pride* magazine).

My first 50 years were a unique journey filled with ups and downs, and as a result this autobiography is peppered with an inventory of business tips, life lessons and references to my nefarious deeds, sexual escapades, real estate deals, dysfunctional relationships, fast cars and charitable works.

Some chapters are comical, edifying and fantastic, while others you may find sordid and shameful. Although several names and identifying details have been changed to protect the privacy of individuals, I assure you that everything you are about to read is, to the best of my knowledge, 100% factual.

Cutting of a feature in the *North West London Press* newspaper on 21-year-old PJ Murray, dated 24 April, 1987

CHAPTERS

CHAPTER ONE
Humble Beginnings
(1966 - 1973)

My first sexual encounter took place in a hostel for single mothers in Willesden Green, northwest London, when I was just three years old. Her name was Kelly Whitehead and she was a tall, skinny, mixed-race girl who lived in the same refuge.

One day, Kelly, who was four or five years older, led me to the communal garden at the back of the house, took down her knickers and told me to play with her vagina, which I did. I'm not sure how long we were there, but after a while my sisters came by and disrupted what was going on. That incident took place in 1969, but the experience has never left me and probably plays out in my relationships with women to this day.

My name is Peter John Murray and I was born the youngest of six siblings at Central Middlesex Hospital in Park Royal, northwest London, in 1966. My Jamaican parents, Hassie Murray and the unfailingly absent John Powell, arrived in England in 1960 to join my maternal grandmother at her home in Cricklewood.

I don't know my grandmother's first name, but remember her surname was Palmer and that people referred to her as 'Lady P'. She was a well-respected landlady with properties in Willesden and Cricklewood who rented rooms to other Jamaican immigrants.

Lady P had two daughters, Olive and my mum, but the sisters didn't 'gree and my mum (who was said to be my grandmother's favourite) believed she was blind in one eye because Olive had worked obeah on her.

During the Windrush in the spring of 1960, my mum left Olive in Jamaica and travelled to England whilst pregnant with my sister Elizabeth. Her boat docked at Felixstowe where she stopped overnight before journeying on to my grandmother's house.

Elizabeth was born later that year, and my twin sisters, Chrissie and Edith, in March 1963. My brother Aaron was born in July 1964. Our eldest sibling William, who never left Jamaica, is around 20 years older than me. Elizabeth is the quiet one, the bookworm. Chrissie and Edith weren't naughty, they just weren't as quiet as Elizabeth. Aaron was the villain and I wanted to be just like him.

While in England, my mum didn't have a job and never worked a day in her life. Her only sources of income were her mother and the pardner she ran with a woman named Anna. That pardner grew to become one of the biggest in Brent after my mum branched out on her own.

The story goes that my mother was saving to buy a house but my dad took all her money when she was six months pregnant with me and she hasn't seen him since. I've never set eyes on my dad and have no idea if he's the father of my other siblings. My mum said so but I don't know and you never do with Jamaicans.

After my mother died I discovered that back in Jamaica she'd been married to a 'Mr Brown' but must have returned to using her maiden name, Hassie Jestina Murray, as me and my siblings born in England all have that surname.

To receive UK welfare benefits and child support in those days, mothers dare not tell the state who their children's father was and babies had to be registered with their mother's surname. Consequently, my birth certificate says 'Father Unknown'. I'm not sure what the situation is now, but that was quite common in the 1960s.

I wanted a dad for the first 10 years of my life, and when kids at school spoke about theirs, if nobody from my ends was in the classroom I'd make up stories and talk about my father that didn't exist. If I'm the only child for my dad, it's bad enough that he's abandoned me. But if you include my brother and twin sisters, he's discarded four young children and never reappeared. What kind of man is that?

I don't know anything about John Powell and have no feeling for him one way or the other. It's alien for the words 'my dad' to roll off my tongue. I don't want them to and when they do I feel pain, negativity and, if I'm honest, a bit of hate.

My mother on the other hand was my best friend up until the time of her passing. She was not judgemental and would inform, guide and counsel me with universal principles.

My mother was almost 40 years old when she found out she was pregnant with me and medics at the hospital told her: 'You're no spring chicken. You've already got four children, you're not working, and you're a drain on the state. You're blind in one eye, you can't read or write and don't have any prospects. Why do you want another child?' They advised her to abort me but she refused, and when I was born the nurses named me after Jesus' disciples Peter and John.

Being the baby of the family I was spoilt rotten by my mother and sisters. I was getting breakfast in bed until I was a teenager, and at mealtimes I was always the first to have my food served; that was my mum's rule. My earliest memory is of my grandmother using a broom to draw the red curtains in the front room of her home in Cricklewood. There was no carpet in those days, but I remember the red linoleum flooring.

I'm not sure exactly how it went, but I think when my mother first came to London she stayed with her mother for a short time, but they fell out and she went to live with a cousin in one of my grandmother's properties.

She moved around a couple of times and by 1969 was living in the hostel for single mothers on Dartmouth Road where Kelly had enticed me into my first carnal dalliance.

We got by on a poor people's diet of mainly cornmeal porridge and I remember my mum, my four siblings and me living in two rooms, one of which had a massive bed. It was probably only a double bed, but as a toddler it looked gigantic.

Later that year, I started receiving therapy to correct a severe speech impediment and we moved into the first of many council accommodations: a third floor, three-bedroom flat at 28 Warwick Court on Curzon Crescent in Harlesden.

My mum had a room, my three sisters were in another and me and Aaron shared the third bedroom. I remember our first Christmas there and sucking on my mother's breast for comfort, which is a bit odd as I would've been four years old at the time.

Truth be told, my family was considered to be dysfunctional, undesirable; and compared to the other families in our community we were poor. So poor that we lived on hand-outs from other people and used to get our clothes from the Salvation Army.

If the neighbours were going to take the piss out of anyone, we'd be in for it. Sometimes, one or two of the older guys would take the piss out of my mum in front of me.

When I'd stay out too late in the evenings, she would come looking for me and because she was blind in one eye they would close one of their

3

eyes and say: 'Peter, Peter, come home,' in a high-pitched voice.

I didn't like it, but you just suck it up and ignore it. Most of them were older so it's not as if I could've beaten them up. I just had to accept it. (Funnily enough, one of them was at my 50th birthday party and I was like looking at him thinking, *'You remember those days, don't you?'*)

We weren't the best family. We were the type that your parents would warn you to stay away from. Nevertheless, every Sunday my mum would compel us to go to church dressed in our best clothes. We walked, oh yes: we walked, to four churches.

First, to a Baptist church on Anson Road near Gladstone Park, and then we'd go to someone's house and rest up for a while before walking back to the Salvation Army church in Willesden.

After that we'd go home and Pastor Moody, who lived on Minet Avenue, would pick us up and take us to his church for a 5pm session. Then he'd drop us home and come back for us at 9pm, and we'd finally get home around 11pm. That was our portion of church every Sunday for a good five years.

Sometimes in church when the pastor sent out the offertory I'd dip my hand in, scoop, and pass it on. Yes, I used to steal the offering.

I'd get away with it at the Baptist and Salvation Army churches, which were attended mostly by white people, but you'd be crazy to try anything like that at the Pentecostal church.

Once I realised other people had more than us, I became determined to change that. I didn't want to belong to the family that didn't have anything. I'd go to people's homes and see they had stuff like peanut butter sandwiches and think, *'Oh my God, why can't I have that?'* Then I'd go home and feel really pissed off. There was a lot of love in our family, we just didn't have much.

Warwick Court was the first of many council homes we lived in. I really enjoyed playing out with the other kids. Some of us would stand on one side of the estate and some would stand on the other side, and we'd go to war by throwing rocks at each other; the kind of rocks that could bus' yuh head. It was a bit sadistic when you think about it, but that was our summer holidays.

The James family lived on the ground floor and their father was the first man I knew to own a car. I had the utmost respect for him, and although I never went inside I remember it was a red Ford Anglia with red seats.

He was in his early 40s, had children the same age as me and my siblings, and was a good, hardworking family man. He wasn't one of those

Jamaicans who went to the bookies. I remember thinking that if I had a dad I would want him to be just like Mr James.

My cousins, Carlton, Paul, Mark and Pepsi (their brothers Colin and Wayne weren't born yet) lived on Curzon Crescent estate near Warwick Court. I don't know what issue my mum had with her brother (their dad, Samuel) but they didn't talk, and so our two households weren't particularly close. Coincidentally, years later the Murray and James families both moved to the Stonebridge Estate shortly after it was built.

When I was four years old I started attending Leopold Infants School, which was around the corner from my house. My class teacher was a black woman, Miss Coco, and I think the headmistress was called Miss Longstaff. At that time, I suffered from two undiagnosed problems. In the summer, my eyes would swell up whenever I played in the grass and on a regular basis I shat myself at school.

Many years later, I realised I suffered from hay fever and was lactose intolerant, which explained why every time I drank milk at school I got diarrhoea and would have to rush to the toilet.

Our council estate was a little community and during the two years we lived there several things happened that shaped me and left a lasting memory. One was an incident involving a neighbour's dog.

I think the dog's name was Danny Larky or something like that, and he belonged to a white family who lived on the ground floor. Their youngest child was a boy named Jimmy who was about my age. I remember we both had the same toy train and would sometimes play together.

Everyone on the estate would tease Danny and run away. But one day the dog saw me as I was going up the stairs on my own. I froze and he just went for me; jumped up and took me to the ground. I remember bawling my eyes out as he mauled my face.

Some neighbours eventually got him off, but I don't know how I've got no physical scarring. That incident happened 45 years ago, but if you bring a dog near me now I'll go nuts. Once, I was dating a girl who owned a dog and I had to tell her: 'Look, forget it. Me and this dog cannot be in the same room,' and that was it. There was no negotiation. It's a phobia I've not really addressed.

Even in my dreams, whenever I see a dog it represents an enemy. So if I dream about a dog I'll consciously try to overpower it and thrust my fist right down its throat, because then I know I've defeated my enemy.

However, if I dream the dog has mauled or overpowered me I know I should watch out in the days ahead because someone's going to try and do something to me.

It's the same thing with police. If I dream I've been apprehended or arrested, I know something bad's going to happen. And it usually does, as sure as night follows day. But if I dream the police are chasing me and I escape and get away from them, I guarantee you within 48 hours I'm going to make some money.

The second notable incident happened when the council were putting lifts into the estate. I was around five or six years old and saw a good friend, who lived in my block and was a year older, fall three flights down to the bottom of the lift shaft. At first we thought he was dead. Then we assumed he must've broken his neck. He survived, but is one of the many people I know with mental health issues.

I really fear mental illness, even though I know it's not right good or fair to think that way. I believe it stems from when my mum befriended a lady called Juliet, who everyone on the estate would call 'the mad woman'.

Whenever she had an episode it would take several car loads of police officers to restrain and take her away in a Black Maria van. My mum was the only person who was nice to Juliet, but me and my siblings didn't like when she came to the house because we were petrified that she might flip.

I really disliked going with my mother to visit Juliet at Shenley Hospital, the local psychiatric institution in Hertfordshire. It was harrowing. I didn't like the smell or seeing all those people drugged up.

I was very young, but knew there was something wrong with the people in that hospital. They didn't talk and moved around slovenly, like zombies. We would go to Shenley many times over the next few years; visiting Juliet, a man called Brother David and a lady called Bonny.

Bonny was a large woman, and I remember whenever she came to the house we'd play the reggae record *Hey Fatty Bum Bum* by Carl Malcolm to try and get rid of her, which was quite wicked.

I'd try to disappear whenever these people came to the house, but I always thought mum was very humane and had a good heart for engaging them. I judged them to be loonies, social misfits and dropouts who were prone to eruptions. That idea was reinforced when I saw them on the streets and heard how the kids at school spoke about 'crazy' people.

In 1971, we moved across the road into 87 Curzon Crescent, a three-bedroom house with a front and back garden. And a white lady from Harlesden, Lesley, donated a black and white television to us.

I remember watching Trevor McDonald present the news, but although my mum and sisters liked it I wasn't really moved by the TV. In the back of the garden was a huge patch of unkempt and overrun grass with all sorts of creatures living inside, including a tortoise. I don't know how it got there, but I was more interested in chucking bricks on the tortoise's exterior to see if it would crack.

I don't know how my mum got to know Lesley, but going to her house was like an outing for me because she had luxuries that we didn't have, like sandwiches with actual jam inside.

I never understood why our family kept relocating, but in 1973 we moved into a four-bedroom house at 17 Chadwick Road in Harlesden where, over the next three years, I would commence a decade-long career in criminality and learn several basic business skills.

Around the same time we moved house, Denmark, Ireland and the UK joined the European Economic Community and I developed a fascination with starting fires. That summer was hot and dry and there was lots of hay and greenery around.

I was about seven years old and remember getting excited after starting a couple of fires in the back garden. But my mum beat me and said: 'Yuh coulda bun dong di 'ouse,' which I interpreted as, '*don't start fires at home*'.

I started doing them outside on a bigger and better scale. It was a very personal and private thing. I would buy some matches or take them from the kitchen, find a dustbin or go to the fields, start a fire and wait for it to really engulf. Then I'd run, hide and wait for the fire engine to come. I found the blaze exhilarating, but watching the firemen put out my work less so.

That September I began attending John Keble, a local Church of England primary school where my twin sisters were in the fourth year, my brother was in the third year. I made a bag of friends including Donovan 'Young Vego' Adams who later died of a drug overdose.

But when Aaron was expelled for fighting, my mum sent me to Oldfield Primary to join him. I was unhappy with the move and felt I had to assert my authority in this new environment. I was a loner and kept getting into fights. It's not that people picked on me, I'd just switch on them for any little thing and because I came from an estate where we used to have stone fights I already had a violent disposition, which I would frequently unleash.

Around this time, I engaged in my first commercial enterprise: raising money begging a 'penny for the guy'. I first got the idea from the Bradishes, a family of five commercially minded Irish brothers who did it and brought my brother in.

He didn't invite me, but I followed, copied what I saw and started doing it with some other kids. We'd come together, make guys and then go off in pairs to different locations.

7

But after a while I became industrious and thought, *'I'm the person who makes the guy and does all the selling, why am I sharing all the profit?'* So I went off, made a slicker and more appealing guy, put him in a pushchair and thought about some good locations. In those days, Brent had a large population of Irish labourers who built roads, buildings, and houses. Every Friday they'd get paid in cash and head straight down the pub. But you'd better catch them before they went inside because when they came out they'd be broke, drunk, and cussing.

Most of the boys I worked with waited outside pubs and earned money from the labourers as they entered and left. But I quickly found a setting that was more profitable. I deduced that going to the Church Road bingo was a better option because even if they didn't win anything, the women coming out would give you something, especially if you looked pitiful or reminded them of their son.

That was the first time I started what would become a lifelong custom: identifying profitable enterprises, improving their operations and business models and then bringing a more polished version to market.

Someone later convinced me that I'd make more money if I stood outside Willesden Junction train station, so I tried and it worked. One day when I was packing up, a tramp called Ginger begged me for money so I bought him a portion of fish and chips and gave him some cash. I can't remember how much.

When I went back a few days later there were other people plotted in the same spot, so I didn't make as much money. Ginger turned up again, but when I told him I couldn't give him anything he called me a 'black bastard' and started throwing bottles and cans at me. That incident was my first exposure to racism, and scarred me quite deeply.

CHAPTER TWO
Beasts, Sticksman and Rastafari
(1973 - 1978)

I first became involved in criminality at the age of seven, when me and Aaron would go to Woolworths on the High Road to steal toys. I remember a middle-aged black woman who worked there would catch us sometimes, bring us back to the shop, take the toys away and let us go.

And if we got away and brought the stuff home, my mum would ask: 'Weh yuh geti fram?' And I'd say something like: 'My friend gave it to me.' But she knew that wasn't true. She'd say: 'A lie yuh a tell,' and would start beating us with anything she could get her hands on usually a long, thick piece of rubber.

When we moved to Chadwick Road, I met people such as David Logan, Winston and Errol Brown and the St Louis, Miller, Pinkie, Brown and Cameron families, who were each like small clans or tribes.

As a result, when things got sticky most of my friends had siblings they could go to. But I had no one because my brother was in care and my sisters weren't bad. So I made sure I was prepared to defend myself using wanton violence if necessary.

Still, things were pretty innocent in those days. Safety only became an issue when I was about 10 years old and we started running into white gangs such as the Teddy Boys and Skinheads.

Teddy Boys worshipped Elvis Presley and were the first British youth group to have an identity. They wore long Edwardian-style drape jackets, skinny neck ties and suede shoes (preferably blue) with thick crepe soles.

They also used a lot of Brylcreem to slick their hair back. Most were peaceful, but if you messed with them they'd pull a razor blade or Stanley knife on you. Skinheads on the other hand were perceived to be racist and ignorant. They wore Doctor Martens boots, Crombie t-shirts and jeans with braces.

Punks were loud, rebellious and in your face, while the Mods, who were among the most tolerable of these groups, listened to ska and The Jam, rode scooters and wore winkle-picker shoes, macs and slick two-piece suits with trousers that came just above the ankles.

In the 1970s, although there were many different white groups there were mainly only two kinds of black groups. You either identified with the conscious doctrine of Rastafarianism or you were a sticksman who was into pickpocketing and other criminality. Whereas the Rastaman was about fighting oppression, the sticksman just wanted cash.

I liked the Rastaman's vibe, but they weren't materialistic and didn't have any money. All they did was smoke ganja and talk about peace. I wanted more than that, so by the time I was 10 I'd already decided to become a notorious sticksman because they were slick and appeared to have everything.

A few weeks after starting Oldfield Primary School I was expelled for fighting and returned to John Keble having been radicalised with a new 'bad bwoy' ideology. I started smoking cigarettes and considered the other schoolchildren to be lambs; they were soft.

I fought regularly and once attacked a student from another school, a white boy with a hole in his heart. Of course, I didn't know about the boy's condition until afterwards but his parents complained and I was excluded.

I was determined to be like my brother Aaron who had by now been taken into care after receiving convictions for bag-snatching and robbery. I spent the months I was out of school learning from the older boys how to snatch handbags.

They taught me how to identify a woman on the High Road, wait until she'd turned onto a side road, run up and push her in one direction, pull the bag in the other direction and run off.

The first time I did it I remember going up to a lady and asking for the time. She told me and I asked for some change. She replied: 'Change of what?' before diving into a large silver handbag. As her hand emerged, I grabbed the purse and ran.

I continued to hang around the Church Road bingo hall, but was now snatching handbags from the same women who'd previously subsidised my 'penny for the guy' venture. I stopped doing any form of legal enterprise and committed to a career in criminality.

Around this time, I remember going on a move to Kilburn High Road with a friend from the area, Winston Brown. I can't remember exactly what went wrong, but we ended up being pursued by some beasts and ran into an enclosure where the only way out was to scale a 10ft-high wire fence.

Winston, who was two years older than me, got over quickly but I struggled to reach the top and was captured. For a long time, I was haunted by the image of Winston laughing and mocking me from the other side of the fence while I was being arrested. Winston's family relocated to Lewisham and he started moving with people from other areas, but we remained good friends for the next 25 years when echoes of this incident would later resurface.

I received the first of many criminal convictions, a 12-month conditional discharge, after robbing some petty change from a young girl around the corner from my house. I was still only 10, and to this day don't remember why I took her money.

When I was re-schooled at Furness Primary, I encountered Martin 'Titch' Raymonds, his older brother Trevor and their next door neighbour Andrew Atkinson. My network of contacts expanded as I delved deeper into the underworld and met more people from large families, including Raymond 'Square Head' Fearon and burglars Delroy MacIntosh and Dennis White, who became three of my closest friends.

I showed Dennis and Delroy, who was two years older than us, how to shoplift and pickpocket, and they, along with Trevor Manning, Dennis's brother Darren and others, taught me about new elements of criminality.

Bag-snatching was already common, but after the racially charged American TV miniseries *Roots* aired on BBC One during Easter weekend in 1977 some people in our community and youth groups evangelised the idea that it was okay to snatch white ladies' handbags. 'Remember *Roots?*' They said. 'This is payback; let's tief from them.' Africans were fair game too because they'd sold us out.

The first rave I ever went to was a street party for the Queen's Silver Jubilee in June 1977. I was 11 years old and Lord Koos' sound system was playing. It was like a carnival contained on Fortune Gate Road in Harlesden. I remember arriving, smelling ganja in the air, seeing lots of people and hearing the song of that summer, *Two Sevens Clash* by Culture, booming out of what appeared to be a dozen speakers positioned along the street. I was in awe.

13

I began raving with a group of around 20 juveniles aged between 11 and 15. At various times some of us would abscond from care homes to join the group and most had elder siblings who were either in care or just entering the criminal justice system. When I really think about it, some of the things we got up to were mad but phenomenal. We'd go to all the local nightclubs, pay our money on the door and rave with the local gangsters like we were big men.

There was The Café in Harlesden and on Friday nights we'd go to the Acorn Club on Church Road. On Saturday nights it would be Fisher's in Neasden, Cinderella's or the Roxy Theatre in Harlesden. Once inside, we'd usually buy a bag of herbs, get a rum and black from the bar and party seriously hard.

If me, Raymond, Cedrick 'Tiny' Campbell and Clive 'Grandfather' McLeod were together and had made money that day sometimes we'd pool together, buy a bag of weed from a guy named Brokie, go to someone's yard, pack a chalice with ganja and smoke.

Or we might just end up smoking and drinking champagne, usually Moet or Lanson, in one of the local clubs where they'd be playing the latest Disco 45 singles, pres and dubplates by revival, lovers' rock and steppers acts such as Gregory Isaacs, Dennis Brown, Jacob Miller, the Mighty Diamonds, Delroy Wilson, John Holt, Ken Boothe, Janet Kay, 15, 16, 17, Tradition and the Investigators.

We rolled heavy. There were people in our group whose names were legendary purely and simply because of the things we did back then. There was no youth group in any part of northwest London carrying on like us, and after a while we started travelling to raves at Villa Road in Brixton, the Crypt in Deptford, and the Sunday session at Settlement, next to Peckham Bus Garage.

After raving, we'd be so knocked out from all the ganja that some people would just lean up right there on the sound boxes and go to sleep. Some of us couldn't go home because the police would be looking for us. Subsequently, when we arrived back in northwest London we'd usually have to sneak each other into our parents' yards.

Sometimes there would be four or five of us sleeping underneath a bed or in a wardrobe. It didn't really matter where, as long as the person's parents didn't find you in their house. Those days were fun and there was a real feeling of comradery and brotherhood.

When we went out we were always dapper, dressed to the nines. And because I was shoplifting daily I'd earned a reputation for never being seen in the same outfit twice. Fur coats and silk, suede and leather suits with either gold tip, or crocodile, lizard, snake, turtle or ostrich skin shoes... yeah, I had the lot.

I remember going to Grants in Golders Green in northwest London, and paying £195 for my first pair of crocs. I was only 12 but no one questioned me, they just took the cash. Similarly, I shopped at the high-end children's clothing store Please Mum, which has branches in Knightsbridge, Golders Green and Wigmore Street, because their silk shirts were branded with the initials 'PM', which I liked to think of as my personal motif.

While I was the man when it came to clothes, Raymond, the youngest brother in the Fearon family, was known for his jewellery. Back then, it was belcher chains with massive gold ducat and Krugerrand coins. But after learning about South Africa's racist apartheid regime we boycotted the Krugs because that's where they came from.

In September 1977, I started secondary school at Aylestone High in Brondesbury but was expelled after just two months for threatening my form teacher. I didn't care. I was a young, prolific, smartly attired shoplifter and budding sticksman with a mindset firmly embedded in gang culture.

I practised my skills on Harlesden High Street until I became proficient and moved on to Wembley High Road, which had more and better shops to steal from including my personal favourite, Dutch fashion retailer C&A.

Then, my brother and some of the boys from the Miller family started talking about London's first major indoor mall, Brent Cross Shopping Centre, which had opened in 1976 on the North Circular Road, just five miles from Harlesden.

We'd go there and tear the arse out of all the big stores; C&A, Marks & Spencer (M&S), Debenhams and John Lewis. Security tags hadn't been introduced yet, so we'd go into a changing room with two sets of clothing, put on one set underneath the clothes we had on, leave the second set behind and walk out. We did that a lot before graduating to the West End: Selfridges, Harrods and then all over Knightsbridge and throughout west and central London. I spent a lot of time in Marble Arch where I remember shoplifting corduroy suits from M&S and velvet suits from C&A in the same location that is now the flagship store for another European fashion retailer, Primark.

But after a while, certain elders started saying: 'What you guys are doin' is some gyal business. Forget about shoplifting and snatching bags, it's all about dropping sticks.'

This was music to my ears because I didn't like robbing women and eventually stopped snatching handbags altogether. However, if I'm honest, pickpocketing is something I truly enjoyed because being able to silently dip your hand into someone else's pocket and remove the contents requires an awful lot of skill.

And there were lots of different techniques and terminologies involved. For example, a front pocket was called a 'front-off' and a back pocket was a 'back-off'. Likewise, an inside pocket was known as a 'breast-off', and the top pocket was a 'top-off'.

Pickpockets like to be in crowds so the elders showed us all of the best locations and I remember making a lot of money from Nigerians at the bus stop outside of C&A in Marble Arch. Nigerians first started coming to London on mass in the late '70s, colonising the Bayswater and Queensway areas. They brought with them oil money, some of which they kept inside the leather pouches that hung from their wrists as they strolled guilelessly along Oxford Street.

We'd just use a Stanley knife, cut around the pouch and watch as a wad of money, customarily folded in £100 bundles, dropped out. Usually, they had so many shopping bags they didn't even notice their cash had gone.

The London Underground tube network, or unda di eart' as we called it, was another prime location for dropping sticks, especially in the West End. Back then, I knew every station platform and all the busiest bus stops like the back of my hand.

But in the late '70s and early '80s there was a squad of corrupt police officers operating in the West End who would take your money if they thought you'd come onto their patch to steal.

If these beasts saw you they'd grab you, take you around the corner and shake you down. And if they had to give chase or you didn't have any money to give them you'd be nicked. They'd say: 'Right, what have you got? No money? Okay, arrest him. Next time, have some money on you.' It was like a game of cops and robbers.

But things were very different for the professional white pickpockets otherwise known as 'dippers'. They came mostly from Elephant and Castle in southeast London and called dropping sticks 'dipping' or being 'on the bottle' because pickpocketing requires a lot of bravery.

They would rent tube platforms and bus stops from the bull who would give them protection and leave them to work the crowds for an hour.

It was really corrupt and some of the beasts working at Vine Street and West End Central police stations were particularly horrible. As a result, a lot of my convictions came from being shaken down when I was working unda di eart'.

We were too young to be tried in a Crown Court so we'd be sent to a Juvenile Court where we were rarely acquitted because there was literally no point pleading 'not guilty', as no one was ever going to believe an adolescent criminal over an officer of the law.

That was the main difference between getting nicked on the ends and getting nicked in the West End. Whereas the beasts in urban stations would beat and bruk you up, it was different in the West End. They just wanted money; give them some dough and they'd let you walk.

In February 1978, I started William Gladstone School but was expelled within a month and placed into care four days before my 12th birthday after being convicted of robbery, attempted theft and possession of a firearm. I'd loaned a handgun from one of the Bradishes (the Irish family) because I wanted to scare Danny Cameron, an outstanding pickpocket and money-maker who earned a living delivering paraffin and gas.

He was my brother's age, but always picked on us. If you went out thieving together you'd have to keep your eye on him because he would skank you and never disclose how much he really made. On top of that, he was a bully.

One evening, we were at the Tavistock Youth Club in Harlesden, a place where we'd socialise and play pool and table tennis after spending the day committing crimes. Danny pissed me off, so I went home for the gun. When I returned at around 10.30pm, the youth centre was closed and people were filtering off. I saw him on the other side of the road, pointed the gun in his direction and shouted 'Danny!' But plain clothes feds were driving past. They saw what I had done, drove back and arrested me.

I was held at the Forbes House Remand Centre in Neasden before being transferred to Redhill Assessment Centre in Surrey where, during my 10-month detention, I absconded for weeks at a time and remember hearing and liking Pink Floyd's *The Wall* and music by British punk bands such as The Jam, Sham 69 and The Clash.

Violent attacks by the local bull increased after I was released. They were brutal back then. If you saw them at night you'd better run because they would stop, arrest and either bring you to the station and beat you up or beat the crap out of you on the road and just drive off.

One time, me and my friend Colin got nicked in Cricklewood under the old 'sus law', which gave the police powers to stop, search and arrest anyone they suspected of committing a crime. I was put in one car with two officers and I think it was the same for Colin.

They couldn't even wait to get us back to the station. As soon as we got in the car, one of the beasts started pushing his hand in my face. He was a big guy and all I remember seeing is a huge white fist landing in the centre of my face over and over again. When we got to Willesden Green Police Station they just carried on.

When Colin's mum came and saw her son all bloodied up she wasn't having any of it: 'A so yuh do mi son? Look pon unu.' She took her complaint all the way to the top in a style similar to the way Doreen Lawrence later campaigned for police reforms following the botched investigation into the murder of her son Stephen by racists in 1993. I had completely forgotten about the incident, but about 18 months later the beasts came to interview me and take a statement. I knew they didn't really give a shit, but Colin's mum wouldn't let the matter rest.

That day was pretty tough. But to be honest, I'd been pursued before. Running from the beasts, getting hit with a truncheon, falling over, getting up and running again; those were regular things for me. That was the cost of being a young, black criminal in London.

We were out on the road after 10pm so when the beasts drove past it was a catch-22. You can either dus or let them stop and search you knowing you'll probably get nicked and beat up anyway. So you just dus, innit? If you dus out and they catch you they'll beat you up and try to stick a charge on you.

This is way before CCTV cameras were installed in police stations and before the Police and Criminal Evidence Act (PACE) 1984, which provided codes of conduct for the beasts to follow and tried to balance their powers against the rights of the individual. Before PACE, the police would literally beat a confession out of you: 'Say you did it.' Bang! 'Say you did it.' Bang! 'Sign here.' Bang! And that's why loathing of the police by anyone who grew up in my era is totally justified.

Back then, the state was vicious and my relationship with its officers was particularly strained. The history books say that was only happening in South Africa, but I can tell you the same thing was happening in Brent, but only to gang members. They wouldn't beat up a normal black guy who was going to school every day, that type of treatment was reserved for repeat offenders.

During this period, I remember there were two well-known police constables in my area, PCs John and Ross. PC John was the local 'bobby' who walked the streets, knew our parents and would talk to us. Don't get me wrong, he would nick you if he had to, but he was cool.

However, PC Ross was a horrible bastard who drove a dark blue Rover P6 and the local station's Black Maria or 'the meat wagon' as we called it. Ross drove because he couldn't run, so when he was in the Rover we all knew he was most likely working with another officer who'd have to get out and do the chasing.

That was cool because if there are three of you running away and one fed jumps out of the car to give chase you know at least two of you are getting away. But if PC Ross was driving the meat wagon, you knew there were pure feds in the back ready and waiting to bruk up man.

I remember one time a few of us were hanging out in Harlesden when someone shouted: 'Bull a come!' PC Ross was driving down the road in the meat wagon. He saw us and sped up, so we all dus out. I found a hiding place in the front garden of a house on Tunley Road and waited.

I tried to be silent, but my breathing was erratic and in the distance I could hear a very distinctive sound that caused my heart rate to increase rapidly; barking. As the dogs approached, my heart banged inside my chest and long before they could get anywhere near me I jumped out screaming: 'Here I am, here I am!' But the beasts still set the dogs on me.

I remember crying and trying to protect myself by curling up into the foetal position. Luckily, a black woman and a Rastaman who lived in the house where I was hiding came out and got them to pull the dogs off.

At the time, I saw police brutality as nothing more than an occupational hazard and didn't realise it was helping to build a lot of hatred, frustration and resentment within me, which is one of the many reasons I was so rebellious. However, when you keep reoffending eventually social services and the State will say: 'His parents cannot look after him,' and commit you into the care of a local authority.

CHAPTER THREE
Predators, Pregnancy and Informers
(1978 - 1981)

Before the Children's Act 1989, which centred on the notion that young people are best cared for within their own family units, whenever a child was placed into care they automatically became the property of the State.

Parents were divested of all legal responsibilities, and Social Services acting as the State's agents became the child's legal guardians.

After being convicted for the Danny Cameron incident, I became a ward of the State on 12th April 1978. I was sent to live with several other young offenders in a children's home managed by the London Borough of Brent.

The State claimed to be taking me into care for my own protection, but with the benefit of hindsight it's obvious there were other factors at play. I suspect some of the care staff were paedophiles who only took the job because it gave them easy access to underage boys they could sexually and physically exploit.

I remember at one Surrey-based care facility when we were in bed at night, some of the care workers would come in to the dormitory and try to fondle and feel us up. Sometimes, they'd pretend to tuck you in then quickly pull down your pyjamas and try to masturbate you. Me and some of the others fought them off, but the weaker boys would just lay there.

If you played up in the dormitory they would put you in either a single room or solitary confinement for the rest of the night, and you really didn't want that to happen.

Naturally, those of us who were brave enough to abscond did, but we couldn't go back to school or home to our parents because the beasts would be looking for us. So we ate and slept rough, and turned to crimes such as dropping sticks and burglary to survive.

We'd stay absent without leave (AWOL) for as long as possible because we knew that after we were caught and brought back, some of the care staff would beat the living shit out of us.

Usually, if I got arrested in London the police would take me to a local facility because it wasn't their responsibility to escort me back to my children's home and my social worker would arrange for a driver to collect me. I went AWOL frequently and spent time in lots of children's homes. I got to know my social workers and all the drivers they used. They'd offer me cigarettes to pacify me because they knew at any point throughout the journey if we stopped at a traffic light I was liable to fly the door open, jump out and run.

When I think about it, I was no older than 13 and representatives from social services were plying me with cigarettes, which was just another form of abuse. They didn't give a shit about my welfare.

In the prime years of childhood development when you're supposed to be met with love, I faced nothing but brutality and abuse: physical, mental and sexual. The whole thing was Dickensian and it was all the State's responsibility.

I remember the principal at the care facility, Jack Jones, and three care workers: Mr Grant, a Trinidadian who restrained boys by bending them up, John Davenport and John Goose, whose wealthy parents owned a house with a swimming pool in Woking, Surrey.

Even though the assessment centre had an outdoor pool, some of the staff would still take us to Goose's house where his white-haired mother would sit silently downstairs rocking in her chair as boys were selected and taken upstairs, into the pool or elsewhere on the grounds. There were hundreds of dolls all over the place and although it all felt very strange I thought nothing of it at the time.

I'm not sure, but I think in some ways those experiences may play out in my sexual behaviour now because I can be quite predatory in bed and like to dominate women sexually.

I've probably slept with more than 500 women, but I don't believe sex and intimacy are the same thing because intimacy is all in the mind. Discussing things, going deep and connecting intellectually is far more intimate than any kind of physical connection.

For me, sex is about power because it's an exchange of energies.

Sometimes those exchanges result in positivity, and other times the energy is negative and comes with baggage that can deplete you.

***

In February 1979, a couple of days after my release from the Surrey-based facility and a few months before my 13th birthday, I bumped into one of my heroes, Michael Jackson, as I was dropping sticks on Marylebone Road. He'd been touring England with his brothers to promote their *Destiny* album and was getting into a big, black Rolls Royce limousine after visiting the Madame Tussauds wax museum. I really wish I'd shaken his hand, but I didn't realise the enormity of the moment.

Later that year, Michael released his breakthrough album *Off the Wall*; Margaret Thatcher became Britain's first female prime minster; and my family moved into our fifth council home, a four-bedroom flat in Clifton Road, Harlesden.

I began attending a local authority-sponsored learning facility, Danesbury Community Boarding School in Hertford, but absconded regularly, preferring to spend my days dropping sticks and chasing girls — a pastime I'd become interested in since losing my virginity a couple of years earlier to Sandra Oke (one of my sister Chrissie's friends).

Sandra was a few years older but I got an inkling that she fancied me, so one night when she was staying at our house I snuck downstairs, went into my sisters' room and slipped into the bed she was sharing with Chrissie. We started having sex but I didn't have a clue what I was doing, so when I was about to ejaculate I thought I wanted to piss and thought, *'Oh gosh, you'd better stop now or you're gonna wet yourself.'*

While on the run from Danesbury, I met a beautiful girl from Stonebridge, Georgina Simmonds, who I really liked. I asked around, but all I heard were unfavourable rumours about her mother and stepfather. They often left Georgina to look after her two younger sisters, sometimes for weeks at a time. One or two of the guys my age liked Georgina, but I got a school friend, Andrew Stevens, who was a real gyalist to introduce us.

I'll never forget, it was November 1979 and my brother and a few guys from the ends were in the middle of a trial at Willesden Crown Court. Georgina and I met up one day and talked for a while before I brought her home and we made love in my bedroom. It was awesome, but I didn't get to see her again.

In the spring of 1980, I started going to John Kelly Boys' School but was expelled within two weeks and quickly found myself in Stamford House Remand and Assessment Centre in Shepherd's Bush after being accused of pickpocketing.

I spent six months at Stamford House where I was joined by Raymond Fearon and introduced to the resident bully, Danny Green, who I would encounter with my old friend Winston 20 years later. Danny was a dark, muscular guy from Tottenham, north London, who had wide eyes, a big head and cropped hair. He was about a year older than me, walked around pounding his feet like a guerrilla and saw the remand centre as a jungle of which he was the king.

Danny personified bullying, and would assert his authority and take your things if he thought he could get away with it. I only befriended him after realising he was one of those people you had to keep onside.

If you showed Danny any sign of weakness or let him get away with anything, he would exploit the situation. He would try and flex with me, but I didn't give him any signs to take advantage.

While incarcerated, I discovered two vital pieces of information that shocked me to the core. First, Raymond announced he was rejecting criminality and encouraged me to do the same. Then, a family friend named Sharon King came to visit and told me that Georgina was pregnant and had gone to my mum's house with her parents who had made a scene and accused me of 'troubling' their daughter. As soon as I was released I went see Georgina but she insisted the pregnancy had nothing to do with me and I had no choice but to believe her.

Then, her stepfather sent a message through one of his friends' sons telling me to stay away from her. He wasn't someone to be messed with so I complied, took Raymond's advice, and tried to find a job.

But with inflation peaking at 22% and unemployment levels rising drastically, 1980 was never going to be a great year for a 14-year-old job-seeker. I returned to dropping sticks and was soon caught and sentenced to three months in HM Detention centre in Send, Surrey.

Detention Centres were like army boot camps for persistent re-offenders aged between 14 and 16, and I think my propensity for discipline, order and punctuality, which perhaps borders on obsessive compulsive disorder, developed during my time there.

We woke up every morning at 6am to make our beds and polish our boots and spent most afternoons on our hands and knees, scrubbing, cleaning and shovelling manure. And we had to march everywhere chanting: 'Left, right, left, right, left, right. About turn.'

It was a tough, hostile and racist environment. For example, the screws loved when a youth with dreadlocks came in because they could cut off his hair. You'd watch as he went in to the room a Rasta and came out a bal'ed. They liked to call black inmates 'Toby' or 'Chicken George', after the characters in Roots. It felt very much like we were slaves on a plantation and the screws were trying to break us.

I refused to break though and actually enjoyed when they came around to inspect our beds, clothing and hygiene kits. I always passed my kit inspections with flying colours because I was and still am fanatical about having everything neat, shipshape, symmetrical and in its place.

I received a letter from one of my twin sisters informing me that on 12th August 1980 Georgina had given birth to a beautiful baby girl, Chineka Eleanor Simmonds.

After my release I went to look for mother and baby, who I found in the Garnet Road Children's Home at the bottom of Church End Estate in Harlesden. Georgina refused to let me see Chineka, and kept saying: 'She's not yours, she's not yours. It's got nothing to do with you.' So I left feeling frustrated and confused. My criminal lifestyle spiralled further out of control, and as a result I spent most of the following year locked up in detention facilities.

Like many people from my peer group and generation, I didn't really have a childhood because we were adults by the time we were 12 and 13 years old. A lot of the girls were pregnant at 15 and 16, because in those days if you had a baby but didn't get on with your parents you could get a council flat.

Things were different for young people back then, but we didn't realise what was going on because it was all new to us. It's important to remember that when the Caribbean people of the Windrush generation first arrived in Britain in the 1940s and '50s, no one knew what to expect.

The Nigerians hadn't arrived yet, so we were the first set of immigrants to go through the institutions and have to contend with racial discrimination. It was our parents and us who opened the doors and instigated the likes of the Race Relations Act 1965.

It was our efforts that forced the government to repeal the sus law in 1981 and it was us who first went through the British education system where, for almost 30 years, Caribbean children were labelled 'educationally subnormal' and diverted away from mainstream schooling.

Nevertheless, I think black people who were born and grew up in Britain during that era really also messed a lot of things up and have a lot to answer for.

***

In the spring of 1981 I was convicted of theft and sent to Latchmere House, a remand centre in Surrey for boys aged 14 to 17 where I spent much of my four-month incarceration writing letters and listening to the radio. On the weekends, I tuned in to Robbie Vincent on BBC Radio London every Saturday afternoon; David Rodigan on Capital later in the night; and on Sunday afternoons it would be Tony Williams back on the BBC.

In jail you were only allowed FM radios, so whenever you were in custody you'd always want to stay local because the moment you were transferred outside of Greater London you'd be disconnected from black music and left listening to Spandau Ballet all day long, whether you liked the Kemp brothers or not.

Around the same time, Aaron was certified mentally ill. He was just 17 and up until that point he'd been my hero. He was my bigger brother and I'd always followed in his footsteps. He was violent, so I was too. When he went into care, I went into care. When he went into the criminal justice system, I followed. When he was serving time in Feltham Young Offenders' Institution, I joined him there.

However, for the past 15 years Aaron has resided in assisted living accommodation where he shares a house with another person suffering with a mental health issue. Prior to that, he spent 20 years in and out of hospital. Although I've always maintained contact with Aaron I don't think I've been very brotherly and I could've visited him more frequently. For a long while I saw his mental illness as a weakness and thought, *'How dare you let the Murrays down like that?'* Previously, I rejected Aaron because I was scared and ashamed of his behaviour. I just couldn't come to terms with it.

I think it started in jail, because back in those days if you attacked the screws they would give you a serious sedative known as 'the liquid cosh'. Prison nurses injected you with it to relax your muscles, sedate you and take away your strength. Over a period of weeks it slows you down, slurs your speech and makes you put on weight. And if you keep attacking screws, they keep coshing you and the cycle repeats.

The elder gangsters explained that it was better to lash out at other inmates instead of screws because sometimes the nurses gave overdoses that turned inmates insane. But Aaron didn't get it and by the time he was 16 the screws were using a straitjacket to restrain him. According to the screws, one morning my brother came out of his cell looking very distressed and hasn't been the same since.

I can remember seeing about four or five guys come into the prison system, attack officers, get coshed up and leave with mental illness. I was violent during my time in youth prison, but I knew how far to go. Every day I pray for healthy faculties and a sound mind.

Before I was sent to Latchmere House, I was pursuing Pauline Joseph, a girl I fancied and had taken to the newly refurbished four-screen ABC cinema on Edgware Road, where we watched *The Blue Lagoon*, a romantic drama starring Brooke Shields that was partially filmed in Jamaica.

Previously, we'd spent hours talking on the phone and I decided to maintain contact by writing to her regularly. However, in one of her replies Pauline revealed she had started seeing a guy named Shane. I wrote back criticising her decision and described Shane as 'grossly obese'. I thought nothing of it, but one afternoon a few weeks after I was released I was getting off a bus in Willesden and bumped into Shane, his friend Roger Pryce and a guy I used to roll with, Tony Blake.

Pauline had obviously told Shane about the letter and he confronted me. Even though he was a bodybuilder and twice my size, I wasn't intimidated and fought back when he tried to manhandle me. We wrestled, but neither of us landed any real blows before Roger stepped in and the two of them got the better of me. I told Roger his cards were marked and that he was nuts for getting involved in the fight.

I knew all I had to do was bide my time because my firm was bigger than his and more importantly we were wild and didn't care about anything or anyone. Our attitude was that even though we're from Harlesden NW10, we were dominant throughout Brent.

About a month later, I was walking with Martin 'Titch' Raymonds when we saw Roger walking up Longstone Avenue, about 200 yards from his home. I called his name, got his attention and approached him: 'Where's your man dem now?' I asked.

Roger, who was about three years older than me, tried to pacify the situation but I saw that as a sign of weakness, which just empowered me. I threw him over a small brick wall and used my Stanley knife to cut him down the side of his face, which I then spat in.

As blood and saliva dripped from his cheek, I said: 'That's for getting involved in an argument that didn't have anything to do with you. You're filth.' And calmly walked away.

I followed Titch to Willesden High School as he needed to collect some homework. As I waited outside the school gates, I saw Roger's younger brother Randy approaching on a bicycle. Although I'd slashed his brother's face less than 30 minutes earlier, I didn't register Randy as a threat. Titch returned around the same time Randy arrived, jumped off his bike, lunged at me twice, jumped back onto his bike and rode off.

I asked Titch if he knew what that was about. He shrugged and replied: 'I don't, I don't, I don't, I don't... I don't know.' Titch and I had awful stammers, so our arguments were always highly entertaining for bystanders. Then Titch said: 'Look at your, look at your, look at your... sweatshirt.' I glanced down and saw my white shirt had turned crimson. I felt faint but managed to reply: 'I think I've been stabbed. Let's go to the ambulance depot around the corner.'

We walked maybe 15 metres before I collapsed to the floor, gasping for air. Titch ran out into the road and stopped a young guy who was driving past in a green Mini Cooper. He drove us to the depot where I was carried into an ambulance and driven to Park Royal Hospital. On the way I remember feeling pain, wearing an oxygen mask and having what I can only describe as an out-of-body experience. I imagined people attending my funeral, and feeling like I was going to meet Sleepy.

Ricardo 'Sleepy' Campbell was a 19-year-old hustler who'd been killed 18 months earlier in a fight over a pair of crocodile skin shoes. Aaron and I knew him through his younger brothers who were our age and had attended Oldfield Primary School with us. While Sleepy was serving time in a borstal, one of his brother's friends had come to their house, nicked Sleepy's crocs and given them to his own brother, a 21-year-old guy named Vince who started wearing the shoes.

When Sleepy came out of prison he got into an argument with Vince one night in a shubeen, and Vince drew a knife and stabbed him in the neck.

Vince got six years for manslaughter, but it was a really big thing at the time because Sleepy was the first person of our generation to lose their life on the road.

It's crazy, but as the ambulance sped down Acton Lane and the paramedics cut away my clothes to get to the wounds, I could see the man dem at my funeral and me going to heaven and seeing Sleepy.

I knew I wasn't dreaming and as perverse as it sounds I felt a sense of achievement and notoriety but also serenity and contentment. I wasn't scared. It was like I'd accepted my fate; I had played the game and this was the consequence.

After arriving at the hospital, I was put on a life support machine and a tube was placed inside me to drain the blood from one of my lungs, which had been punctured. I remember seeing my mum absolutely in bits. I really did put her through a lot of shit.

The police came to see me, but I refused to give a statement. To do that is not in the gangster code. Even if your life depended on it you never spoke to the police, they were an enemy.

Nevertheless, when Randy heard I was on a life support machine and that it was touch and go whether I lived or died, he went to the police station with his parents and told them exactly what happened. I thought the incident was finished, but as soon as I was discharged from hospital the beasts arrested me for the malicious wounding of Roger.

At first, I thought they were joking. But they took me to Kilburn Police Station and started questioning me: 'We know what happened,' said one of the officers. 'We know you slashed Roger, and that his brother, in a rage, came and stabbed you. You might as well just give your statement.' But I declined.

Randy was arrested and initially charged with attempted murder, but the indictment was dropped to grievous bodily harm, to which he pleaded guilty and was sentenced to three months in a detention centre.

If I had made a statement against Randy he would have received a lot more than three months, so when my case eventually came to trial I thought his brother would have given me some leeway. But in addition to giving the police a statement, Roger came to the old Acton Crown Court and committed the most abominable sin imaginable by giving superb evidence in the witness box.

I was astonished and just couldn't believe it. In those days, roadmen operated very differently. Back then, a real gangster would never think of speaking to the police. But for the wannabees, that wasn't a problem.

CHAPTER FOUR
Banged Up, Breaking Out and Jackie Green
(1981 - 1984)

One autumn evening in 1981, not long after I was stabbed, I remember hanging out at Clive's flat on the Stonebridge Estate with Cedrick and Raymond. I was about 15 years old and we were smoking weed and talking about doing something positive with our lives. Clive had just bought a new rare groove record, *Nights over Egypt* by The Jones Girls, which played continuously in the background.

As we nodded to the plucky bassline and saccharine-voiced trio reminiscing about Africa's ancient Nile Valley Civilisations, Raymond said something that made me look at life differently.

Midway through a vibrant debate over the song's lyrics, he said: 'When you think about it, you've got Harlesden, Brent, London; then England, Europe, and the rest of the world. Imagine that? And yet, most people we know will only ever get to see Brent.'

I thought long and hard about his observation, and eventually found a globe, sat down and for the first time looked at the world. I remember thinking, *'Wow, he's right. I don't want to be stuck in Brent. I want to see all the different peoples of the world and where and how they live.'*

Interestingly, Raymond is one of the few friends I've kept from my roots. It's been perhaps a decade since I last saw Clive and after serving two life sentences Cedrick became a martial arts champion in 2011 and moved to Bristol. I used to visit Cedrick in jail during his first sentence in the late '80s and early '90s, but I haven't seen him in a while because our lives went in completely different directions.

I've made a conscious decision to avoid anyone from my criminal past. These days, I won't even let them in my car because I don't know what they might be carrying and I could get stopped by the police. An incident like that could adversely affect my life and I won't create an opportunity for that to happen. It's hard, but you have to break away.

I made new friends in my professional career, but for a while I also held on to old friends, which held me back and by default made me vulnerable to relapsing into criminality. It's almost as though I had some form of misplaced loyalty to my old-time peers and didn't accept that roots turn into trees and trees produce branches which grow out in different directions. That's life.

Raymond was the first one from our group to break out and branch off. He was also the first person to make me think about having a professional career, and was instrumental in helping me make the transition from crime to industry. Ray did his O Levels, some A Levels and became a junior tennis player. After that, he moved into modelling, then acting, and hasn't looked back since.

In 1992, he became the first black actor in more than 40 years to play *Othello* in a major theatre production by the Royal Shakespeare Company (RSC). Later, he became an associate artist of the RSC and was cast in films such as *Harry Potter and the Sorcerer's Stone* and Disney's *Beauty and the Beast*.

Raymond is the youngest brother from one of the most revered families in our area, the Fearons. They were all attractive, slick and well dressed; posh villains if you like. And that legacy transferred to Ray, who had access to all his brothers' clothes. Consequently, he would always be wearing the latest brands, even if the outfits were two or three sizes too big. We became great friends. I'd commit crimes in the day and meet up with Ray in the evenings at a youth club, someone's home or a party. That was the cycle, but he was sensible.

He started behaving differently after his eldest brother Lawrence, who I really respected, came out of jail and started talking about building a more structured life. At first I didn't understand their new mindset, but eventually I began to adopt the ideology and said to myself, *'okay, let's give this a try'*.

Nowadays, Ray and I see each other at funerals and will go out for dinner a few times a year. But we've never lost contact and whenever there's a significant development in my life I'll always meet up with him.

We stayed connected throughout the '80s and '90s when I bought my first home and got an American Express gold card. Back then, he was still an aspiring actor and would talk about his dreams and future plans and I tried to be a living example like he'd been to me.

In 2002, he came to live with me for four years when we were both battling with our own demons. I was going through a particularly acrimonious divorce and a lot of other serious challenges. I remember being flat broke and turning to him for money a couple of times, but I refused to charge him rent. It wasn't about pride. Whether he was staying with me or not, I still had to pay the mortgage. My philosophy is that when you're a guest in my home you're not supposed to put your hand in your pocket.

Raymond moved on after securing contracts to star in *Coronation Street* and *Strictly Come Dancing* and dating Elle 'the body' Macpherson. Ray has always been like a brother to me, and when we lived together he really made me man-up, see sense, and stop making emotion-based decisions. I'll probably always remain close to him because out of a gang of around 30 juvenile delinquents coming from Harlesden in the late '70s, only a few of us made it through.

***

In February 1982, a couple of months before my 16th birthday, I was convicted of malicious wounding with intent and sentenced to serve between six and 24 months of borstal training for cutting Roger's face.

I remember being sent to HM Borstal in Rochester, the UK's oldest youth offending institution, and waiting for two weeks to find out which borstal I'd be allocated to.

When one of the screws finally said: 'You're going to Feltham,' my heart sank. In those days, HM Borstal in Feltham was one of the most racist places on the planet and no black juvenile wanted to go there. Aaron was already in Feltham, but we were placed in separate houses so I rarely saw him.

The facility housed around 250 boys aged between 15 and 20, who were divided into five houses of up to 50 inmates each. However, no more than five black inmates were allowed in a house. So from a racial perspective, we were always outnumbered by at least 10 to 1.

I was placed in South House where white inmates hurled racial profanities throughout the day, and at night they'd shout: 'Nigger, nigger, pull a trigger,' and the Nazi phrase: 'Sieg Heil, Sieg Heil, Sieg Heil'. I quickly grew tired of such hostilities and after speaking with David Miller, a black guy I knew from the remand centre at Latchmere House, we decided to protest by using the shower cubicles that were reserved for 'whites only'.

When David and I first arrived at Feltham the three other black guys in South House told us that at the end of each working day everyone was supposed to wash up and get ready for dinner, but only white inmates were allowed to use the showers. When David, who I called 'Banger', asked: 'So how do you shower?' One of the trio solemnly replied: 'We don't.'

When our three black housemates saw us in the cubicles they must have thought we were mad, but I encouraged them to join in; so they were able to have a shower for the first time since their arrival, albeit reservedly. After a few minutes, some white guys came in and started swearing but we ignored them and they soon left. We exited the cubicles and made our way down a long alcove-style corridor, which ran from the washroom to the residential units, and subsequently found ourselves ambushed by up to 30 white guys.

They apparently wanted to teach us a lesson for using 'their' showers. Our three housemates ran off, but me and David stood together and fought off the racist bullies. After a while an alarm bell rang out and the screws rushed in, but we threw chairs at them, retreated to the washroom and barricaded ourselves in.

'Stop being silly, let us in so we can put a stop to this,' they said. But we knew they were lying and told them: 'No, fuck off. You're just as racist as the inmates.' Eventually, the screws called Aaron who was probably the only person I'd listen to. He said: 'Peter, stop this shit because you don't want to get coshed up.' I agreed, persuaded David to abandon the protest, and we were both sent to solitary confinement for 14 days.

After we came out, David and my brother were transferred to another borstal, Finnamore Wood in Marlow, Buckinghamshire, and I returned to South House where the white inmates continued to dispatch verbal abuse. But it was never anything physical because they knew I'd fight back.

That's how Feltham was: hardcore. But there was one positive experience that came out of my six months there. I obtained my first qualifications - intermediate and elementary certificates in Pitman's Office Practice and Typing. I'd always been impressed by the way the solicitors and barristers who represented me selected and delivered their words in court, and I would imitate their style when addressing adults in positions of authority.

The screws in Feltham were legally obliged to provide inmates with at least a basic level of education and as a result they suggested I take the course to improve my employability.

I agreed and learned office functions such as how to type 40 words-per-minute, filing and writing formal letters. If I'm honest, taking that course was one of the best decisions I ever made because those skills have been hugely beneficial throughout my business career. I think I enjoyed the Pitman's course because I was learning something new that didn't have anything to do with gangsterism. I'd been thinking about Raymond and his plan to go straight and was beginning to understand how I could do the same.

Later that summer, after I passed my exams and started acting like a model inmate, I was sent to Finnamore Wood where I linked up again with David and my brother. Drugs were freely available in Feltham, but they were even more widespread in Finnamore Wood, which was a more relaxed borstal, lots of drugs and music.

There was a guy from east London who played *Never Too Much* by Luther Vandross all the time and I remember 1982 being a great year for soul music. Shalamar had massive hits with *A Night to Remember* and *Friends*, Marvin Gaye dropped *Sexual Healing* and London-based soul acts started to cross over. There was Hot Chocolate with *It Started with a Kiss*, Junior Giscombe's *Mama Used to Say*, Imagination with *In the Heat of the Night* and Phil Fearon's *Head Over Heels*.

They were all local groups who cumulatively sold so many records that mainstream British labels, desperate to capture a share of the market, began promoting their own interpretation of our music; hence the rise of 'New Romantic' and blue-eyed soul groups such as Spandau Ballet, Culture Club and Wham.

In October 1982, during the last month of my sentence at Finnamore Wood, I became eligible for home leave, which is like a five-day parole you use to reacquaint with your family and society. I went home and everything was fine until the fourth day when I got nicked for driving offences and assaulting a police.

I'd been hanging out in Harlesden driving a brown Mini Cooper I had recently purchased when I saw a fed drive past in the opposite direction. I saw him spin around to follow me, so I parked up and quickly jumped out the car.

But the beast, who suspected the vehicle was stolen, followed and tried to arrest me. Although the car was mine, I was only 16 years old so had no licence, insurance or MOT test certificate. We fought and I was arrested and charged. I was taken straight to court, remanded into custody, then sent to Latchmere House. Upon arrival, I revealed that I still had two weeks of borstal training to complete at Finnamore Wood, but the authorities decided that I should serve my remaining time at Latchmere.

A few weeks after I was released, me and my good friend Dennis White hatched a plot to break in to an electrical wholesale store in Harlesden. Dennis was closer to me than my brother Aaron and I learned many valuable life lessons from him. When we were on the road stealing, Dennis always gave to beggars and put money in charity boxes. He taught me that it was good luck and karma to give away some of the money we'd made to people who were less fortunate. I adopted this philosophy. But whereas Dennis would do it after he made money, I tried to give something away before I went out at the start of the day because I've always believed the measure you give is the measure you receive.

The electrical shop we planned to rob was alarmed, but Dennis figured that by taking a sledge hammer to the back wall of the building we could make a hole big enough to crawl through and get access to some video cassette recorders (VCRs). We managed to steal £26,000 worth of VCRs, which were kept at Dennis's yard and fenced out by his elder brother, Dean. I suspected Dean would skank us (which he did) so I took some of the VCRs and hid them at my mum's house, which was a big mistake.

I can't remember how, but Dennis's sister got nicked. Although Violet was a villain, she was a bit simple-minded and basically got everybody, including her brothers, father and me, arrested too. Initially the beasts tried to charge us with burglary, but they didn't have enough evidence to make that stick. So the charge was downgraded to handling stolen goods.

When the case was eventually heard at Acton Crown Court on 16 December 1982, Dennis and I pleaded guilty. By now, I'd been to court many times and knew the procedure. Nevertheless, I was surprised by what happened next.

In sentencing, the judge said that because we remained hardened criminals he was going to detain us under Section 53 of the Criminal Justice Act 1982. My knees wobbled and I could see the blood draining from Dennis's face because we knew that Section 53 sentences were only reserved for the most serious juvenile cases: murderers, arsonists, and armed robbers aged between 11 and 16.

Moreover, the sentences ranged from three years in prison to indefinite detention at Her Majesty's pleasure, which is the equivalent to life imprisonment. Convicts aged 13 and under who received this sentence were placed in care and sent to a secure unit. Then at 14 they were taken to a prison estate like Latchmere House. At 16, like I was, prisoners were sent to young offender institutions such as HMP Prison Aylesbury in Buckinghamshire, before being introduced to adult prison establishments.

You have to understand, the sentencing powers available to the courts at that time were limited when it came to young juveniles. To counter this problem, in the run up to the 1979 general election the Conservative Party had promised to 'experiment with a tougher regime as a short, sharp shock for young criminals'.

After they won the election, Home Secretary Willie Whitelaw targeted persistent offenders aged 14 to 16 by sentencing them to three months of quasi-military training in a detention centre (DC). If they continued to reoffend and were aged between 15 and 20 they were sentenced to borstal training, which lasted anything from six months to two years, depending on your behaviour.

Whitelaw's plan to target young and, if we're completely honest, mostly black criminals with early 19th century disciplinary punishment won approval with the British public. But in truth his policy had dire consequences.

The borstal philosophies and institutions advocated by Whitelaw under Prime Minister Margaret Thatcher did nothing to reduce conviction rates, but helped to create a generation of criminals, bullies and psychopaths whose childhood memories are peppered with State-sponsored abuse and military-style training.

Personally, I learned new skills and passed my first exams during my stints in DC and borstal, but the abuse was terrible and the screws still beat you up. The whole thing was barbarous nonsense.

Subsequently, when the judge said he was sentencing me and Dennis under Section 53, we assumed he was about to hand down a lengthy, draconian penalty. Luckily, he was simply utilising new powers he had access to under the Criminal Justice Act 1982, which had come into law six weeks earlier.

Dennis and I were relieved to discover that we'd only been sentenced to three months; no parole and no remission. Neither of our barristers had ever heard of a sentence like that and it was the same thing at Latchmere House. When we arrived, the screws were so surprised they rang up the court and Home Office who confirmed the sentence was perfectly correct, but had never been passed before.

Later that day, I was also fined £50 for driving offences and possession of cannabis and sentenced to concurrently serve two three-month prison terms for handling stolen goods and assaulting a police officer.

I returned to Latchmere House where I was a model inmate, and after delivering a solo recital at the Christmas church service got to speak with Prince Charles' cousin, Princess Alexandra. I was released in February

1983, but just weeks after my 17th birthday in April 1983 I was again arrested and charged, this time with possession of an offensive weapon.

Me and Dennis had gone to a Maze concert at the Hammersmith Odeon to listen to music and drop sticks. In those days, white people with disposable income were the majority at black music concerts.

Inside, there were some guys from south London doing the same thing but they were acting like they wanted to rob us. Before we had a chance to interact, feds drew down on me and Dennis in the foyer. We hadn't done anything yet, so they could only nick us for the knives we were carrying.

A few weeks later, I was caught running bun and cheese in an off-licence shop in Maida Vale and arrested for fraud. In those days, I'd use bun and cheese to purchase simple things like food and then come back to the ends and shot the produce to local mothers.

The Indian man in the corner shop knew the goods were bought fraudulently, but he'd still take them all day long because once a cheque guarantee card is used the bank is the only entity that takes a loss. Nevertheless, when I attempted to buy a few bottles of high-end liquor using the stolen chequebook and cheque guarantee card, a jackass shop owner on Clifton Road cashed the items, looked at me and said: 'I'm going to make a phone call to check this out.' I dus out of the shop, but the feds were already outside. I got nicked for deception, pleaded guilty, received bail and weeks later found myself facing a robbery charge.

Me, Martin 'Titch' Raymonds and Frankie Wilkins had been travelling from Harlesden on a southbound train when a girl, Jackie Green, who was wearing lots of gold jewellery, got on at Queen's Park.

I didn't know her and thought to myself, *'You're fair game'*, and suggested to the others that we rob her. We all got off at the next stop, Kilburn Park, and moved towards the girl. When I started grabbing for her chains, she screamed: 'I know who you are! What are you doing?'

I told her she was lying and pulled away the jewellery. 'Your name's Peter Murray,' she said. But I kept my composure and calmly replied: 'Okay, so you know me. If you've got man dem send them come, and we'll have it out that way.'

We left the scene, waited for the next train, and went back to Harlesden. Meanwhile, Jackie went straight to the police station. The next morning, bull came to my mum's yard and I was arrested, charged with robbery and after being held in police custody for the weekend, appeared in court on the Monday and was eventually transported to HM Remand Centre Ashford in Middlesex.

I was a reckless, angry, 17-year-old thug. In the 100 days since my release from Latchmere House, I'd picked up a series of charges and was now getting heat from Frankie who was also on remand for the robbery.

Frankie was the youngest in a family of villains and had only just been released from Feltham. He was pissed at being back in jail. He told anyone who'd listen the reason he'd been arrested was that I'd grassed him up and given his name to the feds, which of course was totally untrue.

Man dem in Ashford started accusing me of being a grass and a couple of Frankie's friends were acting like they wanted to beat me up. I liked Frankie. He was a model villain who'd made a name for himself beating up racists in Feltham. But in the end, I had to fuck him up to let everyone know that I wasn't a grass. At the time, my thinking was, *'If I jook you up in your face, all of your south London bredrins will catch a fright and back off,'* so that's what I did.

Around the same time Vanessa Williams became the first black woman to be crowned Miss America and Neil Kinnock took over leadership of the Labour Party, I was placed on 42 days solitary confinement for stabbing Frankie in the face. I began, for the first time, to study English language and literature, another prison experience that proved to be hugely beneficial in later years.

When we returned to court, I got my sister Elizabeth to stand £500 surety to get Frankie released on bail. So when I went back to Ashford, even though I was still in solitary confinement and two of Frankie's mates, King, a brown guy with hazel eyes from Brixton and another man from Tottenham, wanted to beat me up, the situation was far less tense.

A few weeks later in September 1983, the case involving the offensive weapon at the Maze concert came up and I strategically reasoned with my solicitor that if I pleaded guilty I'd probably receive a custodial sentence and be moved out of Ashford, which would make my life much easier.

I pleaded guilty, received a three-month sentence and, sure enough, was transferred from Ashford to Latchmere House. In truth, I should have stayed on remand at Ashford, but the governor at Latchmere House accepted my request because 10 months earlier I'd left his institution as a role model prisoner.

Throughout this entire period I'd been frantically trying to get the man dem to convince Jackie Green to drop the charges. We spoke to her boyfriend, offered to replace the jewellery and buy her stuff, but she wasn't having it: 'It's the principal,' she said. 'I told Peter that I knew him, but he was blasé. Let him stay there and rot.'

By now, I was brimming with anger and frustration because I didn't think black people locked up other black people, and couldn't understand how my bredrins weren't able to find a way to broker a deal with this girl.

After 10 long months the case was finally heard in March 1984, around six weeks before my 18th birthday. I remember the public gallery at Willesden Crown Court was packed with people from the ends who'd come to see me on trial for robbery. When it was Jackie's time to speak, she bowled into the witness box and gave superb evidence. I was stunned and grew angrier after I was found guilty and sentenced to two years in prison. To add insult to injury, the judge also handed down a concurrent sentence of six months for the bun and cheese fraud in Maida Vale.

I was incensed for many reasons, but mainly because I'd just received my longest custodial sentence and was heading to a new place where I'd undoubtedly face many unpredictable challenges. The same location where British comedian Ronnie Barker recorded his 1979 film *Porridge*: HM Prison Chelmsford, Essex.

CHAPTER FIVE
Adulthood, Hunger Strikes and Parliament
(1984)

I arrived at HM Prison Chelmsford just days after the President of the National Union of Miners, Arthur Scargill, kick-started what activist and author David John Douglass describes as 'the most violent industrial dispute in Britain in the 20th century'.

The UK miners' strike, which lasted a year (1984-85) and attempted to disrupt the national power supply, was in response to plans by Thatcher's Government to shut down an average of 23 coal pits annually for the next three years. However, while the strike involved more than 140,000 miners at its peak, their protest was largely redundant since the coal industry would collapse over the next 30 years as British households switched to electricity as their primary source of power.

I'd spent so much time on remand that I only had six months left before I was due for release, so I tried to stay out of trouble and improved my new-found English language skills by writing letters to friends and reading as many books as I could.

Every day I'd read about the battle between Scargill's miners and Thatcher's Government and I bought as many newspapers as possible to get different perspectives on the strike. But I would never buy *The Sun*.

A few years earlier, in the early hours of the morning on Sunday 18th January 1981, 13 black youths died in a blaze at a house party in southeast London - the New Cross Fire.

There was a lot of racial tension at that time because assaults by

43

skinheads and other racist groups were common, so no one could be certain as to whether the fire was accidental or had been started deliberately as a racist attack.

Despite the high death toll, the police's response was at best indifferent, leading to accusations of a cover-up. Two months later, around 20,000 people marched in protest from New Cross to Hyde Park in central London. That was the first act of political engagement I ever took part in and I remember walking past *The Sun's* Fleet Street offices and seeing journalists hanging out of the windows making monkey noises and signs. Furthermore, even though the march was peaceful, the following day *The Sun* covered the story with the headline: *'Day the Blacks Ran Riot in London'*, and for that reason I've never bought that paper again.

***

I was still seething about Jackie Green coming to court, but I tried to forget about her and was pleasantly surprised to hear that I'd been allocated a cellmate. I don't remember much about him, other than his name was Michael. He was white, had brown hair, came from Hertfordshire and was in jail for the first time.

On about the fourth night after he arrived, I remember lying on the bottom bunk talking with him and discovering that we were both 17 and had birthdays coming in the following weeks. I must've dozed off midway through the conversation because the next thing I remember is waking up, looking to my left and seeing his lifeless body hanging from the cell bars. Michael had cut his bed linen into strips, tied them around his neck, secured the other end to a bar, and hung himself.

I never looked at his face, but remember he was wearing a white t-shirt and jeans and there was a puddle on the floor where he'd pissed himself. I pressed the buzzer and banged on the cell door. The screws told me to take him down, but I refused. A few minutes later, the door flew open and a handful of them bundled into the cell and rushed me out to the landing. They could see I was shaken up and took me downstairs where breakfast was being set out.

I remember a screw gently taking me by the arm, walking me over to a tea urn and telling me to make myself a cuppa. About an hour later, the prison Chaplin came in and asked if there was anything I wanted to talk about. I said: 'No.' And that was the end of my grief counselling.

Before the end of the day, I was moved into the cell next door and two new inmates were placed in my old cell. That's jail for you. There are no special days, holidays, or remembrance days. Every day in jail is just another day in jail.

When I think about it now, I probably should have sued the prison service for neglect. But to be honest, the whole thing was so traumatic that it's taken 33 years for me to speak about it.

Michael appeared to be a cool guy, and everything seemed pretty normal when we'd been talking the night before his death. I didn't see that coming at all. If I had any idea that he was going to kill himself I would've talked him out of it, or at least tried to.

Nevertheless, I quickly hardened my heart and tried my best not to let his death affect me. In those days, it was all about bravado and trying to assert your manhood. You weren't supposed to consider certain things or have feelings of a certain type. Well, that's what I thought.

To be quite frank, by the following morning I'd convinced myself that I didn't give two shits about Michael. Yes he was a nice guy, but I didn't know him. I had neither sympathy nor empathy for him, and simply thought to myself, 'Wow, that was an experience!' I looked at it from the perspective of a victim, like it was something that I had experienced and gone through.

On the surface I appeared to be coping, but in reality I was an emotional wreck and in desperate need of counselling and therapy. I'd been locked up for the best part of a year and received my longest custodial sentence just four weeks earlier. I was already incensed and not being able to communicate how I felt about my cellmate's suicide only intensified my frustrations. Consequently, about two weeks later, just after my 18th birthday on 16th April 1984 I became embroiled in an impromptu inmate disturbance.

I don't remember much about how the protest started except that all the inmates were in the exercise yard, and when the screws said it was time to go back inside we refused. Summer had just begun, it was a really hot day and we just said: 'Fuck it. We're not going back inside, we're sitting down right here.' And that's what we did.

The screws accused me of being one of the main agitators, which I expected because a few of them had previously mentioned that whenever there was trouble I was always around, but never directly involved.

They read all my letters and would always say that I was far too mature for my age. So I was initially flattered rather than surprised when the State reclassified me as an adult and I was transferred to an adult prison. Apparently, there is a provision in criminal justice legislation that allows for juveniles as young as 10 to be reclassified as adults. But it's only used when a young person has the mindset and attitude of an adult and is causing a disturbance to the general prison population.

Five months after arriving at Chelmsford, I was transported to HMP Highpoint in Newmarket, Suffolk, a former Royal Air Force base that had previously been used as a transit camp for the Indian refugees Uganda's former President Idi Amin had expelled from his country 12 years earlier.

Life was pretty much the same inside an adult prison. Highpoint had two facilities: a semi-open Category C prison, where I was sent, and a closed Category B prison, which is a lot more secure. I guess the only difference I found was becoming acquainted with men who were doing some real serious sentences. I also met a Ghanaian for the first time; he was my cellmate.

However, within a few days I became involved in another violent incident. Me and a guy from Nigeria got into an argument, so I put a square PP9 battery into a sock, tied a knot in the open end and attacked him. He came running out of his cell and went straight to the screws who transferred me to the closed prison across the road where I caused further commotion by getting into another confrontation with an inmate.

I was placed in solitary confinement, and the following day received a visit from the governor who said: 'Right, you're going. There's a bus waiting for you outside.' I asked: 'Where?' And was told: 'You'll find out when you get there.'

Subsequently, after less than a month at Highpoint I was transferred to arguably the most feared institution in the UK penal system, HMP Wandsworth in South West London, where I shared a cell with three guys. There was a white drug courier, who I think was an ex-public schoolboy, serving five years for smuggling hashish. He was quite intelligent and switched on and would teach me how to finesse my way through the system in a sophisticated way.

There was Bruce, a black guy who'd just started a seven-year sentence for armed robbery. He walked with a limp following a motorcycle accident and was pretty harmless. However, my brother had bruk him up pretty badly with some weapons in Finnamore Wood, so I was always wary that he might attack me as I slept.

And then there was Stevie Sherwood, a white guy from southeast London who was six years in to a 12-year stretch for robbing a security van. Stevie was a short but well-built former soldier in his late 20s who'd just been transferred from HMP Parkhurst on the Isle of Wight to complete the last part of his sentence.

He'd been in the system a while and would tell me how it worked and how far I could go with certain things. Stevie was one of the people who warned me: 'Whatever happens, don't whack a screw because the last thing you want is to get that liquid cosh. That stuff can send you loopy.'

My fear of mental illness and memories of going to visit my mum's friends at the psychiatric hospital in Shenley were enough to stop me from assaulting the prison guards, but Stevie taught me there were other ways to offend and attack the system.

He said that if I really wanted to make a statement I should either barricade myself in my cell or go on hunger strike. This was just three years after members of the Irish Republican Army (IRA), who were in HMP Maze in Northern Ireland, went on hunger strike in protest against the British government's decision to withdraw privileges they'd been granted under the Geneva Convention.

Between 5th May and 20th August 1981, 10 members of the IRA, including the strike's leader Bobby Sands, starved themselves to death. Sands was elected a Member of Parliament (MP) during the strike, which attracted attention from international media and support for the Republican movement.

Stevie explained that as a result, no prison governor wanted a hunger strike in their establishment because the death of the IRA inmates had generated a lot of bad publicity and placed the State authorities in a position where they were unable to claim their usual justification that the prisoner had been killed by screws acting in self-defence.

I began writing a play, *To Be or Not to Be*, about a black policeman who commits suicide after the stress from his job causes him to fall out with his family. I decided that after my release I would try and get the play performed. Raymond's brother David was part of a Stonebridge-based drama group and I knew he'd be supportive, especially as I'd written the lead role with him in mind.

Although I'd been trying to keep a low profile and was only in Wandsworth for about eight weeks, I still managed to find myself in the middle of a disagreement with some guys from Ladbroke Grove. Harlesden and Stonebridge had beef with Ladbroke Grove from when we rushed the youth club on Latimer Road, and caused mayhem. I'd bus' up this big guy called Barrington and remember him staring as if he was memorising my face in case we ever met again.

Ladbroke Grove had the Front Line and was the place where people like soul legend Marvin Gaye used to hang out when they were in London. But we were trying to establish Harlesden as the unofficial capital. The guys at the youth club hadn't really done anything, we were just warmongering.

We gained a lot of respect for rushing that youth centre, especially from the guys living in the surrounding areas, such as Paddington, Acton, Shepherds Bush and Lisson Green, because their situation was similar to what's going on in the Middle East where Saudi Arabia is the powerhouse and all the surrounding states are subservient. The following year, me, Raymond and Cedrick were all dating girls from Ladbroke Grove, and every Sunday we'd go roller skating together at the Hammersmith Palais. One evening after skating some guys from Ladbroke Grove cornered us outside and one of our guys, Dilly, stabbed one of their guys, Lattie, who happened to be good friends with Barrington. I hadn't seen those guys since that night, but remember getting the shock of my life the first time I visited the prison exercise yard. In the far corner I recognised two familiar faces.

They belonged to Barrington, who was serving a five-year sentence, and Lattie, who was doing seven years. I almost shat myself because I was the only Harlesden man in the entire prison.

Luckily, they didn't see me and the following day a big guy from Harlesden, DJ, arrived. He wasn't directly part of my crew, but territorially he was linked to both Harlesden and Grove and he knew Lattie and Barrington.

DJ tried to resolve the issue, but they weren't having it and one afternoon Barrington confronted me in the exercise yard. He said: 'Now that we know you're in jail we're gonna send people 'round to your mum's yard unless you give us Dilly's address, so we can send the mayhem to his mother's yard.'

Of course I knew where Dilly lived, but I wasn't a grass. I calmly explained that I couldn't agree to the deal and recommended that before sending anyone to my mum's house they should first consider the safety of their own families. That set Lattie off and he started to flare up and cause a commotion. Lots of inmates rushed over to see what was going on and the screws came in and separated us.

I knew they'd eventually get to me and was especially concerned by Lattie, a very aggressive bredda who was murdered less than a month after his release. However, neither man got the opportunity to exact the revenge they so desperately sought because a couple of days later, in November 1984, I was shipped out to HMP Camp Hill on the Isle of Wight.

There are three prisons on the Isle of Wight: Camp Hill, Albany and Parkhurst, where Stevie was transferred from. I remembered everything he'd taught me and decided that I was going to make a real nuisance of myself. Within days I got into a dispute with a guy I had a longstanding issue with from Ashford Remand Centre, and one afternoon caused a fracas on the induction wing by barricading myself into my cell, just as I had done two-and-a-half years earlier in Feltham.

The screws came and demanded that I undo the barricade. But I was uncompromising in my contempt and perturbed by the fact that even though I was still a teenager I'd just spent the past three months living without any contact with the outside world, alongside some of the country's most violent criminals.

I told the screws: 'Fuck off. I'm not doing jack shit. I'm only bloody 18 years old and you lot are moving me from pillar to post, up and down the country in all these adult prisons. I'm not doing anything. You can piss off.' I wouldn't relent, but they eventually got in by using a huge vice to pull open the steel cell door.

I was placed in solitary confinement and decided to employ another of Stevie's strategies by committing to a hunger strike. I don't remember exactly how many days I starved myself for, but it was longer than a week. To be honest, it's just brinkmanship. You know the screws and governor have to give you attention because they don't want a death in custody. If you can just bear through it you know that eventually there's going to be a concession.

Stevie taught me how to get noticed and make a statement, but I took it one step further after realising that when you commit to a hunger strike you're actually empowering yourself.

It's a mental thing because they want you to eat, but can't force feed you. The body is weak, but the mind is strong. Your mental wellbeing is strengthened because you've got resolve.

Of course you're hungry. But you don't even watch that because you're in jail and know that once it's over you'll start receiving three meals a day again and everything will return to normal. But for now, your body has to suffer. It's like fasting, there's a gain at the end of it.

The doctors and prison chaplain would come in regularly and beg me to eat, and when I refused the screws threatened to cosh me and feed me via injection. But I knew they were bluffing. Sometimes they'd spit on my food and say: 'Are you hungry now Murray?' But I'd just laugh and tell them I wasn't going to eat it anyway. It was that kind of mind game.

In the end, whenever they offered me food I would just dash it back and tell them: 'I don't want any food, I wanna die. I'm going to starve myself to death right here and it's going to be on your conscience.' Committing to a hunger strike is an awesome feeling when you're being imprisoned by the State, probably because it's the ultimate act of rebellion.

After a couple of days, the prison chaplain contacted my probation officer who revealed that my mother was completely unaware I'd been reclassified as an adult prisoner and had been looking for me in young offender institutions for the past three months. Apparently, the paperwork documenting my status as an adult prisoner had gone missing, and so I'd been floating, lost in the system.

My probation officer brought the matter to the attention of our local MP Royce Boyston who, speaking in the House of Commons, asked Home Secretary Leon Brittan: 'Is my honourable friend aware there is a teenage boy, Peter Murray, from my constituency who is currently on hunger strike in HMP Camp Hill on the Isle of Wight?

'And if he is aware, can my honourable friend please confirm that his conscience will be clear if Mr Murray is successful in his campaign to starve himself to death, having been removed three months ago from a young offenders' institution and unsuccessfully integrated into four separate adult prisons?'

Within 24 hours I was recategorised as a young offender and returned to HMP Wandsworth where I was kept in solitary confinement for a few days before being transferred back to HMP Chelmsford. I returned to Chelmsford in December 1984 and remember listening to the radio and hearing Stevie Wonder's latest album, the soundtrack for the film *Woman in Red*.

A few days after I arrived, my bredrin Lenny from Ladbroke Grove came to visit and brought me half an ounce of hashish packaged in marble-sized balls and wrapped in cling film. I swallowed the packages, shat them out a few hours later and flooded the wing with drugs for Christmas. Everyone was stoned and the place stunk of hash. The screws found out I was the supplier and placed me in solitary confinement. I calmly told them: 'Fuck you; I'm going on hunger strike. I'm going to die in this prison because I want to and I can.'

Later that day, the governor came to visit me in the segregation unit. He said: 'You're a nuisance and I've had enough of you. You are an adult prisoner and I do not want you in my establishment because you're a threat to good order and discipline.'

He tried contacting other youth custody facilities to organise a transfer, but none of them would take me. The following morning, two screws came to my cell carrying a box with all my personal belongings and civilian clothes. I assumed I was being transferred again, but when I reached the reception area I was shocked to discover that I was being sent home.

Even though I had time added to my sentence for bad behaviour and still had around two months to serve, the board of governors had apparently consented to the governor's request to release me early.

On the way out, the prison's Principal Officer gave me a travel warrant to get to Liverpool Street Station and £24, which was the equivalent of one weeks' Unemployment Benefit.

I'd been incarcerated for almost 20 months. During that time, I'd been prematurely thrown into the adult prison system, which I slighted and bucked before being sent back to a youth offender prison. The system deemed me too intellectually savvy and would no longer accept responsibility for containing me. I was released from HM Youth Custody Chelmsford on 28th December 1984 and vowed never to return to prison.

I was hopeful that 1985 would turn out to be a productive and transitional year, but had no idea of the direction I was heading or how long this journey of self-discovery would take. All I knew was that I needed to change my life, find a professional career and stop aspiring to be a criminal.

CHAPTER SIX
Young Offender to Yuppie Salesman
(1985 - 1987)

After being discharged I decided to utilise the English language and office skills I'd acquired, take Raymond's advice and get myself a nine to five job. I was 18 years old and London was full of angry, young men whose frustrations would boil over during the next 10 months leading to riots in Brixton, Peckham and Tottenham.

I could relate to them and understood why they were enraged, but I had another plan. I was trying to push the whole criminality thing behind me and look forward to employment. It was tough and I struggled to make the transition. For six months I scoured the Sales Appointments in the *London Evening Standard*, which had the largest recruitment section of all the newspapers and landed a few commission-only jobs.

I canvassed door-to-door for an east London-based home improvement company; obtained leads via the telephone for a double-glazing firm on the North Circular Road; and sold photographs for two companies in Central London. But each job lasted only a few weeks as I'd quickly become dissatisfied and move on.

Back then, my sister Elizabeth worked as a chambermaid at the InterContinental Hotel in Park Lane and got serious tips, which she shared with me because I had no money to get to work or job interviews. And that's why to this day, whenever I stay at a hotel I'll always leave £20-£30 for the women who clean the rooms. I've never forgotten my sister's generosity. Without those tips, I probably would've gone back to criminality.

Sometimes, the man dem would come look me up and I'd be broke while they would have money, girls, garms, cars and jewellery. They'd laugh, call me an 'idiot' and say things like: 'This road t'ing is the way, because what you earn in a month we earn that shit in a day.'

It's an irresistible temptation when your bredrins constantly flash that shit in your face, but I was resolute that I wasn't going back to jail. I'd been exposed to another side of life and had seen one or two black guys who were making it in sales. They were new, positive role models who I attempted to emulate.

One was a manager who used to bowl around in shiny suits and Bally shoes. I wouldn't have worn the suits, but he was successful, making a little money, and inspired me to get Jheri curls, which gave my road mandem much sense of amusement.

That summer, after a successful interview in Cavendish Square I secured a post as a financial consultant selling Irish Life Assurance products such as life insurance, pensions and saving plans for a company called Cash Safe. Unbeknown to me, I'd entered the market in a boom period. It turned out that 15 months earlier, around the same time I was on trial for robbing Jackie Green, the Chancellor of the Exchequer Nigel Lawson introduced a series of sweeping new reforms that drastically changed the life insurance industry.

As a result, by the time I joined Cash Safe a new type of American product, the Unit-Linked Insurance Plan, had taken the UK by storm. To gain a greater share of this expanding market many of the larger companies began recruiting salespeople and hiring agencies to push their products.Whereas the traditional insurance man had to go to each house every week to collect his £4 or £5 premium, our product targeted the younger generation who had access to new things such as current accounts, standing orders and direct debits.

All we had to say to them was: 'Look, just fill out a direct debit form and pay £20 per month,' and that was it. This was the exciting world I found myself in and I loved every minute of it.

Luckily, I'd landed amongst a group of real professionals. Cash Safe was an exemplary company that believed in exemplary management. The general idea was, 'Do as I do, and you'll succeed. I'm a success, copy me and you'll be a success too.'

In those days, sales managers were given company cars to carry out teams of four salespeople who'd knock on strangers' doors. It was like a numbers game. I knew that if I knocked on 100 doors I'd probably get to pitch four or five people, and get one or two sales from them. That's how

54

we made our money.

But before they took you on the road, you'd receive a week's training and a 550-word script that you had to learn, word for word, without any deviations. It had been 15 years since I'd started speech therapy lessons to help rectify my stutter, but it was learning Cash Safe's script that really helped bring it under control. I was given five days to learn the script. It was do or die. This wasn't a test of my grammar or academic ability because I had none. This was a test of my personal skillset and whether I could speak convincingly.

I blocked everyone out and just committed myself to learning the script. I learned how to use commas and full stops for emphasis, and remembered how I first fell in love with the English language two years earlier at HM Remand Centre Ashford.

I'd been banged up for 23-and-a-half hours a day and decided that I wanted a Certificate of Secondary Education in English. There were no classes, the screws would bring tutorials. I'd go through them and receive a 15-minute roundup session with the prison teacher at the end of each week.

That was the first time I'd studied sentences, apostrophes and how to start a new paragraph. I remember feeling electrified learning about nouns, pronouns and adjectives. For someone whose sum total of secondary education comprised just 10 weeks of schooling, mastering Cash Safe's script was a major milestone.

I remember going to council estates in Elephant and Castle, Stockwell, Brixton, Peckham and Tottenham pitching the script and speaking to many aspirational young people about saving, moving out and buying a home. Back then, selling was an art form that you studied and learned. Salesmen wrote books that you'd read every day like a bible and you went to sales meetings and training sessions to perfect your skill.

If I'm honest, I was never the best salesman. I was above mediocre, but I wasn't great. However, I was organised, consistent and very persistent, and therefore eventually became just as competent as the super sales people. They worked when they wanted to, whereas I worked all the time.

My work ethic has definitely been influenced by the years I spent on the road when I would put myself at risk more than the average man, and the years I spent in prison where everything was routine and systematic.

That's why I have no doubt that prison worked for me. It was doing 'short, sharp, shocks' in detention centres that taught me skills such as orderliness, organisation and punctuality. When I think about it, I'm happy that I was able to get something positive from my time in jail.

When I realised the level of one-upmanship I could score against the system by going on hunger strike, I felt like I'd done the 'prison thing' and it was time to try something else.

I've always said it's not the problem that's the problem, it's the way you manage the problem that becomes the problem. It's all a matter of perception and attitude. A knife can be used for good or bad. You can use it to take a life or cut an umbilical cord and create one. Jail is similar: you can use it to become a better or worse person. It's all about what you do with your time and what you want to get out of the situation.

My formal education took place in jail. I read many books, including the dictionary, in jail. I was still a badman bucking the system, but I also used the time to educate and inform myself. It's all about putting everything you've learned in jail in to practice, and not going back to the same old people if they're doing the same old thing. I had to leave them behind because I wanted more.

I only survived two months at Cash Safe, but established a good relationship with the lady who trained me, a fantastic sales manager named Cathy O'Connor.

Not long afterwards I met an Irish insurance broker, David Byrne, who I persuaded to become an agent for Irish Life Assurance so we could sell their products. He agreed and we set about replicating Cash Safe's business model. I was beginning to establish myself as an effective team builder and started recruiting and training salespeople until I had a team of four.

In return, Byrne gave me a managerial position, a brand new company car and a weekly salary. But he also brought in another sales manager who I didn't get on with, so after four months I left.

I linked up with Derek Brown, an entrepreneurial friend who, like me, was trying to reform his criminal behaviour. He invited me to a marketing event hosted by nutrition and weight loss experts Herbal Life and we agreed to start a business together.

We set up an office in his father's home and I put the Pitman's Office skills I'd learned in Feltham to good use by incorporating a company for the first time. I was hopeful the business would succeed, but for reasons associated solely with greed I relapsed into criminality and was arrested alongside my childhood friend Delroy MacIntosh for pickpocketing in Reading town centre.

In court, I was blasé and thought I'd receive either a fine or a community sentence as I'd pleaded guilty and developed an impressive resume since my last indiscretion. However, the magistrate thought otherwise and sent me to jail. I was flabbergasted. 'Stop worrying, it's only five months,' chuckled Delroy. But I couldn't believe it. 'You don't understand!' I screamed. 'I've got new links and connections. I've turned my life around.' But it didn't make any difference. I was sent to HMP Reading in Berkshire, and then HM Youth Custody Portland, Dorset.

I'd already been in an adult institution so treated Portland like kindergarten, and the screws didn't like it. One day, I took a crap in one of their hats. Everyone knew I did it, but the screws had no evidence. They took me down to solitary confinement anyway.

I threatened to go on a hunger strike, but my appeal came up and I was sent back to Reading Court. The appeal was denied and I returned to Portland where the governor agreed not to put me back in solitary confinement if I 'toed the line' for the remaining four weeks of my sentence.

I agreed, but remember sitting in my cell one night during Christmas 1985 feeling really paranoid. I'd been smoking hashish and thought I was going berserk. It felt like I was losing my sanity and I remember opening the window, grabbing onto the cell bars and gasping for air. I thought about how my brother and many of our friends had fought and lost battles with mental illness, and started praying: 'Oh God, please, please, please let me have my sanity in the morning.'

I was released a few days later but arrested again early in the New Year, this time for pickpocketing in the Sainsbury's behind Willesden High Road. I was released on bail and quickly secured a position as a consultant at Kors Associates, a financial services company based in Shoreditch. When I turned up for my first training session my new manager walked in and I was pleasantly surprised to find it was none other than Cathy O'Connor. She didn't have to teach me much because she was ripping off Cash Safe's business model, just as I had done 12 months earlier with David.

Cathy lived in Essex, but came from a traditional Irish family and you could tell she'd been sold a dream and wanted to run with it. She was in her early 20s, but could've been mistaken for someone five years older because she was so mature. I liked her. Cathy was an organised, results-driven professional, and I knew that if I replicated how she did things I too would become results-driven and successful.

Cathy said if I became her right-hand man and helped her build things up she would promote me, which is how I became a manager and met a fellow salesman who was to become a lifelong friend, Simon Leslie.

I was waiting to be allocated a team of salespeople and Simon, an 18-year-old blonde kid with a Simon Le Bon haircut, was one of the new recruits. One afternoon during his first week I asked where he'd gone for lunch because our team usually went out together.

The smirk on Simon's face turned into a smile as he slowly replied: 'I went to the bookies to put a bet on.' I was taken aback, but asked if the bet had come through, which he confirmed.

That completely amazed me as I'd only ever known old black men to go to the bookies. I immediately requested that Simon be placed in my team and he was, along with an Asian guy, Asif: a black girl Vanessa, from Peckham: and a young Zimbabwean guy named Thulie.

I later discovered that Simon was Jewish, very much into Wham and Duran Duran, and lived in Radlett, an affluent village in Hertfordshire. Every evening between 6pm and 9pm we'd all drive out to cold call in designated areas. One night after we'd finished, Simon was the last person in the car and I asked where he lived. He said: 'Let me show you.'

It felt like we were travelling forever, and although I was driving fast I could still make out that we were entering a posh suburb outside of Greater London. I don't remember much of what happened next, but I continued to speed, lost control of the car and almost killed us - an incident Simon frequently recalls.

We struck up a friendship and when he invited me to his parents' home I was surprised to discover Yazoo singer Alison Moyet was a neighbour and that his house had a swimming pool, sauna and a name (Green Trees) rather than a door number, which was probably my first real exposure to that type of lifestyle. It was a weird relationship, and although I never initially told Simon about my past we grew quite close and he has played a huge role in helping transform my criminal mindset.

Back then, he would say I had no style because I bought suits from high street retailer Principles for Men. So to shut him up we went shopping. In those days, it was all about buying things on the never-never and he really encouraged me to spend. For my suits, I upgraded to Cecil Gee where I had previously shopped during my days of villainy. I also purchased a stereo system. Slowly but surely, Simon introduced me to a new lifestyle etiquette.

He also encouraged me to put the knife in Cathy O'Connor, which is how I got her job as senior unit manager, and how he took over my position as unit manager. It was 1986, the era of yuppies, buppies and Filofaxes. We were shrewd and very ambitious.

Just before I was promoted, my case for shoplifting in Sainsbury's came up and I was scheduled to appear at Acton Crown Court. I revealed to my barrister that in the preceding months I'd turned my life around and become a credible, law-abiding, employed citizen who sometimes earned £2,000 to £3,000 a month.

He attempted to explain my career U-turn, but the judge wouldn't buy it: 'How does a criminal with so many convictions and no education get a job in the City with a financial services company working on investments and start earning that type of money in such a short space of time?' He said. 'I just don't believe it. I'm sending this man back to jail.'

After strong objections, the judge conceded and requested that my barrister get a reference from Kors Associates while he adjourned for lunch and I waited in the cells downstairs. I told the barrister that if he contacted my employers they would provide a glowing reference, but stressed that under no circumstances should he tell them about the court case or make them think I was looking for another job.

When we returned to court, the barrister said he'd spoken with my managers at Kors who confirmed that I had established myself as a hardworking and reputable financial services consultant.

The judge remained unconvinced: 'I don't believe you,' he said. 'But I'm giving you the benefit of the doubt. Judging by your record, you are never out of trouble for more than six months so I'm giving you a six-month deferred sentence. But if you reoffend within that time, Mr Murray, I don't need to tell you that just like in the Monopoly board game: you will not pass go, you will not collect any more £2,000 paycheques and you will go directly to jail.' I am truly grateful for the break that judge gave me because if I'd gone back to jail it would have been all over for me.

The owners of Kors, Ruben Stein and Keith O'Rourke, facilitated my takeover of Cathy's position and I learned a lot from them. Stein was Jewish, O'Rourke was Irish, and they were both in their mid-20s. They partied at West End clubs such as Stringfellows and Tramp, took cocaine, drove Porsches, owned mobile phones and had bought their own apartments. They were archetypal yuppies, products of the Thatcher era, and Simon and I looked up to them. Keith in particular really helped with my personal development. He gave me books such as *You Can If You Think You Can* by Norman Vincent Peale and *Think and Grow Rich* by Napoleon Hill, which I read but didn't really understand at the time.

Because I was 'the black guy', sometimes Ruben would ask me for weed and I would shot him half an ounce. It was cool. We were young. Out of a team of up to 40 people, most of us were aged between 18 and 27. No one in the company was over 30.

I thrived in that environment because it wasn't about your race, background, intelligence or postcode. All that mattered was how many sales you made. We had daily, weekly and monthly sales meetings, and they were just like scenes from the Leonardo DiCaprio film *Wolf of Wall Street*. The whole idea was to 'sell, sell, sell'.

I've still got photos of me collecting trophies for meeting targets and I remember the first time they offered me a company car. I blagged them and didn't reveal that I was yet to acquire a driving licence. After crashing the company's Renault 11 on the way to Simon's house, I got the car repaired but never told Ruben and Keith about the incident. Then, I was involved in another collision when a woman smashed into me. She admitted liability, but the insurance company asked for a copy of my licence.

I went home that evening and was fretting, fretting, fretting, thinking I would lose my job because I couldn't produce a licence. But my girlfriend at the time, Maria Lake, said: 'Nah. Just be honest. You're a high achiever who makes a lot of money for the company, tell them the truth.' So I did.

Ruben and Keith hit the roof and told me to get out of their office. But 10 minutes later they called me back and completely switched, because the truth is I was the company's top salesman. 'You know what,' said Ruben. 'We all make mistakes in life. Everyone deserves another chance, this is yours.'

That car was mangled, but they gave me a second chance. And from that moment on, I vowed that if someone makes an unintentional mistake, no matter how big, I will always forgive them.

I told them I planned to take my driving test soon, and they gave me a red Renault 5 GT Turbo. However, one morning after overdosing on Night Nurse medicine I suffered a momentary blackout while driving and crashed the car about 100 meters from my house. Ruben and Keith were upset, but I got my licence a few weeks later.

Despite these random misdemeanours, I continued to shatter sales targets and was doing pretty well for myself considering that just 12 months earlier I'd been in jail for theft. I flourished after discovering that with sales you could work your own hours and effectively determine your own salary, which for me was hugely motivating.

Eventually, I began earning just as much money as the mandem on road. But I had my liberty and they didn't. In the day, I would go to work and they would go on the streets. But at night, we'd still party in the same places. I no longer had to keep looking over my shoulder, but they did. I could speak a formal type of English and had started going out to restaurants, making friends with professionals and moving in multiple circles.

I spent my days surrounded by white guys who had nice girlfriends, wore Burberry clothes and were into smoking weed, taking cocaine and partying in West End clubs.

And that was the difference: I was in the mainstream, paying taxes, and had become a citizen, whereas they were still operating in the underworld. I could apply for mortgages and car loans, but they couldn't. They paid for everything in cash, but I used a credit card.

My culture began to expand further than sticksman and Rasta philosophies and I found myself in the midst of a merger between the black and white cultures, which took place mostly through capitalism, soul music, fashion and recreational drugs.

It's like the story of the hare and the tortoise, because the people who used to laugh at me when I first tried to go straight are the same ones who, years later, would come and ask for help to complete an application form.

The funny thing is, all the road men who were flossing and at the top of their game are dead, in jail, on drugs or living some type of parasitic existence. I see them at funerals and think to myself, *'Wow, I used to look up to you as a role model.'* Or, *'Did we really used to 'par?'* It's a funny old world.

In April 1987, a few weeks before Tottenham rioter Winston Silcott was falsely imprisoned for the murder of PC Keith Blakelock and Islamic terrorists kidnapped the Archbishop of Canterbury's special envoy, Terry Waite, the *Northwest London Press* newspaper ran a double-page story titled: *Harlesden-Born Murray Making a Mint*, following my lavish 21st birthday dinner party at a new themed restaurant, the Video Café, next door to the London Palladium.

Earlier that year, I had bought my first home, a one-bedroom flat in Kensal Rise, purchased a BMW 525i, become an American Express cardholder and started building a small portfolio of stock market shares. At last, things were looking up and it appeared as though I'd finally turned my life around.

CHAPTER SEVEN
Champion of Champions
(1987 - 1989)

A few months after my 21st birthday, Simon and I were headhunted by sales manager extraordinaire Surjit Shah, a 25-year-old Sikh from Winchester who became one of my greatest mentors.

Surjit drove a bronze Mercedes Sports 500SL, flashed a gold American Express (Amex) card, rolled with an ex-bank manager named Joe who was at least twice his age and used all three of these props to maximum effect. He was of average build, but walked like a penguin and spoke with a cheeky smile as if he was up to no good. I attended his wedding in Southall, and remember he had two ceremonies: a conventional marriage, followed by a traditional Sikh wedding.

Surjit had homes in Winchester and Basingstoke, and drove to London every day. In the industry he was regarded as a flashy wide boy. But I thought he was pretty classy. Throughout the summer of 1987, Surjit wined and dined Simon and I in fancy restaurants and explained how we could earn a lot more by cutting out the broker and working directly for a life assurance company.

He told us how much he was earning, acted as a referee to help upgrade my Amex from regular to a gold card and promised me a managerial position if I brought my team of salespeople over to his company.

This obviously excited me. I persuaded Simon to come on board and he convinced one of his work colleagues, Bernie Stein. Together, we amassed a team from Kors Associates and went to join Surjit. Ruben and Keith, the bosses at Kors, were livid. It was like a Premiership football team losing half of its squad.

We joined Surjit's Wimbledon-based company Gresham Life Assurance, but the project flopped after a couple of months so me, Simon and Surjit secured positions selling life assurance products for Citibank Financial Services in Eastcote, Middlesex.

I took 10 new recruits with me and they did some really good business. Surjit, who was a regional branch manager, kept his promise and at the age of 21 I became the youngest assistant branch manager in the history of what was then the world's largest bank.

I was on top of the world; living large and thanks to my new job had a net worth fast approaching £250,000 in properties, shares and other financial products. Simon, however, was less interested in management and found a profitable niche supplying Citibank's consultants with mortgages for their clients.

I partied regularly during this period and one of my favourite West End spots was Legends nightclub on Old Burlington Street. There, I became friends with another insurance salesman who was four or five years older than me; a well-to-do, and probably blue-blooded, cokehead.

One night in October 1987, as the unsigned pop group The Pasadenas performed on stage, he introduced me to a girl named Lucy Sanders. They were around the same age and of similar ilk, but for some reason Lucy and I just took to each other.

All three of us went into the toilets and snorted a stupid amount of cocaine and my friend went off with a girl he'd met, leaving Lucy and I alone. Apparently, they worked together but she was concerned that his drug habit had gotten out of control and was affecting their profits. I told Lucy that if things got worse she could come and work with me. We drank several bottles of champagne, and she agreed to come back to my place.

We jumped into my BMW, and as I flew past Edgware Road underground station I remember excitedly thinking that I'd never shagged a posh totty before and was just minutes away from changing that. I was drunk as a coot and speeding down the bottom of a hill on Willesden Lane when I lost control of the vehicle and crashed into another car. Lucy was taken to hospital in an ambulance and I wroteoff my 5 Series, but thankfully no one was injured.

The police charged me with driving under the influence, but when I visited my local lawyer he told me I was no longer eligible for Legal Aid and recommended an expensive specialist barrister who I hired.

When the case was heard at Brent Magistrates' Court, my barrister's performance was dazzling. He managed to persuade the magistrates that I wasn't wholly responsible for the crash, even though a breathalyser test found me to be two times over the limit.

'Peter Murray is clearly a product of Thatcherism,' he told the court. 'And while he may be guilty of an overindulgence of exuberance following a long and stressful day at work, should we really punish him for that?

'Taking into account his background and professional track record, surely no reasonably minded person could determine that responsibility for this accident rests solely on his shoulders?

'This young man is not a petty thief or a criminal. He's a hardworking salesman who got taken in and consumed by his environment; a situation any one of us could quite easily find ourselves in.

'If anyone's to blame, it's [Prime Minister] Margaret Thatcher and [Conservative MP] Norman Tebbit who told Mr Murray to sort himself out, get on his bike and get a job. Because that's exactly what he did.'

I was facing a two-year driving ban, but thanks to my barrister's sensational performance only received a hefty fine and the minimum sentence, a 12-month driving ban. That's when I learned that once you have money you can buy justice. And just like any other tradable commodity, the quality of that justice is directly related to the amount you can afford to pay.

About a week after my car accident, the Great Storm of 1987 tore through London and three days later, on 19th October, the stock market crash known as 'Black Monday' wiped out my portfolio of shares and pushed me to the brink of bankruptcy.

I had almost £70,000 of debt, which was a lot of dough in those days. But I still had my flat, which was worth £60,000, a couple of grand overdraft in the bank, and a few credit cards such as Amex and Diners. Even though my debts were huge, I wasn't worried because I knew that I'd be able to work them off through Citibank.

All I had to do was recruit more people, and that was my specialty. Surjit had taught me how to go into the offices of rival companies, recruit their best staff and bring them to our team. He told me that as soon as I brought the new recruits over I should gain the group's loyalty, and then cut off their head by sacking the manager. I bought into Surjit's philosophy 100%. But then, that's exactly what he did to me.

In a sales meeting just before Christmas he accused me of disrespecting him and fired me. I could've kicked myself because even though he'd always taught me to kill off the chiefs and keep the Indians, I hadn't seen it coming. I was pissed, but had to acknowledge that Surjit was a super tactician who played the game well. He had an enormous impact on my career and I enjoyed working with him because I learned so much.

One of the first things he did after we met was take me and Simon away to a country retreat for the weekend. There, he stripped us of everything we knew about insurance sales and taught us everything we needed to know about recruitment sales, which fascinated me because all my training up to that point had been product based. Surjit taught me many things I still use today. He was a numbers man who believed the more salespeople you have, the more products you're going to sell.

'Don't sell products, sell people,' he would say. 'I can't tell you anything about these products. Don't ask me, I'm not interested in what they can or cannot do; I recruit people to do that. My job is simply to recruit.'

On another occasion, he explained: 'Recruitment is legalised prostitution. As managers, we're legalised pimps and your salespeople are your prostitutes - and they should be treated as such.

'In life Peter, you're either a pimp or a prostitute. If you work for people, you're an employee, and employees are prostitutes. Pimps are employers. If you want to be a pimp, be an employer.'

But most importantly, Surjit sent me on reconnaissance missions so I could learn how to recruit without a budget. We'd ring up brokers who had placed job vacancies in the *London Evening Standard* newspaper and pretend to be salespeople with no experience of the insurance market.

They'd call us in for an interview, which I'd attend and use as an opportunity to gather information. I'd quiz them about their best performers, look out for their production board (usually placed somewhere prominent in the office) and memorise the names of their top salespeople.

Then, I'd wait a couple of days to phone the company and ask to speak with either their sales manager or one of the top performers. I'd say something like: 'I've heard lots of great stuff about you. Come and meet me for coffee and I'll show you how to double your income doing exactly what you're doing now.'

In those days it was all about building teams. But traditionally that meant advertising, screening and training new recruits, and having to wait two or three months to get them up and running. But if you poach the competition's best people, who already have product knowledge and sales experience, they can be up, running and selling your product within a week without you having to spend a penny. That's what we did, and I acquired a reputation for going into insurance companies and ripping away their best salespeople. Surjit did that where he lived in the south of England, but that shit was unheard of in London. So I got known in the industry for being 'that guy'.

He also taught me that when someone's coming to you for a job, hold the first interview on neutral territory. But keep the second interview in your office. When the salesperson is sitting down in front of you, phone their manager and say: 'Hi, I'm calling for a reference. Can you tell us about this person?' Or you might even say: 'Hey, I have your boy in my office looking for a job.' That was Surjit.

When he fired me from Citibank I must've drank half a bottle of vodka, and remember being flat out in my yard. My girlfriend and family all thought I was going to commit suicide because my world had collapsed.

My mum came over and kept asking: 'Ow much 'im drink? Ow much 'im smoke?' She was right to be concerned. I was crying and in a really bad way. I phoned Surjit saying: 'Why have you done this? You knew I was wounded after Black Monday.'

His response was calm, firm and unforgettable: 'You've had too much to drink. I understand your distress, but c'mon Peter you know the game. I taught you, weren't you listening? It's your turn now. You're fired.' And I had to take it.

Irrespective of how our relationship ended, I still rate Surjit, and funnily enough over the next year both he and the Kors directors offered me new jobs, which I turned down.

The fallout from the previous year's setbacks was extensive. But in December 1987 I was headhunted by 26-year-old insurance salesman and entrepreneur Larry Moore. He called one day and said: 'Listen Peter, I'm not gonna bullshit you. I'm a friend of one of the owners at Kors [Keith] and he told me about your story. I've got an opportunity. At least let's meet up and hear me out.'

Larry was a skinny, East End wide boy who wore big-rimmed glasses and was the manager at the Chingford branch of Cannon Lincoln Assurance, a UK-based insurance company owned by the American corporation Lincoln National. He had patches of hair on either side of his head, but was completely bald through the middle. He lived beyond his means, but desperately wanted to be known as the man with the cash.

Larry was cool though, and one of the first people I knew to own a BMW convertible. He reminded me of the cockney boys I'd known in jail and we immediately struck up a good working relationship. I met his area manager Ken, and visited their offices where I observed that Cannon employed mainly older men in their 30s and 40s. I was still only 21 years old, so Larry was clearly taking a risk.

I agreed to work with him, but was unhappy about the three-hour commute between Harlesden and Chingford that I endured each day. I had no choice though. The commissions and bonuses at Cannon were too attractive to overlook and NatWest bank's investment arm, County NatWest, and several credit card companies were hounding me for money.

I suffered racist abuse from an instructor during Cannon Lincoln's week-long residential training course, but still passed top of the class. I went back to the Chingford branch and sold a lot of good business. Larry was pleased, but hungry for more money.

Throughout the autumn of 1988 I began to realise that even though my sales were stupendous, the branch was failing and Larry was relying on me to prop up his operation. A couple of months later, he admitted: 'Peter, I'm gonna leave Cannon Lincoln. I want my own agency.'

***

In December, Simon and I travelled to Florida on the first of many holidays and bought a pair of adjacent condos in Breakers, Fort Lauderdale. I was 22 at the time and looking for new real estate opportunities. I'd just made a tidy profit trading up my one-bedroom apartment in Kensal Rise to a two-bedroom flat in the neighbouring but more upmarket area of Cricklewood.

I really liked the guy who sold us the condos and he convinced me to follow him to Miami for a seminar being held by Tom Hopkins, a man he described as 'the godfather of real estate sales'.

Simon was more interested in hanging out on the beach, so I drove to Miami with this guy, paid an $89 entrance fee and sat down for the presentation. I was absolutely hooked. I bought Hopkins' book, *How to Master the Art of Selling*, and the audio version on 12 cassette tapes, which I listened to regularly in the car and at home to vibes myself up and get indoctrinated.

When I returned to London and started implementing some of Hopkins' techniques, sales went through the roof. Nevertheless, Larry resigned a few weeks later and set up a meeting with executives from one of Britain's biggest insurance companies, Guardian Royal Exchange Assurance (GRE). He was looking for funding to set up his own brokering agency, the Moore Group, which would earn revenues by sending business exclusively to GRE.

Larry persuaded me to join him and write and present a proposal detailing how I could quickly develop a first-class sales team at a cost of £20,000. When I tried to explain that we didn't need £1 let alone £20,000 to start the business, he insisted and promised to 'sort me out' if the deal went through.

The GRE meeting took place at the historic Royal Exchange building in the City, and proved to be somewhat of an informal introduction to freemasonry. Upon arrival, we were shown into a room where huge chandeliers hung from a high ceiling and the walls were adorned with pictures of eminent bankers, insurers and industrialists. This was the core of the British Establishment.

Waiters with white gloves invited me, Larry and four GRE executives to eat lunch, and we were ushered towards a massive oak dining table that could've easily seated 20 people.

I eased myself into a comfortable leather Chesterfield chair, and observed the grandeur. Even the crockery was enormous. We ate steak, and I learned that red wine was to be drunk with red meat and white wine is for fish and white meat. After lunch, I delivered my presentation and remember at the end of the meeting one of the executives did something funny with his fingers when we shook hands.

I didn't understand and thought to myself, *'Hang on a minute, this guy's missing part of his finger.'* I just didn't get it, until later when I told Larry who laughed and started talking about freemasonry. He told me I wasn't ready for that yet and I had no choice but to agree.

GRE gave Larry £60,000, and in January 1989 he set up a beautiful office at 5 Hackney Road, close to the junction of Shoreditch High Street, Old Street, and Kingsland Road in east London.

I was appointed chief operations manager, paid a weekly retainer of £500, and given an expense account to cover the cost of hiring a chauffeur-driven Rolls-Royce strictly for the purposes of recruiting (as I was still banned from driving). I developed a strategy for the business and began to find salespeople.

By combining the discipline I had learned in detention centres with the Cash Safe script and everything that Surjit Shah, Keith O'Rourke and Cathy O'Conner had taught me, I was able to create an entirely unique sales strategy.

I targeted young, mostly black guys and blew their minds by taking them out to eat, pitching them, flashing the gold Amex and offering them a lift in the Roller. We opened for business with 12 salespeople in February 1989, and hit the ground running.

Every morning at 9am the main doors closed and any member of the team who wasn't suited, booted, on the sales floor and ready for the daily meeting was sent home. After the meeting, which lasted around 45 minutes, everyone went back to their stations and started hitting the phones. Salespeople had to make at least 60 calls a day and weren't allowed to sit down or visit the restroom until 1pm. They were expected to book at least four appointments a day, which they tried to convert into sales by going out on the road after lunch.

I calculated that out of four appointments, one would blow out; the salesperson would pitch and miss two; and close at least one sale. That was the formula. Anyone who'd failed to secure four appointments by lunchtime had to stay in the office and start booking for the following day. It was a tough, militaristic and regimented operation. But it worked well.

The cash rolled in and Larry bought a house in Buckhurst Hill, Essex, and a Z1 - the first model in BMW's line of two-seat convertible roadsters. Similarly, after my driving ban was lifted I hired a cherry red Toyota MR2 at a cost of £400 per-week and brought Simon and his mortgage business on board to further strengthen the project.

Around the same time, Simon hired a plump but attractive American personal assistant who dreamt of becoming a singer and would leave work most nights to record at various music studios across London. Lo and behold, about five years later he called and told me to turn the TV onto a music show on Channel 4. When I did, he asked if I recognised anyone on the screen. It was his PA, Deborah Cox, who'd lost weight and hit US charts with the r&b classic *Sentimental*.

To celebrate my newfound success, in April 1989 I held an extravagant 23rd birthday dinner for 75 guests. I decided to host the event at Bridge Park Complex on the Stonebridge estate in Harlesden. I'd held my 21st party at a top West End venue, so this time I wanted to do a large-scale event in the ends.

Bridge Park Complex was the perfect location because it had been established a few years earlier by a group of reformed gangsters, headed by a man named Leonard Johnson and Raymond's brother Lawrence. The consortium secured funding from the government, local council and Prince's Trust to renovate a disused bus depot into the first community complex of its kind - a multimillion-pound centre offering education services, business units, social spaces and sports facilities.

My party comprised a three-course meal with bottles of champagne and wine on each of the tables, which were set out in the shape of a horseshoe. All of my professional friends were seated on one side and my hood friends were on the other. At the head table was me, Simon, my cousins, Mark Richards and Laurel 'Pepsi' Gregg, then Dennis White and his partner Samantha and some other close friends.

We had a sound system playing and after we'd finished dining all the tables were taken away and everyone partied until the early hours of the morning. Nobody did parties like that back then. It was a beautiful occasion, like a wedding.

Over the next few months the number of employees under my responsibility swelled to around 30 support and sales staff, who I recruited, trained and managed. I also drafted in my cousin Mark, who took on board everything I taught him, ran with it and started making proper money as Moore Group's top salesman.

After the Surjit situation I was understandably protective of my sales team, which made Larry unhappy. He wanted to penetrate them, but because the majority were black he knew they'd be loyal to me. We'd made a lot of money together, but Larry was fearful it could all end at any time because he had too little control over the business. Eventually, he and I fell out after I disrespected him in front of everyone.

We had an argument and I squared up to him, started pushing up my chest and said: 'What do you tek dis t'ing for? Have you forgotten that I'm the one putting money into your pocket?' He laughed and fired me on the spot.

After realising that Larry wasn't going to re-employ me, in December 1989 I returned to Florida to recuperate with another of Raymond's brothers, David, who I left in my condo for a couple of days while I travelled to Scottsdale in Arizona where Tom Hopkins was hosting a sales conference in his hometown.

I'd introduced myself to Hopkins in Miami and he was surprised to see me again. He even spoke to his audience about how this young salesman had come all the way from London to attend his conference.

I bought more of Hopkins' material, returned to London and decided to mimic his business by setting up my own sales training company, Champion Results. But whereas Hopkins hosted seminars and conferences in massive auditoriums, I would target companies with bespoke training courses.

I looked to exploit all the knowledge and experience I'd gained working in sales and financial services over the previous five years, and started binge-reading personal development and self-improvement books to further enhance my skills.

I read *How to Win Friends and Influence People* by Dale Carnegie, *Unlimited Power* by Anthony Robbins (who was the hot new author on the scene) and anything I could get my hands on by W. Clement Stone. However, the book that resonated most was *Think and Grow Rich* by Napoleon Hill, the paperback Kors director Keith had given me three years earlier.

In *Think and Grow Rich*, Hill claims that willpower is the primary factor that determines whether a person achieves their goals and sexual energy can be conserved, controlled and channelled to help people increase creativity and production levels.

He called this process 'sex transmutation' and believed that sexual desire is the most potent form of human aspiration and '...when driven by this desire, men develop keenness of imagination, courage, willpower, persistence, and creative ability unknown to them at other times'.

I'm a living example of how Hill's theory can be successful if diligently applied, because I read his book during a 10-month period of celibacy and became a millionaire in less than 18 months, simply by channelling my sexual energy into building my business. Both men and women kill, steal and do all sorts of things for sex because it truly is an awesome energy.

As a teenager, I remember my mother warning me to be careful who I slept with because bad energy and evil spirits can manifest in a woman and attach themselves to her partner when they have sex. But I was too young to understand what she meant.

Hill's book also taught me that if you have a goal you want to achieve, you should write it down on a piece of paper, look at that piece of paper every day, visualise, memorise, chant over and put all your energies into that goal and try your best to make it happen. And that's exactly what I did.

I devoured self-help books, became imbibed, and started embellishing their ideologies and combining them with my own expertise to develop a new philosophy for my training programme, which was very exclusive and required a lot of research.

First, I would study the company, pretend to be a consumer, do some ghost shopping and summarise my experience in a detailed report, which was sent to the company's chairman. Then, I'd design a course focusing on the company's specific needs and get them to send 10 of their best salespeople for me to train.

I got the idea after watching an interview with Derek Hunt, the chairman of British furniture retailer MFI on BBC Two's finance and business show *The Money Programme*.

While Britain had enjoyed a period of enormous prosperity in the mid-'80s, by the end of the decade the economy was in decline and as a result Hunt was complaining that sales were stagnant.

I felt his pain and decided to call and pitch him first thing Monday morning. I got through to his office and they told me to speak with his sales director. I called the sales director and told him: 'Derek said I should set up a meeting with you.' He agreed and a few days later I drove to MFI's head office near Staples Corner in northwest London.

But when the sales director and his colleagues came downstairs and saw me waiting in reception, their sense of shock was palpable. They were absolutely gobsmacked to discover a 23-year-old black guy with a Mohican hairstyle and permed, slicked-back ponytail. I ignored their surprise, focused on the task at hand and pitched.

I didn't get the contract, but going through that process gave me a huge confidence boost. I subsequently became the doyen of sales training and started making serious money travelling all over the country selling my courses.

Over the next 12 months I taught salespeople from BT (the UK's largest telecommunications provider) how to sell £60,000 products; trained estate agents from the UK's largest building society, Halifax; and secured contracts to train staff at DIY chain Texas Homecare and shoe retailer Faith.

I tried to persuade some of the salespeople at the Moore Group to come and join me, but they were reluctant as Larry had increased their salaries and given them bonuses. Still, two guys, Kim 'the Viking' Olsen and Leroy Morgan, did slip away.

Kim was a short, stubby Norwegian who wasn't the best salesman but wanted to be my right-hand man. He was in his early 20s, academic, proactive and generally quite adorable. He liked doing presentations and really enjoyed pitching at the boardroom level.

Leroy, who became a lifelong friend, was a black guy from Harlesden. He was three years younger than me and we'd both attended John Keble Primary School. However, when Leroy started getting into trouble, his parents sent him away to a private school in Somerset.

He scored good grades and spoke well, but was completely removed from black culture and found it difficult to fit in when he returned to London. I recruited him to the Moore Group when he was 17 years old and noticed how he loved that I was from Harlesden and had made something of myself.

I remember watching Leroy interact with the other black guys on the sales floor and thinking how the situation was something of a homecoming for him because he was meeting peers from the ends who were doing something positive: earning money, but weren't involved in criminality.

I was making up to £10,000 a month with Champion Results, and over an 18-month period bought and upgraded three Toyota sports cars including a brand new second-generation Toyota MR2 and a brand new, navy blue, fifth-generation Toyota Celica.

It was all over the hood that I was bathing in money. So whereas parents had previously told their children to stay away from me, now those same people and others from my local community were suddenly much friendlier.

CHAPTER EIGHT
Fatherhood, Culture and Pride
(1990 - 1991)

Sometime in the early part of 1990, I went on a date with Jennifer Vandy who had a child with my friend Winston Brown's brother, Errol. Our date was platonic and I had no idea she was also a good friend of Georgina Simmonds - the girl I'd slept with once back in 1979, when I was a wild and delinquent juvenile.

Jennifer and I only went out a couple of times, but apparently every time we did she would tell Georgina about the fantastic time we had. I think the gossip must have riled something inside of the girl I'd made love to when we were both 13, and who was now my sister Edith's hairdresser (unbeknown to me), because a few days after my 24th birthday in April 1990, Georgina posed a question that would change our lives forever.

On a warm Thursday afternoon, as she gently massaged shampoo into Edith's hair Georgina asked very matter of factly: 'Did you know your brother is my daughter's father?'

I was at the Champion Results office in Kilburn when I received the call, and remember jumping into my Toyota Celica and racing to the salon in Willesden where Georgina worked. I demanded to see my daughter. Georgina agreed and we arranged to meet later that night at Pizza Hut on Kilburn High Road. My mother and sisters were sceptical and suggested I abandon the meeting.

I went anyway and that was the first time I met Chineka Eleanor Simmonds. I was introduced as a family friend; eased myself into a chair opposite mother and daughter and attempted to engage in small talk.

But as soon as Chineka opened her mouth to say: 'Hello,' I had to excuse myself and rush to the restroom downstairs. I burst into tears and was crying uncontrollably. The instant I heard her speak I knew Chineka was my blood. It was a life-changing moment, but I managed to compose myself before returning to the table, ordering some pizzas and continuing the conversation as if nothing had happened.

After that day, Georgina allowed me to take Chineka out on my own. So I took her and my nephew to places like the wax museum Madam Tussauds. Although Edith remained enthusiastic, the rest of my family encouraged me to get a blood test to prove that Chineka was mine.

Nevertheless, I bought her loads of toys and we were getting on fine until one day she asked her mum: 'Why does this man keep taking me out, buying me stuff and introducing me to his family?' Apparently, Georgina replied flippantly: 'Well, he is your father,' which naturally came as a shock to nine-year-old Chineka who'd been calling another man 'dad' all of her life. I initially had no knowledge of this conversation, so was surprised when Chineka refused to see me for several weeks.

I begged her mother to arrange another meeting and invited Georgina to the three-bedroom mews house I'd just bought in Hampstead to show her how I had refurbished one of the bedrooms for our daughter.

But Georgina, who'd been drinking heavily, got upset and posed another momentous question: 'What about me? You've ruined my life. I had dreams. I wanted to be a photographer. Instead, I ended up being a 14-year-old gymslip mum, living with my baby in a children's home.

'Nine years later, you want to waltz in and take care of Chineka and I don't have a problem with that, but what about me because we're a package?' I thought long and hard about what she said, but already had a partner and wasn't about to sabotage my new relationship. I did, however, persuade her to get Chineka back on board and the three of us started going out together, which I wasn't really comfortable with but nevertheless enjoyed because I was getting closer to my daughter.

My partner at the time, Faye Williamson, was a few years older than me, of Jamaican parentage, and lived around the corner from my flat in Cricklewood. Faye wasn't glamorously attractive, but she was sophisticated, stylish and headstrong and I really liked her.

She worked as a marketing executive for the Holiday Inn hotel chain, spoke fluent Italian, dressed in Aquascutum and was the type of woman who made her man feel like he could take on the world and win. It was through her that I was able to claim on my marketing paraphernalia that

Champion Results had 21 training centres across the UK, whereas in reality they were the conference rooms I had access to at various Holiday Inn hotels.

Faye wasn't from the hood and didn't know anything about that lifestyle. She was Eurocentric and enjoyed taking short breaks at stately homes and castles where we'd act like king and queen for the weekend.

The late '80s and early '90s was an era of real estate acquisition, and by this time I'd already bought and sold my first property for £64,000, and put the £14,000 profit towards an £80,000 two-bedroom flat in Cricklewood.

Champion Results was making money hand over fist, so in 1990 I decided to take advantage of my good fortune, work closer with Simon (who was now a mortgage broker and estate agent) and buy more properties. He introduced me to a network of young Jewish guys and that's when I started to realise that business is very much about who you know and are connected to.

We already owned the adjacent condos in Florida. He later hooked me up with a mortgage for the flat in Cricklewood and helped my mother buy the family home in Harlesden.

With my mortgages, Simon's guidance and links to developer Franklin Steinberg, over two years I was able to build a portfolio of properties worth more than £1million, including the mews house in Hampstead, two three-bedroom apartments in Swiss Cottage and a five-bedroom detached house in Oxhey, Hertfordshire.

Mortgage fraud was rampant at the time and although I didn't indulge everybody was doing it, including some older ex-gangsters I knew who'd elevated themselves out of the streets. To get a mortgage in those days all you had to do was prove your income. So people would use a mailing address to set up a fake company and start applying for 100% mortgages. On receipt of the application, the lender wrote to the fake company requesting confirmation of income and then someone would respond on letter-headed paper with the required information. And that was it. Once the loan was obtained, the buyer would purchase a property, start paying the mortgage and rent out the house.

Although the modern 'buy-to-let' mortgage didn't exist yet, competition was fierce so lenders rarely shared information with each other. As a result, it was possible for one person to obtain multiple mortgages, which made it easy to acquire several properties in a short space of time. That's what the guys from my ends were doing. Simon and I got mortgages for them, but we had to withdraw the service after a while because sometimes they'd stop paying, which was problematic as the lenders were people

Simon had personal relationships with.

During this period, I helped to lift a lot of people in my area out of council housing and into homeownership. Very few would've been able to obtain a mortgage ordinarily, and to this day some will remind me how I helped them to purchase their first home. In August 1990, for Chineka's 10th birthday I arranged for me and her to go to Disney World, Florida, along with a friend, his partner and their two sons. I rented a huge villa with a private swimming pool in Kissimmee, a small city close to the theme park.

On the tram to Disney World, several passengers complained of losing their purses and wallets and I knew that my friend and his missus, being kleptomaniacs, were responsible. I was horrified and feared their petty pilfering would get us all nicked and banged up in a Florida jail. Thankfully, that didn't happen and in the end we enjoyed a wonderful, fun-filled holiday.

When I returned to London I began feeling torn, as I was in a serious relationship with Faye but had started sleeping with Georgina who kept asking if we were going to try and be a family.

Faye was understandably concerned about my relationship with Georgina and my mother and sisters were all telling me to stay out of Chineka's life. I decided to silence them once and for all by doing a DNA paternity test.

Today they cost less than £100, but in 1990 when the technique was still new I paid £4,000 to confirm what I'd already known instinctively - that I was Chineka's father.

Around the same time, Faye came up with a brilliant idea to create a magazine, *The Connoisseur Guide*, which would include advertiser-friendly content, a four-page service directory and be distributed to four-and five-star hotels across London. I agreed to fund the project and when Faye ran into problems with sales I formed a publishing company, Champion Media Services, and seconded Leroy and Kim to work alongside her.

I was concerned that my love affair with Georgina was affecting my relationship with Faye, and decided to take another holiday to clear my head. I invited my good friend Dennis to come and stay at my apartment in Fort Lauderdale over the Christmas period.

He agreed, but after a few days we grew bored so I hired a white, 5.0 litre convertible Ford Mustang, and drove 30 miles south to Miami. As soon as we arrived we headed straight for Luke's (the nightclub owned by 2 Live Crew rapper Luke Campbell) where we lived the highlife and partied all night.

When the girls started flocking and asking questions I accentuated my English accent and boasted that we were from London and I was a sales trainer. That didn't seem to grab their attention, so I told them I was publishing a magazine that would be distributed in four-and five-star hotels.

None of the girls were the least bit enthused. Then, one said: 'So you don't do anything for black people?' Another asked: 'What are you doing for your own community? Who do you employ?'

A third girl started grilling me about my Mohican hairstyle and eventually they all drifted off leaving me utterly flummoxed. I didn't get it. I was young, black and successful. How and why was this happening?

It burned me and I started thinking, 'Wow, I must be really out of kilter.' Dennis said I'd probably be more successful in another environment and suggested that we fly to the Caribbean. 'Come on man, let's go to Jamaica,' he said. 'I know you'll have a good time and it's only a 45-minute flight from here.' I thought about it, agreed and on Boxing Day 1990 flew to the land of my parents' birth.

We landed in Montego Bay, drove for two hours along the picturesque north coast and booked into a hotel called the Dibby Dibby in Ocho Rios. Something about the beauty and vibes of Jamaica really touched me, especially when I went back to Mo Bay a few days later and spent a day at the beach.

That day was a real eye-opener because all I could see was black people, which is the opposite of what I was used to in urban areas such as London and Florida where people of Caribbean and African descent make up between 13% and 17% of the population respectively. It was even less back then.

At first, I felt a little overwhelmed and out of place. But when I looked at all the black skin, the sun, swimsuits and people having fun, it began to dawn on me that Jamaica was paradise.

I phoned my mum and she suggested that I look for my eldest brother William who lived in the district of Gayle, 20 miles southeast of Ocho Rios. A few days later, we charted a taxi and stopped in Gayle on our way to the capital, Kingston. I asked around for my brother, and at first people were reluctant to talk. Eventually someone took me to his house. It was a small, board shack where I met William's wife who was sick in bed, his two sons (who were around my age) and their three younger sisters.

His wife said my brother had left the family home and relocated to Spanish Town a long time ago. I stayed for a while, took photos, gave them some money and promised to keep in contact. But never did.

I fell deeper in love with Jamaica when we returned to Ocho Rios and really began to consider that paradise could be my home. There were normal, happy, black people everywhere. After climbing Dunn's River Falls I felt elated and inspired, but kept thinking back to the girls in Luke's nightclub and the question they'd asked: 'What are you doing for your people, the black community?'

I remembered that when I mentioned publishing one of the girls assumed I was a British version of John Johnson, the founder of African American culture magazine *Ebony*.

But when I explained further, she was genuinely horrified by the idea that I would create a publication that wasn't for black people. When I reached the beach at the bottom of the falls, I experienced something of an epiphany and thought to myself, '*P, you've gotta do a magazine for black people.*'

A fisherman took me out sailing, and as I smoked marijuana and thought more deeply about the magazine I concluded the team working on *The Connoisseur Guide* could also be used to develop a publication targeting black people in Britain. As the sun set and the ocean waves caressed the boat, I started reassessing the feasibility of the guide. Three months earlier, Iraq's President Saddam Hussein had invaded Kuwait and the US were pushing for a coalition of allies to retaliate with military action.

I decided to abandon *The Connoisseur Guide* after theorising that America would probably strike back early in the New Year and the inevitable war would cause hotel occupancy to fall, thus making it harder to attract advertising revenue.

By the time the boat returned to the beach I'd already come up with a name for the new magazine, *Pride*. I'd found my identity in Jamaica and that's where the name came from. It was just about me being proud of who I am. I'd never really had any problems in terms of understanding and knowing who I was as a person, but the blackness only came in Jamaica. Before that, colour was never an issue.

If you'd asked me to describe myself, I would've said: 'A young, up-and-coming business or salesman.' And if I was still on the road, I would've said 'gangster' or 'villain'. But never: 'I'm a black man.' I don't think I was in denial. I'd just become detached from my blackness, and it took a trip to Jamaica for me to recognise that.

Like many young British-born blacks, I was very conscious in the 1970s but my consciousness started to recede in 1978 after I was placed in care and became enveloped by the young offender institutions.

As a minority in care, especially when you're very young, you end up adopting the culture of the majority or at least taking on their way of life. You don't give up yours, you just learn another way.

I lived one type of life when I was at home and another when I was in care and I didn't think anything of it because that's what I was introduced to from a very early age. It's important to understand that although I was poor, black and from Harlesden, I grew up in a mainstream way.

I remember in boarding school where it was all about tea and biscuits, cutting toast into four equally sized pieces and not putting butter and marmalade on the same slice of bread. I was exposed to the English way of life, so naturally picked up all sorts of etiquettes.

In the early 1980s when I went into criminal institutions, I was with white guys who were the majority. And when I turned my life around I found myself working mostly with white people, so for the most part I've existed in a dual world. I'm not complaining. My approach has always been, '*This is how it is, let's just get on with it.*' That's what I did when I was taken from my mother and placed into care at 11 years old.

My life changed, but I didn't complain. I embraced it and that's how I respond every time my life changes. It's not as though I made a conscious effort to adopt British culture, it was just a natural reaction.

I guess years of sustained victimisation and racist abuse, particularly in detention centres and at HM Borstal Feltham, led me to subconsciously internalise whiteness and repress my blackness. No doubt, that process accelerated when I began to pursue a life in industry because I welcomed the fact that I was a product of the Thatcher era. In addition, I'd embraced two icons, Michael Jackson and Prince, who were perceived to be colourless.

I'd been trying to form a colourless identity, but my trip to Jamaica brought me back to reality like a cultural baptism. In Jamaica, I could look around and see where my family came from. My roots. Everyone spoke like my mum and the food I tasted, music I heard and culture I'd previously experienced in small amounts back in England was now tangible and visible for as far as the eye could see. Even though there was a lot of poverty, it looked heavenly to me.

I returned to London during the first week of January 1991, cut off my perm and observed as US-led allied forces launched Operation Desert Storm, an extensive aerial bombing campaign in Iraq that kick-started what would later be known as The First Gulf War.

Champion Results was a cash cow making shit loads of money, but I kept thinking back to the girls in Miami and asking myself: '*What's more important Peter, profit or your conscience? If it's about profit, keep Champion. But if it's about your conscience, do something for your people.'*

I convinced the sales team at Champion Results to abandon *The Connoisseur Guide* and started telling them about my plan to launch *Pride*, a black British culture magazine that I planned to pump all of my money in to.

Actually, all I had was a vision and a name. But I spoke emphatically, as if I had a blueprint, and told them we'd be competing against *Ebony* magazine and launching in five months. Kim, the only white guy, left. But the rest of the team were excited.

I took the helm as publisher and set out looking for designers and printers. Faye was appointed as editor and I asked Leroy, whose parents were from St Kitts, and William Ansong, a British-born Ghanaian and former Moore Group employee, to become the project's respective sales and marketing directors.

I decided I no longer wanted to help corporate Britain make money and succeed. *'I'm about my people'* was my mantra. I was so full of myself that I completely abandoned Champion Results.

I had good rental income from my properties and presumed that as long as *Pride* launched quickly the profits generated would replace any lost revenue. The magazine had to prosper because it was the only commercial entity I had.

We started researching the market and learned about *The Voice*, a newspaper founded in the wake of the race riots that broke out across England in the early '80s and Choice FM, a radio station that had just launched in south London. Leroy and I secured a meeting with one of the station's founders, Neil Kenlock, at their office in Brixton.

At that meeting, as I told Neil about *Pride* I remember him leaning back in his chair and staring at us for a while before slowly bending down, opening a desk drawer and pulling out a bundle of old magazines. He proceeded to explain that he was a photojournalist by trade and in 1979 alongside Choice FM's managing director, Patrick Berry, had launched a black British culture magazine called *Root*.

I remembered the publication and asked about its relationship with Barclays bank who usually advertised on the inside cover. Neil said that between 1969 and 1987, British students had led a high-profile campaign to boycott Barclays because of the bank's longstanding association with South Africa's racist apartheid regime, and the advert was simply a token gesture to clear their conscience and gain favour in the black marketplace.

He told us that black publishing was notoriously difficult because sales and advertising revenues were traditionally low, which eventually led him and Berry to sell *Root* in the mid-'80s to Hansib Publications, owners of *The Caribbean Times* newspaper. Neil recalled how *The Voice's* founder Val McCalla (RIP) tried to sabotage *Root* by launching a rival magazine, *Chic*, which split the market. Neil considered this to be an underhanded move as there was clearly only room for one magazine.

Moreover, he noted that because equal opportunities campaigners such as Sir Herman Ouseley and Linda Bellos OBE had pushed for local government jobs to be advertised in black and Asian media platforms, when Ken Livingstone became leader of the Greater London Council in the early '80s he arranged for all local authority advertising to be coordinated with Val's newspaper.

Neil observed that one peculiar consequence of Livingstone's media policy was that for many years *The Voice* was able to operate as a virtual monopoly, collecting advertising revenues directly from local government without ever having to work for them.

I told Neil about my plan and he was appalled that I was attempting to use the same staff from *The Connoisseur Guide* to develop *Pride*. 'No mon, no mon, dat nah go work,' he said. 'Yuh need black people on board; black writers, black photographers and black designers. Oh lawd! And yuh a launch magazine?'

He kept asking how I was going to fund the venture and almost fell out of his chair when I told him that I was going to use my own money: 'Nooo. Yuh cyaan do dat!'

Neil spoke like a father figure and tried to convince me to abort the project, but I was determined. 'Bwoy, alright,' he said. 'I'm telling you now, don't do it. But if you go ahead, I'm here for you.'

Neil was horrified by the fact I could be so bold, and still not have a clue. He never said it, but I'm sure in the back of his mind he thought, 'you're going to squander £50,000 very quickly and won't have anything to show for it because you have no idea what you're doing'.

Those words never came out of his mouth, but I sensed that's where he was coming from because for the next few months, every time we spoke he'd say: 'Look Peter, I like you and think what you're trying to do is a great thing. But I'm telling you, go back to where you came from - sales and sales training. This is not for you.'

CHAPTER NINE
Black Media, Birth Control and Beethoven
(1991)

On numerous occasions over the next few months Neil Kenlock tried to get me to abandon the *Pride* project. But I wouldn't listen. Instead, I spent time considering strategies that would introduce the magazine to the marketplace.

I quickly learned that the black media market was run by a small, tightly knit and hugely competitive fraternity of experts. But, couldn't decide on the best method of approach. Eventually, I said to myself: *'What would Surjit Shah do?'*

I phoned *The Voice* newspaper and told them I was looking for some publicity to help promote a black magazine that I was launching. A receptionist took my number and said that someone would get back to me shortly. After two days of waiting I said to myself, *'Time's running out. Use your skills and go to the top.'* I contacted *The Voice*'s editor Winsome Cornish, but she wouldn't take my calls so I blagged the deputy editor, Joseph Harker.

I told him: 'I've just spoken with Winsome's office who said that I needed to deal with you.' I spun him a couple of lines about my exciting, new magazine designed specifically for British blacks and he said: 'Yeah, that sounds like a great story. Come and see me.'

Pride's sales director William and I met Joseph at *The Voice*'s offices in Brixton. He asked some basic questions and suggested we go out for lunch later that week. With the benefit of hindsight, I think Joseph (who

87

went on to launch *Black Briton*, an aspirational, but short-lived rival to *The Voice*), was considering leaving his job and defecting to our editorial team and used the second meeting to suss us out.

We talked for a while. He was pushing for me to launch a monthly publication, whereas I'd already planned to start off quarterly and gradually increase frequency. We couldn't agree, but parted on good terms. He later became *The Guardian* newspaper's deputy opinion editor.

I phoned and pitched another of *The Voice*'s best writers, Ron Shillingford, who agreed to meet for lunch. Ron, who later became editor of the *Caribbean Times* newspaper and a best-selling author, was indifferent and a little dismissive.

'I can't see how you're going to succeed,' he said. 'You've got no experience or background in media - you're not even a journalist.' Nevertheless, he perked up when I offered to pay 30% more than the standard National Union of Journalists rate he usually charged.

Ron looked surprised and asked how much of *Pride*'s editorial content he would be expected to write. 'All of it,' I replied. He laughed heartily: 'No, no, no, it doesn't work that way. I can't do it all. You need more writers.' He agreed to bring in more contributors and introduced me to another of *The Voice*'s top reporters, Brenda Emmanus, who went on to enjoy a lengthy career as a BBC TV presenter.

When we met, Brenda appeared a little puzzled. She said: 'I hear you're paying 30% more than the standard rate. That's more than we get at *The Voice*. Are you sure you want to pay that much?' I explained that I was willing to pay top prices for quality content and Brenda also agreed to bring in more writers for the first issue.

Neil wasn't surprised by *The Voice*'s unwillingness to support *Pride* and suggested the paper's owner would see any new publication as a threat: 'Mi did tell yuh seh, yuh nah get nutt'n from *The Voice*. Dem nah gi yuh nutt'n. Val a go try destroy yuh.'

He advised me to book an appointment to see public relations specialist Yvonne Thompson, who ran Britain's first black marketing agency WM&P, alongside a camp black guy, Werbayne McIntyre, who had experience working for a mainstream advertising agency.

WM&P targeted African American companies that were trying to reach black British consumers, and channelled them through to *The Voice* and Choice FM where, unbeknown to me, Yvonne held a post on the executive board as one of the company's founding directors.

I asked Yvonne to hook me up with some of her American clients, but she was reluctant and only seemed interested in getting me to rent a stall at an exhibition taking place later that year at the Islington Design Centre in north London, the Afro Hair and Beauty Show.

I purchased a database of black businesses from Werbayne for around £500 and a stall for the show, which was to be held on the Spring Bank Holiday weekend a few weeks after we were scheduled to launch *Pride*.

Still, I left the meeting feeling a little dismayed. Yes, some headway had been made. But in all honesty, trying to break in to the black media network reminded me of my time in jail where everything was tribal. WM&P, *The Voice* and Choice FM were all based in south London. But I was launching *Pride* from northwest London, and subsequently was very much an outsider.

The general vibe and attitude was that everyone was willing to take my money and sell their services, but no one really believed *Pride* would make it past the first issue.

My affair with Georgina continued and Faye kept asking: 'Are you really going to let this woman come in and start changing your life?' I tried to explain that to maintain a relationship with my daughter I had to accept Georgina as part of the package, but she disagreed and we separated. My relationship with Georgina was always complicated. Just weeks later, I remember spending the night at her house, stumbling upon her birth control pills and discovering that she'd stopped taking them. I became very angry and briefly considered strangling her when she came out of the bathroom.

I couldn't believe it, and said to myself, '*You bitch. You're trying to get pregnant again and make a unilateral decision that's going to affect me for the next 20 years. Who the hell do you think you are, and what gives you the right to do that?*'

I'd convinced myself that trying to build a relationship with Georgina was the right thing to do, but in truth I was only with her because of Chineka. After that night, I became less trusting and started to wonder whether Georgina might be setting me up because at times it honestly felt like I was negotiating with someone who was trying to consolidate a deal.

I reduced the time I spent with her and she responded by twisting our daughter against me to the point where I did not see Chineka again for the best part of a year. During this period, I remember reading a feature in *The Voice* about a guy from Birmingham, Karl George, who ran a networking organisation called Black Link, and was one of the youngest qualified accountants in the country. I was impressed with his story, got his number and called him. Karl invited me to his house and I drove up to Birmingham the same day.

89

We talked about working together and he agreed to help me build a national distribution network by taking care of Birmingham, linking me up with a Pan-African group in Manchester and connecting me to his contacts in Leicester, Nottingham and Leeds.

Instantly, we struck up a great professional and personal relationship that has endured for almost three decades. In the years ahead, Karl became a corporate governance expert, a happily married father of three, a Christian minister and one of my most trusted confidantes.

As launch day approached, the *Pride* team expanded with a new designer and sub-editor alongside Faye, Leroy, William and myself. Journalists would post us a Jiffy bag containing a hard copy version of their story and a floppy disk wrapped in foil to protect the magnetic data inside. We'd save the article on an Amstrad PC2286 computer where it would be edited then printed with double-line spacing for the designer to cut and paste around some photographs on a board. Absolutely everything was done by hand.

Besides my fledgling publishing empire, I had several other issues to contend with. I hadn't seen Chineka in months and as interest rates climbed I haemorrhaged cash so it was becoming increasingly difficult to hold on to all of my properties. On top of that, we began hearing rumours about two new magazines, *Origin* and *Candice,* which were both launching around the same time as *Pride.*

I think the publisher of *Candice,* which targeted black women, had some link with former *Eastenders* actress Judith Jacob. While the team behind *Origin* had supposedly received a grant from the Prince's Trust charity, which they'd used to purchase desktop publishing equipment.

Origin only had a mock-up version of the magazine with dummy copy inside, but the design looked modern and professional. People were saying they were going to annihilate us because their publication was slick and they had media connections.

Then, Ron, Brenda and some of the other writers from *The Voice* asked if their names could be removed from the features they'd written because they were scared Val would punish them for working with us. No one wanted to be associated with *Pride.*

Initially, the idea of two rival magazines concerned me. But after a while, I realised that all we needed to do was play to our strengths. While it's true that we didn't know anything about publishing or black media, we did have something that gave us a huge advantage over our competitors - my sales experience.

Up until this point, Leroy had been responsible for sales. But he wasn't doing well, and as the launch drew closer I began to realise that my core skills were also *Pride's* key assets. I picked up the phone, called some potential advertisers and started selling.

It didn't take long to bring in some revenue, but I kept facing the same objections from people who'd say things like: 'How do we know this is going to work? Black magazines are notorious for nosediving. They don't succeed and you haven't even launched yet. Why on earth would we advertise with you and pay before the launch? You must be joking.'

Despite these reservations, I managed to generate a decent amount of pre-and post-publication income. Neil could see my determination and mentored me as the weeks passed.

Then one day, he said: 'How are you getting into the newsagents; who's doing your distribution?' I told him that we'd planned to visit every newsagent and give them copies of the magazine. But he replied: 'No mon, a nuh so it go. Yuh affi get a distributor who will supply the newsagents. And when dem sell di magazines dem pay di distributor, who then pays you.

'It's a long process and you probably won't collect all the revenue from the first issue until you're working on issue three. And by that time, you've already paid out expenses for two publications. So yuh betta av plenty a cash, a dat mi a tell yuh.'

I did some research and discovered that although there were a few small independent distributors, about 80% of the UK market was controlled by just two companies: WH Smith, who were strong in the south, and John Menzies who covered Scotland and the north of England.

None of the independents wanted anything to do with *Pride* and John Menzies said that before offering us a deal we'd have to pay for TV adverts and give them either £50,000 for a national marketing campaign or 100,000 copies of the magazine.

As the traditional method of distribution wasn't available, I instructed William to travel to all the relevant areas in London and get orders from every newsagent. We developed our own marketing campaign and recruited vendors who were placed strategically at all the major train stations in black communities: Seven Sisters, Brixton, Harlesden and Hackney.

Then, one Sunday evening a few days after my 25th birthday and a few weeks before launch day, I was almost killed in a car accident. I'd just left the office to go meet Chineka and was speeding northbound along Cricklewood Broadway when a drunk-driver pulled out from a side road. The force of the collision spun my £26,000 Toyota Celica and lifted all four wheels off the ground.

When the car eventually stopped in an embankment on the other side of the road (just outside of the Royal Mail sorting office) I was thrown out of my seat and smashed the windscreen with my face.

I shattered the nerve in one of my front teeth, wrote-off my car, almost lost an eye, and for weeks after the accident remember pulling lumps of windscreen out of my hair and finding tiny glass splinters embedded in my skull and above my eye. Remarkably, the last fragment was removed with a pair of tweezers 21 years later after I discovered a small but sharp object sitting underneath a scar on my eyebrow.

Thankfully, within minutes of the accident I was rushed to Edgware General Hospital. But I refused to stay, and against the doctors' advice discharged myself and returned to work.

I was functioning on automatic pilot, and it took another three days and a heart-to-heart conversation with Lawrence Fearon at the *Pride* office before I acknowledged the full effects of what happened. Lawrence seemed very concerned and started talking about how I could've lost my life and an eye. I guess that was the first time I really considered how close I'd come to death because I broke down and cried.

I was under pressure and anxious about the magazine launch, which was less than two weeks away. Talking to Lawrence felt good, but as soon as the conversation ended I returned to autopilot and went straight back to work. I was determined and nothing was going to stop me from completing my mission and defeating the army of critics who were saying that *Pride* was going to fail.

Around the same time, I met a radical Muslim convert who had, coincidentally, changed his name from Ron Shillingford to Shabazz Lumumba. Shabazz had a team of graphic designers and we began discussing and planning the layout for the magazine's second issue. He knew a lot about history and began schooling me on legendary African Americans such as inventors George Washington Carver and Garrett Morgan, and human rights activist Harriet Tubman. I was blown away with his encyclopaedic knowledge and invited him to write a column in the magazine.

In addition to competition from *Origin* and *Candice*, a third publication targeting British blacks, *Sphinx*, launched into the marketplace. None of us had distribution deals and I realised that if *Pride* was really going to set itself apart and get people talking we'd have to find an exclusive story for the front page of our first issue.

I spoke to Shabazz who recommended the launch issue include a feature revealing how some of the most famous icons of European culture were black people of African descent.

He told me Queen Charlotte, who was born in Germany but ruled Britain for 57 years until her death in 1818, was black and claimed that legendary composer and pianist Ludwig van Beethoven was a descendent of the African Moors who travelled Europe between the 8th and 15th centuries.

He explained that Charlotte was Queen Victoria's grandmother; Queen Elizabeth II's great, great, great-grandmother, and the first queen to live in Buckingham Palace.

I didn't believe him, so called the other senior managers to my office and listened as he talked about the evidence documenting how Queen Charlotte was responsible for introducing maternity hospitals and Christmas Trees to England and helped to establish the Royal Botanical Gardens in Kew, South West London.

Shabazz tried to convince me to run both stories in the launch issue, but I thought they were far too radical. However, the rest of the team disagreed with me and we decided to run with the Beethoven story.

To get some additional publicity, I approached one of Choice FM's DJs, Lawrence's brother-in-law Daddy Ernie, who I knew from the ends. I asked if he'd like to be interviewed because I knew that if he was on the front page he'd talk about it on his radio programme, which was more free promotion from Choice.

The Voice were still refusing to give me any coverage and Brenda (who'd started presenting BBC One's fashion programme *The Clothes Show*) and Ron continued to say: 'If anyone asks, please don't tell them we wrote for you.' That really pissed me off and I thought to myself, *'I'm gonna publish your names alongside your stories because that's what Surjit would've done. And if you get sacked, guess what, you're going to need me.'*

I then decided we needed to bash someone. So I put some names in a hat and pulled out Diane Abbott, the first black woman to hold a seat in the House of Commons. I got the designers and a writer to create a feature questioning whether the four years she'd spent in parliament had been of any benefit to British blacks. It was a cheeky move, but we desperately needed some controversy to raise awareness.

Pride hit the newsstands on Friday 10th May 1991, the same day a landmark comedy show, *The Real McCoy* (which helped propel the careers of several black and Asian performers), made its debut on BBC Two. We launched as a quarterly, general interest magazine covering various aspects of black culture because, as Neil had explained, the key to publishing is the ability to create content that advertisers want to be associated with.

Working with the same £2 cover price as *Ebony*, Leroy and William spent the first couple of days driving around in the company car distributing *Pride* on a sale and return basis to all the major newsagents in Greater London.

In terms of promotion, *Pride* didn't get much mileage out of the Afro Hair and Beauty Show as our stand was undressed. I hadn't been told the booths needed electricity and decorations. Everyone else's stand was kitted out and fresh, whereas ours looked naked. I felt low and discouraged, but used the opportunity to sell subscription packages and network with the advertising executives from all the hair care companies.

I sent a copy of *Pride* to John Johnson, founder of the world's largest black-owned publisher, the Johnson Publishing Company. At the time, he was one of America's richest men and had been publishing *Ebony* for almost 50 years.

Attached to the magazine, I sent Johnson a letter asking if he would pay for me and my team to come to Chicago so he could teach us more about publishing. About a week later I remember Faye called me sounding very excited. She explained that John Johnson's office was on the other line and they were waiting to put his call through to me.

Faye transferred the call and I heard a woman with a Southern American drawl say: 'Hi there, are you Peter Murray? I'd like to connect you with the president of the Johnson Publishing Company, Mr John H Johnson who would like to speak with you. Are you ready to take the call?'

I said: 'Yeah, sure, go ahead,' but was shocked to discover that Johnson was not very happy with me. 'Mr Murray,' he said: 'How do you have the audacity to send me a magazine and ask me to pay for you to come to America so that you can learn how I run my business. Are you crazy?'

I didn't understand and tried to explain that I was simply seeking support and advice from one of my heroes. 'I'm not your hero,' Johnson countered. 'I'm your competition. Why on earth would I want to help you? 'We sell to black people. Who do you sell to Mr Murray? We are selling to the same market. When a black man or woman goes in to that newsagent with their $2, they've got-ta make a choice between *Ebony* and your magazine, and that's when you become my competition.' I noticed that he never once mentioned the name *Pride*. 'Frankly, you're a threat so I have nothing further to say to you,' he added. 'If, as you say Mr Murray, you really wanna know about me and how I run my business I suggest you go and buy my book,' he said before slamming down the phone. I felt dejected and distraught, and to make matters worse I was running out of money.

Just before I went to Jamaica the previous year I'd leveraged all of my properties against a big deal with Simon, which had backfired. Now, the lenders were looking for their money. I didn't have any to give them, so one by one I started losing my properties.

About a month after the launch date I remember feeling extremely stressed and agitated because a huge amount of work had gone into the *Pride* project, and yet we hadn't received any publicity.

I sent copies of the magazine to *The Sun*, *Daily Mirror*, *The Times* and *The Telegraph* newspapers, with a cover letter highlighting the story about Beethoven's ethnicity.

But aside from a freelance journalist who called to say she'd come across the magazine and was interested in doing something for *The Guardian*, we were ignored by the mainstream papers. And only Choice FM gave us some additional publicity.

I remember sitting in my house in Hampstead one morning feeling totally disheartened. I was running out of money, my properties were being repossessed left, right and centre and I'd been dissed by John Johnson. As I sat at the dining table eating a bowl of porridge and trying to come up with some inventive ways to get more publicity, I remember looking up and seeing the presenters of *BBC Breakfast* discussing the headlines from that day's newspapers.

One of them picked up *The Guardian* and on the front page was a picture of *Pride* magazine alongside a story about Beethoven's skin colour. I jumped out of my seat and screamed: 'Yeeesss!' I couldn't believe it.

I ran outside to my local newsagent and bought a copy of *The Guardian*. There it was: Beethoven, *Pride* magazine and publisher Peter Murray all on the front page. As I raced to the office in Cricklewood, I could hear presenters and callers talking about it on all of the major radio stations. I called the team and told them: 'Get into the office now. We've got to plan!'

The phones were ringing off the hook, and one of the first people I spoke to was a representative for legendary broadcaster Michael Parkinson who wanted me to come on his LBC morning radio show. We had no clue about how to manage the media firestorm we'd created, so I called Joseph Harker panicking: 'Joe, what do we do, what do we do?' To which he replied: 'Calm down. You've got to do the interview with Michael Parkinson. Just relax. Parky's going to attack and come at you, but whenever you respond just say "Michael" before answering the question. Peter, you've had a phenomenal response. This thing is going ballistic, you've got to control it.'

Our office was now under siege from couriers sent to collect the magazine by staff at the mainstream publications who'd obviously thrown away the copies and cover letters that I'd sent them weeks earlier.

I did the interview with Michael Parkinson, but decided that Shabazz was the best person to conduct future interviews on the story as we had NBC News from America, the Canadian Broadcasting Corporation, German TV stations, the Armed Forces Radio and radio stations from all over Europe trying to contact us.

The Voice called for a story, but we ignored them and recorded an exclusive interview for Choice, which ran every 30 minutes on their news bulletins. Then, we received a call from an Austrian media outlet requesting that someone from our organisation come to Vienna where Beethoven lived, worked and died, to explain our theory.

I said: 'No, we can't come right now, we're too busy.' But the voice on the other end of the line said: 'You have to come.' I continued to object until they said: 'Name your price.' I told them £5,000, and they replied: 'Send me your bank account details, you're coming.'

They agreed to provide a first-class plane ticket, security and five-star accommodation. I sent William to do the interview and observed the media frenzy that ensued over the course of the following week.

The Establishment were upset that we were questioning Beethoven's ethnicity, and the Americans picked up on that and ran with it. As a result, all 10,000 copies of *Pride* we printed sold out in weeks. We received global TV, radio and newspaper coverage, and all the newsagents were phoning us saying: 'Please, please, please can we have some more magazines?'

Ron and Brenda were now happy to be associated with the magazine. Although, *The Voice* did publish a story, which rubbished *Pride* and implied the mainstream media hadn't taken our story seriously because it was poorly written and we were inexperienced. However, what their piece failed to mention was that I initially took the Beethoven story to *The Voice's* deputy editor, but he wasn't interested. The simple truth is, the publicity garnered from that first issue had a value well in excess of £1million and made us appear bolder, brighter and more in touch than our contemporaries. Naturally, neither *The Voice* nor its owner liked that.

Pride was now established and we used the publicity generated to sell advertising for the second issue. Ron returned to write some more features, so I gave him the Queen Charlotte story and tried to replicate the public relations strategy.

The second edition didn't receive anywhere near the same coverage, but obviously that was to be expected after the fantastic sales of our first edition of *Pride*.

CHAPTER TEN
Women, Money and Making New Friends
(1991 - 1992)

In May 1991, one month after my 25th birthday, Leroy, William, Faye and I launched what is now known as Britain's most successful lifestyle publication targeting women of colour, *Pride* magazine.

I was young, happy, on top of the world and, although I'd lost some properties due to the rising interest rates, earlier that year a consultant from investment company Hill Samuel valued my assets at £1.3 million.

I remember driving every evening after work from the *Pride* office to my mum's house in Harlesden, where she'd give me a plate of food and we'd talk. Afterwards, I'd cruise through the area along Church Road then through Willesden and Cricklewood (the places where I reigned during my days of criminality) before entering a new world: Golders Green, West Hampstead and Hampstead, where I now lived.

I'd frequently pinch myself and wonder, *'Is this real?'* Everything happened so quickly that I hadn't seen it coming. Five-and-a-half years earlier I'd been in prison, serving time for pickpocketing. But things were different now. Sometimes I'd think about all the people who'd doubted me, and the parents who told their children not to play with me because my family was poor.

There were other routes I could've taken to get home, but I wanted to drive through the hood. That drive was like a homecoming for me every night; my self-promotion. I wanted to experience that feeling of elation.

My single biggest aid in becoming a millionaire at 25 was Napoleon

Hill's *Think and Grow Rich*. I took that book very seriously, imbibed every page and would chant a daily mantra of self-affirmation:

'I, Peter John Murray born 16th April 1966, do declare that I shall, by 16th April 1991, have in my possession £1million. This £1million shall come to me as a result of sales training and property dealing. I can see, sense, smell and touch this £1million with my hand; it's coming to me now.'

You have to involve all your senses and try to step within yourself because that's where the ultimate power is. I did that every morning and night, and guess what? In less than 18 months I was worth £1.3 million.

I also adopted Hill's 'six feet from gold' theory, which is about never giving up because the moment you're ready to quit is when you're actually closest to victory. Success is on one side of a coin and failure is on the other side. Life is just about flipping that coin.

Think and Grow Rich was instrumental in my success and I remember being so focused that even though I was prosperous and had properties and fast cars, I didn't realise how much money I was making. I was so focused that I didn't look up to take a breath.

In 1991, I met and established relationships with three women who would profoundly impact my life in one way or another: my ex-wife Donna Walker, *Pride*'s 17-year-old office junior, Marcia Abbott (who remains my trusted assistant) and a very special girlfriend, Michelle Kelly.

The longest relationship I've had with a woman other than a blood relative is with Donna, who I met through Dennis the same week I launched *Pride*. Dennis was seeing a girl, Sandra Barrett, and wanted to introduce me to her best friend.

We all met up at a party in Bridge Park Complex, and I remember finding a quiet place to speak with Donna as *Bandelero* by Pinchers blasted out of the sound system speakers nearby. She was beautiful, curvy, five foot three, elegant, reserved and about to turn 20. I thought she was very intelligent and enjoyed her company, chocolate-brown skin and gorgeous mane of long, thick hair.

Donna had a great sense of style, so when I was driving around in a convertible with the roof down and blasting music, she would say something like: 'Oh Peter, you're so crass. Don't you know less is more?' But the thing that impressed and attracted me most of all was that she was mature beyond her years. Back then, we were producing *Pride* on a shoestring budget and because I was so fanatical I'd do the final editing, subediting and proofreading before the magazine was sent to the printers. But it was Donna who schooled me on English grammar. I reminded her about it recently and she doesn't remember, but it's true.

Over the next 13 years, Donna and I lived together, married had three children, separated and divorced. She is a fantastic mother and I love her dearly, but for periods in our relationship I was unfaithful because I felt unloved. I had my own issues, and she wasn't the type of person to initiate affection, give you a hug or say 'I love you.' As a result, it often felt like there was an absence of love in the relationship. That's one of the reasons why I started to play away, which quite naturally led to the breakdown of my marriage.

In August 1991, a few months after I met Donna and around the time we published the second issue of *Pride*, I became involved with Michelle, a hairdresser from Bristol who relocated to southeast London and set up a beauty salon.

Michelle was athletic, caramel complexioned, about five foot six and very pretty. But most significantly, she had a huge appetite for risk, loved fast driving and was absolutely fearless.

Michelle was very entrepreneurial and I'd often see her networking at the same events I attended to promote *Pride*. We clicked instantly. I quickly discovered that our birthdays were just one or two days apart and she was an absolute freak. We linked on an impromptu basis for about five years and throughout that time she always had this amazing hold over me, almost like a spell.

I considered her to be more than my equal and together we were like a modern-day version of American armed robbers Bonnie (Parker) and Clyde (Barrow), who became famous for their criminal escapades in the 1930s. I remember being in the passenger seat of her Black Volkswagen Golf Mk1 as she raced down The Mall - the road leading to HM Queen Elizabeth II's official residence in central London.

In the '90s we didn't have suicide attacks in the UK, but London was nonetheless held under siege by the IRA who, in an attempt to end British occupation of Ireland, planted and detonated dozens of bombs in public places all over the capital during the first half of the decade. As a result, the security forces were particularly nervous of attacks on the Royal Family, which must've slipped Michelle's mind because on this particular night she was driving at top speed and heading straight towards Buckingham Palace.

Michelle was driving so fast the soldiers stationed on the roadside drew their guns and trained them on her car. When she finally realised they were about to shoot us to pieces she braked and brought the skidding car to a standstill. That was Michelle. She loved speed and danger.

On several occasions she and I would be driving on the motorway at some crazy speed, touching and kissing each other and then we'd pull over and have sex on the hard shoulder. Or I'd see her at public events and concerts and she'd just grab me and take me to the fire exit for sex.

Another time, I'd just started dating Donna and brought her with me to a dinner and dance held by African-American hair care company Luster's at the Hilton Hotel on Park Lane. Donna and I were getting to know each other and having fun, but then Michelle appeared and sat down at our table. I got up so we could speak privately and remember her ushering me quietly but firmly out of the room towards the building's staircase. After a particularly intense making-out session, she took out a mirror, fixed her hair and makeup then said: 'Now, you can go back to your table.' No woman, before or since, has ever had me like that.

A lot of people knew her as a sassy businesswoman, but I don't think many knew that sexually Michelle had a seriously perverse and controlling side to her character. She introduced me to my dark side and would say things like: 'Look, relax and just float...'

One evening, towards the end of our relationship she invited me to her home in Lewisham where we talked in the kitchen about hair and fashion. After I agreed to have a cup of tea, Michelle got up from her chair, reached into the cupboard above my head and took out a pair of white, ceramic jars. One marked 'tea', the other 'sugar'. She opened the sugar jar and slowly pulled out two black plastic bags wrapped tightly in brown masking tape. Then, she looked into my eyes and said: 'There are one-and-a-half kilograms of cocaine here Peter. Can you get rid of this for me?'

I told her: 'Fuck off, I don't do that. I'm a magazine publisher.' To which she smiled and said that despite my persona as a media professional, she could sense I was from the streets. She went on to reveal that she was a drug courier who flew to Brazil at least twice a year, returning to London with approximately two kilos of coke wrapped up in her hair.

I was shocked, but continued to listen as she told me more about her background. In the end, I told her: 'I'm sorry Michelle, but I've got to let you down. That's just not me,' and left.

Later that evening, I was rolling in the West End with my bredrin and started telling him about this wild girl I was seeing and the proposal she'd put to me. He said that I was 'stupid' and urged me to tell him exactly where she kept the drugs. I foolishly agreed.

Two nights later, I took Michelle out and we had a beautiful meal at an Italian restaurant on Old Burlington Street while my friend burgled her house. It sounds pretty twisted, but I vividly remember her giving me head as I sat in the back of *Pride*'s company car waiting for a phone call confirming that my friend had procured the cocaine and left the premises safely.

The following morning, Michelle called me fuming: 'Peter, you've robbed me.' I lied: 'No Michelle, I haven't robbed you.' But she was insistent: 'I know you've robbed me because you're the only person I told about my stuff. You've robbed me and you took £10,000.'

I maintained my innocence, and even though I knew Michelle didn't believe me I eventually got her off the phone and raced over to Kensal Green to see my friend, who confirmed that he'd stolen the drugs but claimed to have taken only £2,000 in cash. I tried to persuade him to give the cocaine back, but he was reluctant and accused me of being 'wet'.

Subsequently, the following afternoon three masked gunmen burst into *Pride*'s office in Cricklewood, shouting: 'Who's Peter? Where's Peter?' I almost shat myself when I heard them barge in and start calling my name. I immediately crept upstairs to the landlord's flat, which was located on the top floor. The door was unlocked, so I went inside and discovered a small, sparsely decorated room with a window, refrigerator, bed and two-burner electric stove. I climbed out of the window and waited.

Although sales director Leroy initially held them off, after a minute or so they pushed past him and started to search the building. They walked into every office, opened doors and looked under desks and inside cupboards. Eventually, I heard one of them come into the room and walk back out. He'd failed to notice that I was hanging out the window using my fingertips to grip the edge of the windowsill as my feet dangled three floors above the ground.

I waited for as long as possible before climbing back inside to my office downstairs. I peeked out of a window and watched as they sped off in a black BMW 3 Series with tinted windows.

That evening, when it was time to leave the office I was petrified as I knew Michelle's gunman friends would still be looking for me. I drove slowly through Cricklewood and checked my rear-view mirror intermittently. As I crossed Willesden Lane I spotted a black BMW two cars behind and pressed down firmly on the accelerator. They pursued and I engaged them in a high-speed chase for a good few miles along Brondsbury Park.

I couldn't shake them and decided to seek refuge by pulling over outside Queen's Park Police Station. I hoped the gunmen would drive past, but they parked right behind me and turned off their lights. I thought about the responsibility I had to protect my staff and considered going into the police station to make an official report, but couldn't bring myself to be an informer. The gunmen must've tried to read my mind and wrongly assumed that I was going inside because a few seconds later my mobile phone rang and a deep voice on the other end said: 'Don't be stupid man, don't be stupid.'

After what felt like an eternity, they drove off. I sighed and concluded the best thing to do was convince my bredrin to return the stolen merchandise.

I drove to my mum's house and when I arrived, she said: 'Peter, some people came here looking for you earlier.' I left quickly, making sure I wasn't followed, and went to find my friend. I told him: 'Listen, this is getting crazy. These people know where I work and have been to my mum's house. You really need to hand that shit back.' He did, albeit 250 grams short. But Michelle didn't seem to mind. I guess she was just grateful to get her product back. In fact, she couldn't have been that pissed off because the next time I saw her she gave me a threesome.

Michelle made my heart race, and although it was exhilarating I knew I couldn't live like that permanently. When she heard I'd gotten married, she was livid: 'Peter, you've settled for the three-up, two-down house and 2.5 kids. Why did you do that?' We talked for a while, but she was so upset that I didn't stay for long.

I went to visit her again about a year later in the spring of 1995, and discovered that her salon had been taken over by a new owner. When I asked where she was everyone looked at me strangely.

One lady brought me to the back of the shop and said: 'Don't you know?' I replied: 'Know what?' And that's when I found out that Michelle had died after sustaining fatal injuries in a high-speed car crash.

I was devastated and felt cheated because we'd made a pact that when it was time to go we'd die together, racing at top speed. To this day, thinking about Michelle still upsets me because her impact was so great. She's the only woman I've ever met who actually scared me to the point where I thought: 'I can't deal with you, you're really just too much for me.'

***

Another colourful character I connected with in 1991 was Stephen Davis, a well-spoken, black salesman and marketing agent from Slough who I'd met almost a decade earlier as an inmate at Latchmere House.

One Wednesday afternoon, while I was sitting in my office at *Pride* I received a call from a guy who was trying to sell a product to the magazine. His pitch grabbed my attention, we talked for a while and then he said: 'I used to know someone called Peter Murray, but I know it's not you.'

I asked how he could be so sure and the man replied: 'Trus' me, the Peter Murray I'm talking about is a completely different guy. You and him are like chalk and cheese.' Our distribution was still patchy and I knew there was no one selling the magazine in Slough, so I sent him a copy.

About a week later the same man called back, introduced himself as Stephen Davis and said that after seeing my photograph in the magazine he'd realised that I was the guy he'd been talking about.

Stephen came to the *Pride* offices and told me he'd always assumed the Peter Murray he'd met back in 1982 must be either dead or serving life in prison.

We spoke about how we'd turned our lives around, and Stephen revealed that he'd made his money selling double glazing but wanted to get into black media. He asked if he could manage *Pride's* subscription sales, but I'd already given that task to my cousin Mark. We parted on good terms and agreed to keep in touch.

Over the next two years, *Pride* flourished and we became known for being original, independent and fearless. I didn't give a damn, which meant the magazine operated with a freedom our competitors could only envy. We had to go out and seek advertising revenue that was mostly consumer-driven, so at *Pride* we published whatever we wanted. In contrast, *The Voice* had to be far more restrained because the majority of their advertising revenue came from local authorities. Their editorial content was rarely controversial and tended to follow the government line.

We developed and introduced a whole new approach to publishing that helped re-shape the black media landscape. We were the first people outside of America to interview Oprah Winfrey, and scoop exclusives with Denzel Washington and Spike Lee during the filming of *Malcolm X*. Additionally, because a lot of the British celebrities disliked *The Voice* we were able to get big interviews with people such as supermodel Naomi Campbell, musician Jazzie B and heavyweight boxing champion Lennox Lewis.

We broke new ground in the advertising world too, securing a pioneering contract worth £6,000 with national high street retailer Miss Selfridge. That contract included a caveat insisting all the adverts used in the campaign would feature black models, which was another first.

Working in media expanded my network exponentially and I made contacts with hundreds of new people. However, by far the most flamboyant individual I met during this period was Zimbabwean businessman and politician Dr Alfred MKondo who, in the summer of 1992, attempted to purchase a 50% stake in *Pride*.

I first remember hearing his name one morning when Faye came to my office talking about an eccentric, African-sounding man who had called making ludicrous statements and wanted to come and meet me. I said I trusted her to screen my calls and visitors and thought nothing more of it until later that day when she returned to say the man had arrived and was insisting that I come next door to meet him immediately. I asked: 'And what makes this guy so important?' Faye smiled and calmly replied: 'He says he's in business with Tiny Rowland.' I was astonished and heard the words: 'Piss off,' stumble out of my mouth.

I'd told Faye on numerous occasions that of all the tycoons, entrepreneurs and businessmen living on the planet, the three that inspired me most were financier Sir James Goldsmith, Virgin Group founder Richard Branson and corporate raider Tiny Rowland, who I'd long admired as an icon of British business.

I followed Faye next door and found an overweight but seemingly untroubled black guy with a full set beard sitting in her office. In his hand was a slim, black, leather-bound contacts book and he was trying to impress Faye with its contents. Alfred looked at me, smiled, introduced himself and asked: 'Sir, are you the owner and publisher?' I confirmed that I was and he said: 'I'm interested in the magazine and think we should do some business.'

I didn't understand what he meant and invited him to look at some paraphernalia with our advertising rates. 'No,' he said. 'I wasn't really thinking about advertising. I'm just passing and have my chauffeur waiting downstairs. Can we go out for dinner later? Why not bring your team with you?' I told him we worked until late, but would try and come if we weren't too busy.

At 5pm, Alfred called to find out if we were coming and when Faye told him we weren't sure he called back every 15 minutes until I eventually gave in and said to her: 'Find out where he is and tell him we'll be there.'

He directed us to the London Metropole, a four-star hotel on Edgware Road owned by the London and Rhodesia Mining and Land Company (Lonrho), the conglomerate where Alfred held a seat on the executive board and Tiny Rowland had been employed as chief executive for more than 30 years.

When Faye, Leroy, William and I arrived we were escorted up to Aspects, the restaurant on the 23rd floor, which overlooks London. Alfred invited us to dine with him and about seven guests, including oil ministers and other dignitaries from various African states. The conversations taking place around the table were pretty straightforward and matter of fact, but midway through the meal Alfred turned to me and said: 'I'd like to buy *Pride.*' I looked at him and laughed. He corrected himself. 'No. I mean, I'd like to buy in to *Pride.*' I told him the magazine wasn't for sale and started talking about all of the hard work we'd put in to the project over the previous 18 months.

I could feel the rest of my team staring at me and knew what they were thinking, 'Are you crazy? You've got us on some pitiful salaries and this man is telling you to name your price. Take the deal'! They were right of course, the deal made perfect economic sense. But what they didn't realise was that any sale would probably cost them their jobs.

Alfred thought I was simply playing hardball and suggested that I come with him to Zimbabwe for a few days. I asked: 'Why would I do that?' He replied: 'I understand that maybe you think I'm some crazy African. So if you come to my home in Zimbabwe and I introduce you to my family you will know there is no hiding place for me.

'I'm trying to help you understand that if we get into bed together you will not catch fleas. And if you did, you will know where to find me because, as you know, when a man is on the run he runs straight home to his family.'

I was reluctant, but Faye convinced me by tactfully implying that failure to accede might suggest that I was a weak leader who was too scared to accept an invitation to the Motherland. Additionally, she pointed out that I'd been perfectly willing to send William to Austria to deal with the media storm that our Beethoven story had created a year earlier.

I sheepishly agreed to travel with Alfred on Friday that week, and remember that as I packed my suitcase the night before, his chauffeur came to the office and delivered a first-class British Airways ticket to Harare, Zimbabwe's capital. The following morning, my team dropped me to the airport and I met Alfred in the first-class lounge. 'I've got you now,' he said looking genuinely relieved that I'd accepted his offer.

As we entered the plane's first class area and Alfred was ushered upstairs, it quickly became evident that he was a frequent flyer who was popular with the cabin crew. I stretched my legs, prepared for the 14-hour flight ahead and only then began to consider that I had no real knowledge of who Alfred Mkondo was, or even what he really wanted from me.

CHAPTER ELEVEN
Africa, Brazil and the Sale of Pride
(1992 - 1993)

I'm not usually into films, but during the outbound flight on my first trip to Africa I remember thoroughly enjoying the action-comedy *Lethal Weapon 3*, starring Danny Glover, Mel Gibson and Joe Pesci.

When the plane touched down in Harare I was whisked through immigration and retrieved my luggage almost immediately. There was a police and military escort waiting for Alfred, and I followed him into a black Mercedes limousine.

It took around 30 minutes to reach his house, which was nestled in the upmarket suburbs of Harare. I can best describe it as a blue palace with a tennis court, swimming pool, team of staff and fleet of luxury cars. He had everything, including security guards patrolling the perimeter of the property and prison-style exterior walls that were so high you couldn't climb over. On the plane I'd asked myself: 'Who is this guy?' But now I really started to wonder, as it dawned on me that Alfred was tremendously wealthy.

The next morning we went to his office located in a large town house similar to the type of buildings you see in Ladbroke Grove or on Caledonian Road in London, but his was for commercial purposes. He introduced me to his personal assistant Grace and told her to make sure I got whatever I wanted.

The following morning he took me to a hotel where he had a substantial interest. We sat down for breakfast and started speaking with a black

American who was attracting a lot of attention from the hotel's guests - for some reason, they kept coming over for his autograph. I continued chatting normally, but towards the end of the conversation I heard him say that he'd come to Zimbabwe to shoot *Bopha!*, a film about a black police officer working in South Africa during the apartheid era. I remember replying: 'Good for you,' and asking Alfred who the man was as we exited the hotel. He laughed and said: 'You really don't know who that is?' I had no idea: 'Enlighten me,' I quipped. But even when he replied: 'That was Danny Glover,' I was still clueless. 'Who's Danny Glover?' I asked.

Alfred let out a full belly laugh, put his hand on my shoulder and said: 'You don't know who Danny Glover is, even though on the plane you spent two hours watching him in *Lethal Weapon 3*?' We both laughed at the irony, and when I returned to the hotel the following morning I spoke to Danny about *Pride*. He promised to let his friends and colleagues know about the magazine so they could use it for publicity whenever they came to Europe.

Alfred took me to the rural town where he came from in Mount Darwin, about a 90-minute drive northeast of Harare. He told me he'd sent members of his security ahead to inform the villagers that he and a special guest were coming to visit. Nevertheless, when we arrived I was stunned to see all of the villagers lined up along the main road with men on one side and women on the other.

They were clapping, chanting and singing. I was overwhelmed. Tears came to my eyes as I got out of the car, fell to the ground and kissed the earth. The villagers danced and cheered around me and I was escorted to a hut where I sat with some elders and drank homemade beer out of a wooden bowl.

Alfred said they had slaughtered a cow, a goat and some chickens for me. When I told him I didn't eat meat, he replied: 'Nonetheless, as you can see these people are dirt poor, but they still brought out the very best they have for you.' He had houses in the village, so we stayed there for a couple of days and I remember being shocked at having to use a pit latrine whenever I wanted to go to the toilet.

Driving back to his house in the city, Alfred revealed that although he enjoyed a luxurious lifestyle and ran several businesses (including a Tesco-style supermarket chain), less than 15 years earlier he'd lived a much humbler existence as a life insurance salesman and pirate radio DJ.

We shared jokes and stories about selling life insurance, and he explained how his big break came in 1979 when rebel forces led by African independence leader Robert Mugabe overthrew Ian Smith's racist government in Rhodesia to establish the Republic of Zimbabwe.

Apparently, when Mugabe's administration came to power one of the first people they called for was Alfred. He had no idea what was going on and thought he was going to be executed. But it turned out the head of Mugabe's army wanted to speak with him. When they met, the General said that listening to Alfred's music on the radio had kept the spirits of him and his soldiers alive during their four-year battle to end white majority rule in Rhodesia. To show his gratitude, the General (whose army had control of all the government's assets) agreed to endorse Alfred's cultivation of maize and tobacco, which is where much of his wealth came from.

When he'd finished telling his story, Alfred paused and said to me: 'Part of my wealth can be your wealth. If you do business with me I will change your life forever. I want half of your business. Give me half of *Pride*.'

I explained that I only owned 70% of the magazine; Leroy (20%), Faye (5%) and William (5%) had the remaining shares. Alfred urged me to buy their shares and go 50-50 with him. But I told him that I didn't do business like that and was loyal to my team.

He smiled and said: 'You do not understand. I can get you a meeting with any African Head of State within 48 hours and major corporations like Coca-Cola to advertise in the magazine.' He tried to persuade me further by bragging about his vast network of contacts and seat on Lonrho's executive board. But I remained steadfast.

Although we were unable to reach a deal, Alfred made sure I enjoyed the rest of my stay. A couple of nights before I left Zimbabwe, he invited me to a special dinner banquet where I was the guest of honour. I bought a new suit and attended wearing African attire. It was a really beautiful event where I got to meet dignitaries from all over the continent.

The following day, Alfred told me: 'I'm changing your life forever. When you leave Zimbabwe, you will leave a different person. You will not leave the way you came.' He was right, but when I returned to London and thought about his offer I just couldn't bring myself to do the dirty on Faye, Leroy and William.

He flew to London twice to sign a deal, but I kept making excuses. On the third occasion, I tried to encourage Alfred to buy Choice FM and introduced him to Neil Kenlock. But Neil wouldn't go for it. By then, I'd concluded that for Alfred *Pride* was just an ego thing. He had money and wanted a publication to circulate throughout Africa. I don't think he understood that *Pride* wasn't just about money - it's a black British thing. So unless his cash was also going to allow us to retain control of the publication, it wouldn't really be worth it.

Still, I learned two valuable business lessons from Alfred. First, every morning when I was staying in his palace he'd get up and go to work while I'd stay in my room, bun ganja and use the phone to call Donna and the office. Back then, internationals calls were a nightmare because there was no direct line. To make a phone call I had to go through an operator who eventually became concerned and started asking: 'Do you realise how much all of these calls are going to cost?'

The weed and phone were part of my daily routine, and Alfred must've known what was going on because when I asked why he'd flown me all the way to Zimbabwe and brought me into his home, he replied: 'Peter, when you have to do a deal you do a deal, whatever it takes. Sometimes things are uncomfortable and don't sit right, but you overlook them in the spirit of getting the deal done.

'Sometimes, someone may transgress your principles, values or way of life. But you have to ask yourself, what's important? And keep your eye on getting the deal done. And in the spirit of getting the deal done, you let them carry on with whatever they're doing.'

I knew he was talking about me smoking and running up his phone bill. From that, I understood that whenever you're doing a deal just remember what's important because it's easy to get sidetracked. The person you're negotiating with may behave in a certain way that pisses you off and makes you want to scupper the opportunity. But really, you overlook everything, all the transgressions, and just do the deal.

The second custom I've adopted from Alfred is the rule that you should avoid any deal where you end up with less than 50% of the business. When he initially talked about buying into *Pride*, I offered him a 30% stake and remember the tone of his voice changed: 'Listen, don't insult me,' he said: 'If I can't get a 50-50 deal where we're equal, I'm not interested.'

***

Later that year, I launched *Pride Fashion* magazine and travelled alone to San Francisco and Oaklands, California. Then, in 1993, Dennis and I decided to take another holiday together. We spent a few days in Portugal where we were racially abused by local police, before flying on to a city famous for its Copacabana and Ipanema beaches - Rio de Janeiro in Brazil.

At that time, the authorities were trying to clean up Rio's seaside areas and had introduced a policy of murdering the kids who were begging and hustling tourists along the coast.

We stayed there for around 10 days, visited Sugarloaf Mountain to see the 30-meter Art Deco statue 'Christ the Redeemer', and spent most of the time partying and bar-hopping. But as someone who doesn't eat meat, I remember having difficulty with the food because just about everything contained pork.

One of the first things that struck me in South America was that Brazil has the largest population of black people outside of Africa. It was a real eye-opener to see descendants of Africa speaking Portuguese. I'd previously thought about the black experience from the African, Caribbean and African American perspectives, but this was something different and it took a while to get my head around the idea that we all came from the same place.

For me, it was another cultural enlightenment because as the son of Jamaicans whose ancestors came to the Caribbean from Africa over 400 years ago, it was interesting to see and understand the experiences of other African descendants who were also struggling to survive in the 'civilised New World'.

I noticed the same light-skin and dark-skin issues that exist in other black cultures were prevalent. I guess it's the same racist bullshit everywhere; the light-skinned Africans work front of house and the dark-skinned Africans are nowhere to be seen.

***

Another influential entrepreneur I had dealings with during this period was *The Voice* newspaper founder, Val. I learnt how to buy a business simply by studying how Val operated when I sold *Pride* to him in the autumn of 1993. He didn't sit me down and teach me anything. I just observed how he did business.

I decided to sell *Pride* for a number of reasons, including a slump in advertising revenues and stress from people who were trying to blackmail me over an allegation of sexual harassment. I must admit, one of the things I enjoyed most about being a publisher was being approached by beautiful girls at nearly every business-related function. They would seek me out for work at the magazine, either as a model or part of the advertising and production teams. They were flattering and I was flirtatious, but we generally kept things professional.

However, on one occasion I overstepped the mark and abused my power. I'd been in my office interviewing a lady for an advertising sales job, but it quickly became clear that she didn't have enough experience.

After the interview was over, I told her she wouldn't be getting the job and suggested we get to know each other personally. She continued to pitch for a job, but I moved towards her and slipped my arm around her waist. She made her excuses and left.

The following day, I received a phone call from a man I assumed was her boyfriend who accused me of acting inappropriately and threatened to go public with his allegation of sexual impropriety. We met and he demanded that I give him money to resolve the situation. I refused and he repeated his warning about going to the media, which was the last thing I needed. I asked for some time to think about it and left.

He called back, but I kept stalling. I had other concerns. My mind had become wholly consumed by thoughts of my mother who'd suffered a series of strokes over a four-week period. I found myself plunged into a tailspin of anguish and resolved to sell the magazine within a month.

Prospective buyers included the owner of *Vogue* magazine, Condé Nast; the owner of *Harper's Bazaar* magazine, the National Magazine Company; maverick businessman and hair care specialist James Kimber (who offered £50,000); and *The Voice* founder Val McCalla.

It was an exciting opportunity, but I was mentally unable to engage in any serious business affairs. So I placed my faith in Neil to advise me and coordinate the sale. He said: 'Peter, do the deal with Val because whatever you do in life you'll always want to keep your reputation intact. You'll always be known as the one who didn't sell out to a mainstream organisation. You kept *Pride* in the community. You kept it black.'

I thought Neil was right and agreed to sell the business to Val, but he was only interested in *Pride* and not our publishing company, Champion Media Services. He sent in his accountant to depress the assets and business valuation, then took me to new offices in the London Docklands and said: 'This office is yours, just take it. After the deal, bring *Pride* here. I'm not going to interfere. Just do your thing.'

I was concerned about having to make the long journey from northwest London every day but agreed, as the alternative involved sharing office space with *The Voice* in Brixton, which was totally out of the question.

Val eventually agreed to buy *Pride* and Champion Media Services for £100,000, but was quick to have me dismantle the magazine's offices in Cricklewood, disconnect the phone lines, cut off the gas, serve notice on the landlord and fire my team.

On more than one occasion, my accountant asked if I was sure I wanted to do the deal. I told him to go ahead, but in all honestly my mother was my primary concern at the time. As soon as I'd shut down my office, Val told me the money for the sale would have to be delivered in instalments and I was to receive £10,000 immediately, and £10,000 per month for nine consecutive months providing that I met certain targets.

Then, after we'd done the deal, signed contracts and shook hands, he shifted tactics and said: 'We'll place the *Pride* staff in *The Voice's* office in Coldharbour Lane.' All of a sudden, the sparkling new offices in the Docklands were off the agenda. Instead, my team would be stationed in Brixton, alongside the staff from our main rivals.

I felt humiliated. I tried to work alongside *The Voice's* staff, but quickly became frustrated and walked out of the office after a couple of days, never to return. With the benefit of hindsight, there's no doubt in my mind that if my mum hadn't suffered those strokes I would have fought for and kept *Pride*. Yes, advertising revenues were down but the hospitalisation of my mother was the real issue.

My biggest mistake was to dismantle the business so swiftly because I would've had more bargaining power when negotiating with the other potential buyers. But I'm glad things panned out the way they did. Even with the benefit of hindsight, I think selling to Val was the best option. Who knows what Alfred Mkondo or the likes of Condé Nast would've done? But it's unlikely *Pride* would still be running today.

I later knew I made the right decision because when I returned to the media industry almost a decade later, I was dealing with a much younger generation of people who'd never heard of Peter Murray. But when I told them I founded *Pride*, everyone showed me love and respect. That's when I thought, '*Yes Neil, you were right. Thank you.*'

Val improved the magazine but couldn't sustain it financially, which vindicated me because he owned *Pride* for a shorter time than I did. He sold the magazine to City financier and fellow Jamaican Carl Cushnie, who was reportedly worth £200million. Carl pumped the magazine up, turned it into a monthly publication, added more pages and sustained it, which wasn't easy because *Pride* is a tricky commercial product. To make money, you've got to get your distribution and advertising numbers just right.

I'm truly proud of our many innovations and achievements during this period, and the more I review my life the more it becomes obvious that *Pride* magazine was probably my career pinnacle.

We launched in the middle of the longest economic depression Britain had experienced for more than 60 years, with interest rates at 15%. We weren't supposed to succeed. But we defied the odds, and that's why almost 30 years later *Pride* magazine is still on the newsstands.

While our editorial content remained uncompromising we also made it cool to embrace pop culture, which was unheard of in black media. We were different, but the truth is we were simply trying to show that it was possible to produce a non-conformist black magazine and still attract mainstream advertising. We developed concepts such as a ban on the advertisement of skin-lightening products, and the *Pride Directory* where businesses paid a £200 annual fee to have their contact details appear at the rear of the magazine.

Similarly, the introduction of a regular space dedicated to fostering and adoption services was something we pioneered. After conceiving the idea, we simply contacted social services and encouraged them to utilise the space by filling it with targeted and bespoke advertorial content.

Pride Fashion was another apex. The magazine launched in 1993 with a ground-breaking show, *Fashion Noir*, which was held at the South Kensington Hotel and attended by designer Vivienne Westwood, shoemaker Jimmy Choo, Wayne and Geraldine Hemingway of the Red or Dead brand, and Premier League footballers John Barnes, Ian Wright, John Fashanu and Les Ferdinand.

Pride Fashion, which aimed to bring couture clothing to the black community, became the first black media outlet to secure an advertising deal with Italian fashion brand Benetton, supporting the launch of their women's fragrance, Tribu.

Essentially, my time at *Pride* taught me something very few people knew: that black media can be profitable and sustainable, but access to distribution is essential because without that you can't get your message out. If you're trying to make money in publishing, distribution and advertising revenue are the two biggest challenges. Eventually, I began to generate income by grabbing market share from *The Voice*, Choice FM and *Black Hair and Beauty* magazine, which was a popular advertising platform among the hair care companies.

Personally, I found black media to be a cutthroat but profitable business. It should be flourishing in the internet age because the barriers to market no longer exist. Online magazines don't need distribution, and services such as Google's AdSense programme makes it much easier for independent publishers to generate revenue.

Around the same time I was selling *Pride*, the magazine's fashion editor Kim Menzies (who was also contracted to the UK's leading makeover company Cover Girl) suggested I establish a photography and portfolio company. I'd previously sold photographs in the West End and could see how adopting and modifying Cover Girl's business model would be profitable.

I did the deal with Val during the same week my mum went in to hospital, and after careful consideration launched a photo and portfolio business, Distinctive Images, with one of *Pride*'s former sales agents, Alissa Rhodes.

We opened an office behind the John Lewis department store on Oxford Street, at the top of a multi-storey building at 26 Harley Street. We targeted women and actors by placing adverts in *Stage* magazine and three publications - *9 to 5*, *Where to Go* and *Girl About Town* - which were distributed freely in central London train stations.

We offered a free makeover and complementary photo, which brought in floods of mainly white and Indian women. Afterwards we'd develop the photographs, create an album and tell the customer to come back for a viewing about a week later.

Alissa was a brilliant saleswoman who offered a high-quality service that resulted in a complete transformation for our customers. As a result, she often persuaded them to purchase the full photo package for £500 (the equivalent of around £900 today). Many of them couldn't afford it and would pay with post-dated cheques. But we didn't mind because the business was flourishing and we were all making money.

My only issue was I didn't necessarily trust Alissa to handle all the cash sales. As the only male in the business I'd have to exit the office and leave her with the customers when the service was being delivered, which made me a little uneasy.

On the surface things appeared to be going well, but in truth my mother's condition had broken my heart. She was wheelchair-bound, couldn't speak and one side of her face was drooping. One day she was happy and 24 hours later she'd be down. I was an emotional wreck and had no idea my mother's condition had become so serious. The woman who'd been my tower, my strength, my everything, would never return home.

CHAPTER TWELVE
Bereavement, Marriage and Back in Business
(1994 - 1997)

My mum passed away on 5th November 1993, and I was greatly affected by her death. I was sad, lonely and battling to stop her pardner (a community saving scheme) from collapsing. My mother's pardner was the biggest in Brent and paid out £6,000. A full hand was £100 a week. Some people would pool together with three friends and contribute (£25) each to make one hand, while others might throw as many as three hands.

I remember my mum used to count notes really quickly, and swore blind that simply by touching someone's money she could tell if they dabbled in witchcraft. 'Don't touch dat money,' she'd warn. 'Dem tink mi no know seh dem put obeah pon it.'

There were more than 50 people in the pardner and although my mother may have been illiterate and blind in one eye, she knew her operation inside out - including the exact amount each participant had thrown, and the date they were due to collect their draw.

Newcomers usually had to throw all of their hands before receiving a payout, while the elders got their draws earlier. My mother usually received a tip of one or two hands. She knew exactly what she was doing because when the pardner restarted, those who tipped best found themselves receiving early payouts.

When I think about it, my passion and aptitude for manipulating business systems and formulas probably comes from my super numerate mum who was also the conduit through which I received the entrepreneurial spirit of my grandmother, Lady P.

The pardner paid out every Monday, so from Friday through to Monday evening there'd be a steady stream of visitors to the house as people threw their hands. I knew people who used their payouts for a deposit to buy a home and others who used it to pay their mortgage for the year.

My sisters and some of our friends were in the pardner, which was hugely successful until after my mum's funeral when some people stopped throwing hands - including my mum's good friend Lou Graham.

A few nights after my mum died I dreamt that Lou hugged and kissed me, which was concerning because my mum always said that when someone kisses you in a dream it means betrayal. My mum really respected Lou who was a local councillor, magistrate, and supposedly upstanding member of the community. She also had the biggest hand in my mum's pardner.

I remember crying at the funeral, looking up and seeing her. She glided towards me, gave me a hug and kissed my cheek. After that day, Lou stopped throwing pardner hands and I never set eyes on her again.

At the time, all I could think about was how my mum used to always say: 'When I'm dead and gone you're going to cry at my graveside. And you're going to cry a lot.' She was right. I went to her graveside and I bawled: 'Mum, look what they're doing! Look at how Lou Graham is carrying on.'

I'd be there for ages, collapsed by her graveside. In between sobs, I'd ask: 'Why did you have to go? I'm sorry for all the wrong I've done. I'm sorry for everything I put you through.'

She'd always say certain things would happen when she died, and I'd shrug it off. But many of the things she talked about really did come to pass. Crying helped ease the pain and although the sense of loss assuaged over time, I don't think it's ever truly left.

Sometimes, when people of my age group talk about losing parents I find it difficult to empathise because I'm thinking, *You're lucky you had a mum and dad for such a long time.* I never had a father and my mum died when I was 27, so from then I've had to get through life on my own.

My sister Elizabeth and I agreed to put all of our money in to the pardner to ensure that everyone who continued to throw hands got paid out. We knew that if it collapsed people from our community would say: 'Look how Ms Murray's children took the pardner money and used it to bury their mum.' That's what they're like.

While still grieving the loss of my mum, I gave my shares in Distinctive Images to Alissa and left the business after six just months. Yes, it was a lucrative venture that needed little hands-on management. But I'd grown bored of marketing and selling consumer products, and was desperately looking for something more challenging to sink my teeth in to.

I rekindled my relationship with Stephen Davis, the former inmate who I'd befriended at *Pride* three years earlier. We went for lunch and I told him about my mother's passing.

He was making good money working for Legal and Commercial (L&C), an insolvency, debt recovery and sales agency, which was run by one of his business associates, Clovis Cameron, and based in Whitechapel, east London. Stephen took me on the road, showed me how he was making money and threw me a lifeline. He got Clovis to give me a car, gave me a day's training and sent me on my way.

Meanwhile, Elizabeth had run out of funds and stopped contributing to the pardner. But thanks to L&C, within seven weeks I'd made enough money to pay out all the remaining draws.

It was 1994 and Londoners were experiencing their first days of joyous summer sunshine. I'd just turned 28, and times were changing.

We were fast-approaching the 21st century, and Britain was becoming a very different place with the opening of the Channel Tunnel, new laws enabling retailers to open on Sundays and the election of Tony Blair as leader of the Labour Party.

I was also in a state of transition. I had a new idea and could foresee huge profits. My mind raced and I was excited. Stephen and Clovis were both master salesmen, better than me. They were making a lot of money. But I saw flaws in their business model and knew I could develop a better, glossier and more profitable operation. Consequently, around the same time I finished paying off my mother's pardner I left L&C and decided to set up a copycat company.

Stephen had originally introduced the business model to Clovis who set up L&C with Gerry Turner, a young white guy from Liverpool who he permanently fucked over. Gerry was unhappy, so when I approached him about setting up a rival business he jumped at the chance. We hijacked Clovis' best salespeople and operations manager, and I retained the services of *Pride*'s former office junior, Marcia.

Later that summer we launched a London-based insolvency and debt collection business called Legal & Financial (L&F), which started to fly and later expanded with offices in the Midlands and South West England.

Gerry brought in his cousin Phil Duncan, and we built the business up until they tried to rob me and I was forced to outmanoeuvre and get rid of them.

***

By the time Donna and I had our first son Darius in June 1995, it had been almost 18 months since I'd seen Chineka. One day, a short while after I'd fallen out with her mother she came with a friend to visit me at the *Pride* office.

I took them to an Ethiopian café nearby and ordered something to drink for the three of us. Once we were settled, Chineka looked me in the eyes and said: 'I don't ever want to see you again. Leave my mum, leave me, leave us alone and get us out of your life.'

She absolutely ripped the stuffing out of me, but what could I do? I spent the next few months begging to see her, but Georgiana claimed Chineka was adamant and would not be changing her mind.

Occasionally, I'd call and ask Georgina to help fix the situation. But I never got anywhere. Then, I was told Chineka was having psychiatric issues. Neither she nor her mother ever mentioned anything, but I heard through a friend, Valerie Brooks, whose friend Jenny Pecco (to whom I'd previously sold life insurance) knew Chineka.

***

Clovis, who was a former Jehovah Witness, rated me for how I'd set up L&F but probably figured I was vulnerable because I was now on my own. He came to visit and said: 'You've annihilated my business. Let's team up because you're strong on the front end and I can do the back end.'

I have the utmost respect for Clovis and remember him as a black, wide boy from Ilford and a fellow Aries who loved roots reggae and dated a middle-class white girl, Hannah, whose family were against the relationship.

We agreed to structure the new enterprise around two key elements whilst delivering a service to help businesses retrieve unpaid debts from directors of companies that had closed down.

At the front end, salespeople would visit the client, sell the service and take an advance fee. At the back end of the business we'd act on the client's behalf to negotiate deals with company directors.

Clovis and I worked out an agreement where in return for shutting down L&C and joining me at L&F we'd share 50% of all profits. In truth, I had no intention of giving up half of my business and was simply biding time to gain more control of the situation.

I did exactly what Val had done to me 18 months earlier and made Clovis dismantle his operation. Then, on the day he came to move into my offices with Hannah and his team, I told him: 'I've changed my mind.

I don't want to do the deal anymore.'

Clovis went berserk: 'I've decimated my business for you!' he barked. I stayed cool and just kept repeating: 'I don't want to do the deal anymore. I'm entitled to change my mind. We haven't signed contracts.'

I kept him at bay for about five days before offering him 20% of the business with an opportunity to earn more over time. Having already disassembled his business, Clovis had little choice but to agree to the deal.

I rolled heavy during this period and remember giving Karl George a Mercedes Benz when he became L&F's financial director. I only travelled first class and drove a brand new, £47,000 blue Mercedes Benz E220 Coupe, which I upgraded on a whim one day when Stephen and I were driving past the Mercedes showroom in Park Royal.

When we walked in we were treated like timewasters. Even when I told the staff I was interested in purchasing something from the SL Class range, the only response I received was: 'Sir, that's a £70,000 car.' To which I replied: 'I didn't ask how much the car was, just tell me what I need to do to secure it.'

I was told to pay a 10% deposit, so I called L&F's financial controller Karen Jones and told her to courier a £7,000 cheque to me immediately. When the biker arrived I gave the cheque to the sales manager who said I could come back in a few days after the financing had been sorted.

Later that week, Stephen and I drove off the showroom forecourt in a brand new Mercedes Benz SL, which attracted an equal measure of attention from females and envy from males.

Months earlier, I'd shown my cousin Mark the same business model and he'd gone off and set up his own company, Net Alliance, which Clovis and I bought out. I merged L&C and L&F, and ran Net Alliance independently.

The new business was a novel idea because whereas the L&C salesman took advance fees but had no real interest in delivering the back-end service, we worked with lawyers and utilised provisions in the Insolvency Act to claw back considerable sums for our clients.

The expanded business prospered, and later that year I moved in to a rented two-bedroom penthouse on the outer suburbs of northwest London in Harrow-on-the-Hill.

Moreover, after a three-and-a-half-year courtship I married 23-year-old Donna Walker during a beautiful ceremony at the luxurious all-inclusive Sandals hotel resort in Montego Bay, Jamaica.

Ironically, although L&F had been inspired by three successful black salesmen (Stephen, Clovis and myself), I had great difficulty finding African Caribbeans who could goin to the field and take new business.

Almost every black person I'd hired for field sales failed miserably. Subsequently, while the staff who handled the back-end calls were almost entirely black, all of our field salespeople were white. I made a white guy, Bob MacDavitt, the face of the company. Bob was in his late 50s and sharp as a razor. He'd worked for Clovis, but came over to L&F and was our best salesman by far.

As the company's sales director, Bob was responsible for managing the sales team and proved to be a valuable asset. I eventually gave him 5% of the business.

L&F opened an office in Birmingham which employed one black guy, Gary Mills (RIP). I expanded my network through Simon who introduced me to textiles merchant Alan Goldberg and criminal solicitor Alistair McIntyre, who in turn introduced me to commercial solicitor Bob Jackson.

Business was good, and to celebrate our first wedding anniversary I flew with Donna to Acapulco in Mexico where we stayed for 10 days at the Sheraton Hotel.

By 1997, L&F was still doing well but Clovis wasn't satisfied with his 20% stake and kept pushing for a greater share of the business. I foresaw trouble ahead and decided to split the company into three.

I'd acquired the assets of L&C, but the company remained dormant while L&F and Net Alliance traded independently. The organisation had been set up that way because I was using the 'sweep up' model where salespeople from one business (L&F) are sent out to pitch a high-priced service. Customers that decline are passed on to a second business (Net Alliance), which pitches the same service at a lower price and 'sweeps up' the customers who are completely unaware they'd been dealing with the same organisation all along. L&F had a flagship office in Knightsbridge, but Clovis and I shared space at the main office in Wembley. As time passed, his frequent calls for greater control became more vocal and annoying. Previously, he'd only pushed for pay rises which I'd consented to. But now he wanted to increase his stake in the business from 20% to 50%. Clovis was learning my negotiating skill and wanted to know everything I was doing.

To give myself some space I incorporated a third company, Corporate Financial Management (CFM), and moved Clovis and his team to new offices I'd rented in Harrow, leaving them to manage the backends of all three companies through CFM.

I also sent Marcia (who'd become my senior account manager) with Clovis and his team to help make a smooth transition and keep me informed of their progress.

In the three years since its formation, L&F had grown rapidly and was now generating an annual turnover of more than £1 million and employing close to 70 members of staff. However, despite its success the company imploded because we made too many deals with company directors that we shouldn't have, and I let costs run out of control.

Eventually, L&F was placed under investigation by the Office of Fair Trading (OFT) - the UK government department responsible for regulating the economy, protecting consumers and managing competition. In response, I hired a solicitor from a company in Gray's Inn Road, Barry Brooks (who in the following weeks joined Mishcon de Reya - the law firm that represented Diana, Princess of Wales in her divorce the following year).

For £5,000, Brooks sent the OFT a substantive letter, and advised me that because the agency's powers were limited to companies handling consumer debts they'd been operating outside of their jurisdiction by engaging with L&F.

I attempted to wind down the now insolvent company; firing all staff except Bob, Marcia and Karen. However, almost immediately I was contacted by the UK government's Department of Trade and Industry (DTI) who said the Companies Investigation Branch (CIB) had launched an inquiry following allegations made by the OFT that L&F had been acting against the public interest. The CIB investigation lasted several months, but was dropped due to lack of evidence.

***

After a three-year hiatus, Chineka was back in my life. We started going out again, and she spent time bonding with Donna and her baby brother at the penthouse. Aside from the fact that Chineka was still very much controlled by her mother and insisted on calling me 'Peter' rather than 'dad', we got on well and I enjoyed her company. Still, I sensed that something was making her unhappy.

By the time the CIB launched their investigation, I noticed she had started questioning Donna's authority and was developing issues with her mother who I suspected of working as an organiser in the sex industry. My suspicions were confirmed during a conversation with Georgina about Australian rock singer Michael Hutchence, who'd allegedly killed himself by accident the day before while practising erotic asphyxiation.

We talked more about sex, and Georgina revealed that for a good while she'd been running a home-based call centre for a brothel frequented by several well-known Premier League footballers. I concluded that if the call centre was being run from Chineka's home then she probably knew what was going on, and this was the source of her distress.

Although Georgina and I briefly became intimate during this period, I didn't share my concerns with her. I probably should have, but simply couldn't bring myself to burden her any further because deep down I still felt guilty and partly responsible for how her life tuned out.

Around the same time L&F started to collapse I began an ill-fated relationship with G&K Fabrics and Furniture, a wholesale firm based in Surrey that was introduced to me by Alan Goldberg - a stocky, dark-haired textiles merchant who I'd met through Simon a few years earlier.

Alan was a Jewish wide boy who was four years younger than me and drove an £80,000 blue Mercedes Benz SL 500. He owned a profitable warehouse in Rotherhithe, southeast London, and was alleged to have some gangster connections.

Even though I'd lost L&F, I still had staff to pay and a lifestyle to maintain. I searched for new opportunities and on several occasions spoke with Alan about establishing a new, legitimate business. But things didn't work out like that. The long and short of it is that after offering corporate secretarial services to G&K, I found myself at the centre of a long firm fraud.

The scam, which was allegedly created by the Kray twins in London's East End, occurs when a fake company is set up and run for a period of time as an apparently legitimate business in an attempt to build up good credit. Once this has been established, the organisers collect as many goods from as many suppliers as possible before secretly closing down the business, relocating, and taking any profits. A new business is quickly set up, and once all the goods are sold the organisers pocket the revenue and walk away without having to pay back the original suppliers.

Following my appointment as G&K's company secretary, I set up new bank accounts and made the necessary filings at Companies House. Suppliers were contacted and told the business would be selling home furnishings from a warehouse in Acton. There was a 90-day window to receive as many deliveries as possible. Generally, suppliers start chasing for payment 30 days after delivery so the operation had to be swift and efficient.

Deliveries worth between £5,000 and £30,000 started arriving at the warehouse. Over the next two months, G&K received a consistent supply of bed linen, curtains, crockery, cutlery, microwaves, TVs, computers and around £400,000 worth of fabrics and soft furnishings.

However, the scheme began to unravel when a supplier became suspicious and contacted the police. The warehouse was placed under surveillance and early one morning, about a week later, the feds made their move. They raided the warehouse and arrested one of G&K's drivers. It was game over and only a matter of time before I'd be hauled in for questioning.

CHAPTER THIRTEEN
A Slippery Slope
(1997 - 2000)

By the autumn of 1997 I knew the police investigation into G&K had started because two unnervingly polite detectives turned up at my office in Harrow and began asking general, but carefully worded questions about the business.

Although I tried not to think about it, the prospect of returning to jail hung over me like a thick, grey rain cloud. I decided to clear my head by flying to San Diego, California, where I stayed with Stephanie, a stunningly beautiful half-Italian and half-Sri Lankan lady I'd been seeing the year before.

Stephanie fell for me quite hard and the affair caused her such distress that she eventually immigrated to the United States to join her sister Trudie, who'd relocated from London with her husband a few years earlier. Stephanie had established herself and was making shitloads of money. I told her about the investigation and she begged me not go back to London. I considered her proposal, but returned home after 10 days because I simply wasn't prepared to leave Donna and two-year-old Darius.

Before G&K collapsed I'd launched a utilities company called Utilico Ltd, which provided least-cost routing services for cheaper landline telephone calls. I secured contracts with Energist, a Reading-based firm that used the national grid to operate telephone amenities, and City of London Telecommunications who offered a 30% saving on local and international calls.

I resold both services to the Quality Inn and Comfort Inn Hotel chains and expanded into gas and electricity, supplying customers across southeast England through a contract with Beacon Gas. A company in Yorkshire, Northern Energy, gave me permission to supply customers in Sheffield, which was too far away so I subcontracted the deal to former L&F salesman Gary Mills.

Additionally, I threw myself into a series of new ventures including Golf Unlimited, a company that sold businessmen low-cost access to dozens of golf clubs across the country. I got the idea after an impromptu meeting with Douglas Hippolyte, an entrepreneurial and articulate young black guy I'd recruited to L&F a few years earlier.

During a brief conversation over coffee he explained how the golf club membership company he worked for generated revenue. As a result, Douglas's employer's operation became one of the many business models I copied, enhanced and made more profitable.

The startups kept me busy as did Dionne Short, a Golf Unlimited saleswoman who I began having an affair with. She was younger than me, attentive, business savvy, creative and going out with a guy called Pierre who was a lot younger than her.

I was making money and working hard to steer my thoughts away from the police investigation, but my mind was nevertheless plagued by distant memories of prison life.

Around the same time G&K collapsed I moved Donna and Darius into a three-bedroom, semi-detached house in the leafy northwest London suburb of Pinner Park in Harrow. We were a young couple, Donna in her mid-20s and me in my early 30s, with a nice lifestyle. She worked in the City and drove a Rover 216 Cabriolet, while I worked locally, drove a £70,000 SL280 Mercedes Benz Convertible and was responsible for mortgage, au pair and nursery school payments comprising around £3,000 each month.

After Donna gave birth to our second son, Dillon, I told her the full story about G&K and the police investigation. Naturally, she went nuts: 'That was stupid,' she fumed. 'Why would you do something like that? You're gonna get convicted. You're going to jail.'

I disagreed, saying: 'No, no, no,' and tried my best to convince her that I could still walk on water, even though deep down I was beginning to question my own abilities and decisions.

Shortly after we moved into the new house and a day before I was scheduled to fly to South Africa with Simon, Dennis came to visit. He told me about some Cameroonian guys he'd met who claimed to have access to money-printing machines and were looking for investors.

I'd been friends with Dennis for almost 20 years, and although he was probably closer to me than my own brother I was beginning to see that we were slowly drifting apart. He asked me for £50,000 to help finance the scheme and appeared confident that my investment would generate at least £150,000 in profit.

I told Dennis I didn't believe the story he'd been told and warned him against investing any money in the scheme. But he was determined. I suspected that something was wrong with the deal, but was too caught up with my own problems to give it any further thought.

In the months that had passed I'd kept abreast of the G&K investigation through some of the people the police contacted, including a girl at my local bank and Nick, a likeable friend of Alan's who prepared the accounts for G&K, drove a Ferrari and hailed from Gants Hill, east London. By the time the police called me in for questioning nine months had passed since the warehouse raid and G&K had fallen into compulsory liquidation.

Sometime during the summer of 1998 I appeared at Holborn Police Station alongside Alistair McIntyre, the criminal solicitor I met during the L&F days. Alistair, who was Scottish, had made a name for himself working at a small, Liverpool-based law firm.

In the previous years, my personal assistant Marcia and I had given Alistair plenty of work, including a high-profile murder case. So he was my natural choice and first port of call for criminal legal matters.

Prior to our arrival at the station (which specialised in white collar fraud crimes), Alistair had instructed me to give a 'comment' interview. In retrospect, that advice was unwise because it changed the focus of the police investigation. After my interview, all the police had to do was find evidence to contradict my statement and every time they did their case appeared stronger than mine. I was pissed at Alistair, and he knew it.

My businesses were functioning, but the new mortgage payments and hefty childcare expenses were depleting my finances. I turned to Alan who agreed to drip-feed me £2,000 a week for the next year, which allowed me to pay off Bob MacDavitt, give Marcia some money and continue funding my lifestyle.

Still, even with the additional funds I became increasingly stressed as the trial date grew closer and remember asking myself, *'Peter, how did you come so far and still manage to end up in the same place?'*

I needed more money and decided to seek help from Alfred, the Zimbabwean millionaire who'd attempted to buy *Pride* magazine in 1992. I went to his London office and spoke to his PA.

After a brief wait, Alfred whizzed into the reception area where I was sitting. We spoke briefly and he suggested that I call him later that week. When I did, he told me to meet him at what is said to be London's most expensive hotel, The Lanesborough in Knightsbridge.

We sat down and had a single malt whisky before he turned and asked: 'Well, what do you want? I wanted *Pride*, but you didn't give it to me. Now you don't have it. So what do you want from me?'

I was taken aback and in that moment realised I'd made a mistake in seeking support from Alfred. 'Never mind, it's alright,' I said before leaving swiftly.

In February 1999 me, Marcia, Alan and two of his drivers stood trial at Southwark Crown Court on charges of conspiracy to defraud. The case was declared a hung jury and everyone, except me, was acquitted. Alan collapsed in the dock when he was found not guilty and celebrated by taking everyone out to Sir Terence Conran's restaurant, Quaglino's, in St James's.

I was happy for him, but my delight was tempered with the knowledge that according to British law when there's a hung jury the judge can either dismiss the case or order a retrial.

Even though I hadn't been found guilty the judge ordered a retrial, which I faced single-handedly in June 1999. Alistair was out of the country at the time, which left me feeling lonely, isolated and totally pissed off.My barrister said I should expect to receive four years in prison, but I got a huge boost when the jury came in and I realised half of them were Africans. 'Yes!' I secretly screamed. *I've got my people here. I'm going home.'*

The trial was short and ended unexpectedly. On the morning of the verdict, Donna and I had a massive argument that had started the night before. We were quarreling as I left the house and shut the front door. It simply didn't occur to me that many months would pass before I'd see that door again.

The jury was sent out at lunchtime and I thought they'd take all day like the jurors in the first trial. But these guys were back in less than an hour. I was called in for the verdict and stood in the dock trying to exude confidence. All I needed was for three jurors to find me innocent, which would result in another hung jury and an instant acquittal. I was devastated when they came back with a guilty verdict.

I turned and looked at the black people on the jury and silently screamed, *'Why did you do that!?'* But they just stared back with blank expressions on their faces.

I assumed my legal team would be given time to prepare our next move, but the judge said: 'Right, time is pressing and I want to get on with sentencing. Remand the defendant into custody.'

I couldn't believe how swiftly things were moving. I asked my barrister: 'Isn't the judge going to adjourn for three weeks while the sentencing reports are compiled?' His response was swift and cutting: 'He doesn't need to. You are, Mr Murray, an established and prolific criminal.' I couldn't believe my ears: 'How dare you call me that,' I bellowed. 'I've been an industrious person and kept out of trouble for a long time. Do you know how many businesses I've run, people I've employed, and taxes I've paid? I genuinely got caught up in something that went out of control.'

My barrister was unimpressed: 'Well Mr Murray, you're going to be sentenced now so I suggest you just take it like a man. Chin up old boy. I said you could expect four years, but I'm going to do my best. I know this judge. Don't annoy him, and let's see what we can do.'

He asked for the case to be adjourned for three weeks so we could collect some references to show the court that I was an industrious professional. But the judge said: 'No, I don't believe it. This man is a prolific offender. He's a gangster. He just hasn't been caught for 14 years.'

The judge gave us 24 hours to get as many references as we could. I was remanded into custody and sent to HMP Brixton for the night. I remember driving in the sweatbox (prison van) across the Elephant and Castle roundabout, fretting over my fall from grace and the possibility of receiving a four-year prison sentence at the age of 33.

However, within minutes of arriving in Brixton I saw Dennis and another friend from the ends, Andy Roberts, whose legal problems were far more serious. Both men were furious with each other because they'd lost more than £400,000 investing theirs and other peoples' money in the money-printing venture. Unsurprisingly, the business turned out to be a scam and the Cameroonians disappeared with all the cash.

However, about a year later Andy and Dennis tracked down one of the scammers, held him captive and now stood accused of torturing the man in an attempt to retrieve their money. They'd contacted the Cameroonian gang and tried to get them to pay a ransom in exchange for their friend's release. But the scammers, fearing for their lives, called Interpol who in turn contacted the Metropolitan Police who stormed the building in northwest London where the man was being held.

Andy and Dennis were both looking at 12 to 18 years in prison. The four years I faced paled in comparison and gave me some context of the severity of my situation.

When I arrived at court the following day I could see Donna, my sister Elizabeth, Delroy MacIntosh and Stephen Davis in the public gallery. I remembered the last time I was in this situation during the summer of 1986 when I'd received a six-month probationary sentence because the judge had been impressed with my employment references.

Sadly, history didn't repeat itself and after my barrister made his plea the judge said: 'Before I pass sentence Mr Murray, I must say having read all of your references it is truly remarkable that you've managed to stay on the right side of the law for the past 14 years.

'I take note of the businesses you have engaged in during that period, and the fact that you are a married homeowner who lives with your wife and young children. I have to say that does not speak to me of a criminal. That speaks to someone who has really tried to turn their life around.

'Mr Murray, this morning I had every intention of sending you to prison for a period of no less than four years. But no. I want to see you re-engage with the community and pursue an industrious life at your earliest opportunity. 'However, I must be seen to be applying justice so I'm sending you to prison for 18 months. If you're good, obviously you should know this by now, you can be out in nine months. Take him down.'

I returned to HMP Brixton. Prison life had changed quite a bit since I left youth custody in December 1985. Now there were TVs, Sony PlayStations and toilets in the cells. Buying confectionary from the canteen was like shopping at Tesco Express. It was nothing like I remembered.

I felt like shit. All I wanted to do was keep my head down and get out. I knew I didn't belong there and no longer considered the other inmates as peers. They were criminals and I was a businessperson. I had no association with them and would walk around the exercise yard with my glasses on. I stayed by myself, didn't socialise, never visited the TV room and wasn't part of a clique.

Some inmates thought I was a geek or a weirdo, but a few people from the ends who'd just arrived would hail me up and tell the other prisoners: 'Yo, don't look at him and think he's an idiot. That's an old-skool OG.' And every now and again I'd get some respect.

I was with Dennis and Andy for about a week before I was moved to another wing where I was supposed to get privileges, including a job in the kitchen. But that changed after I had a fight with my cellmate, a French-speaking African.

Apparently a screw told one of the prisoners that someone on our wing had raped a girl and given her a sexually transmitted infection, before pointing to our cell and saying: 'He's in there.' There were only two of us in the cell, and because he'd assimilated into the population but I'd been reserved and solitary some of the inmates assumed I was the rapist.

Greg, a prolific pickpocket from Kensal Rise who was serving a short sentence, told me what was going on: 'Yo, I've already told the man dem that it ain't you,' he assured. Nevertheless, I was on the verge of depression and extremely angry with myself for getting sent back to jail.

I really didn't need a false accusation of rape lingering over my head. The following day when my cellmate started throwing his weight around I got vexed, put a battery in a sock and beat him up.

As soon as the cell doors opened he ran outside and made a whole heap of noise to attract attention from the screws who came over and nicked me. I denied any wrongdoing but was transferred the following morning to HMP Belmarsh in southeast London.

I remained in Belmarsh for a few months before being relocated to HMP Weare, a prison boat docked in Portland Harbour, Dorset, which the UK government purchased four years earlier from the New York City Department of Correction.

There, I prepared myself for the 21st century by studying an Information Technology course that taught me how to use a personal computer. I learned about Microsoft Office applications such as Excel, Word and PowerPoint, and experienced a faint scene of déjà vu when I thought back to when I'd studied an office practice and typing course at HMP Borstal in Feltham 17 years earlier.

As I've said before, prison time can be helpful. It just depends what you do with it. A lot of people slip into bad habits and forget what they've learned when they come back out. Not me though. I was determined to improve all aspects of myself and my environment.

Chineka, who at long last started calling me 'dad', came to visit and it felt like our relationship was finally improving. She was 19 years old and living on her own in a flat in Tottenham having fallen out with her mum.

After serving seven months of an 18-month sentence I was released from HMP Weare on 15 January 2000 and spent two months on tagged home curfew probation before my world began to disintegrate further.

I was trying to enrol on to a master's degree course in either business administration or music management, and had started hanging out with Alan who gave me a job collecting (legal) debts from some Jewish and Asian market traders who owed him money. He'd put the frighteners on them and I'd follow up, usually with a telephone call or meeting. That became a nice little earner as the traders would cough up £5,000 here and £10,000 there, and I'd split whatever I collected 50-50 with Alan.

On 22nd May 2000, after a trip to get information about a master's course at City, University of London in Clerkenwell, I bumped into someone I'd known for more than 25 years but hadn't seen in a while - Winston Brown, who was living nearby in Hackney.

Although Winston had previously received four years in prison for entering a Turkish fast food shop and using the owner's kebab skewers to stab a man on the street, I still considered him a good friend who'd attended Darius's christening and always shown me love. I was happy to see my old friend and had no way of knowing that in the coming days our chance meeting would place me at the centre of a murder investigation.

Winston and I went to a wine bar in Hoxton and after a few drinks decided to go to his apartment, which was at the top of a small block of flats a short distance away. We drank a few beers, smoked weed and continued to reminisce about old times. I met his partner, a white girl named Janice, and their two-and-a-half-year-old daughter, Camille.

According to court documents and eyewitness statements taken by the police, later that night Winston and a neighbour got into an argument that escalated into a deadly altercation. According to the police report, Winston ran out of rolling papers and went across the landing outside his apartment to ask neighbours Keith McMann and Laura Hanson if they had any Rizla.

By some freakish coincidence on that same day, Danny Green (the dark, muscular bully I'd met at Stamford House Remand Centre 20 years earlier) was staying with Keith, who happened to be his brother-in-law. Danny had just returned to Keith's flat after visiting a heroin dealer, but had forgotten to shut the front door. Subsequently, when Winston stepped inside to ask for Rizla, he found Keith and Danny preparing to smoke the drug.

It was an awkward moment. Keith and Danny were clearly embarrassed, so Winston took some rolling papers from Laura, made his excuses and returned to his own flat. However, Danny was angered by the intrusion and went outside to protest. Winston stepped out of his flat and the men argued and fought briefly on the landing before Keith and Danny returned to their flat and shut the door.

Winston went inside his flat, armed himself with two large knives, returned to the landing and shouted for the men to come back out. Keith opened the door and Danny must have seen the knives in Winston's pockets because he pulled his brother-in-law back into the flat. At that moment, Winston stabbed Danny in the abdomen. The 20-centimetre blade entered Danny's liver, severing his intestines and portal vein.

Danny staggered backwards, screaming: 'Keith, he's done me, the bastard's stabbed me,' before collapsing on the floor. Keith shut the front door. But Winston kicked it down, stabbed him in the chest and side, and attempted to wound Laura who received a cut on her wrist.

After returning to his flat, Winston came to my house with Camille and Janice, who used the landline to call her father. That's how the police traced Winston to my house, which was full at the time because Donna's family from Jamaica and Canada had come to stay with us.

By the time the police raided our home the following morning, Winston, Janice and Camille had gone. Unfortunately, Donna's mum, aunt and uncle were still in the house. I wasn't home and didn't go back. I'd been one of the last people inside Winston's flat before the killing and wasn't sure if I'd left a DNA sample or some other evidence behind. I'd only been out of prison for 125 days and was petrified that if I handed myself in the police would take one look at my record and throw me back inside. I decided to run until I worked out my next move.

I was scared, confused and angry with myself. I just couldn't understand how over a three-year period I'd gone from being the director and owner of a £1 million company to a prime suspect in a police murder investigation.

CHAPTER FOURTEEN
Descent into Hell
(May - August 2000)

Winston and I spent a couple of days at a flat in west London, which belonged to a cousin of his friend TC. Winston was convinced that we had to find and kill his neighbours Keith and Laura because they were the only witnesses to Danny's stabbing.

My friend Delroy visited and tried to persuade me to leave on several occasions. He said: 'Peter, this is nuts. You need to break away from Winston. You do not want to go on trial with this guy because he's going to sink you and you're going to find yourself doing some serious jail time.'

One morning we awoke to see feds searching the street and decided it was time to move. TC suggested we travel to Bath in South West England and stay with some family he had there. Winston and I agreed, but quickly found ourselves in a dangerous and awkward dilemma. TC suggested we go for a drive in his cousin's car, an old, blue, two-door Vauxhall Nova that had half of its front number plate missing.

I didn't feel comfortable sitting in the back seat and refused to get in. But Winston insisted: 'Get in the car, get in the car,' he kept saying. 'I'm God-blessed. Nothing's gonna happen to me.'

After Winston and I got into the back, TC sat in the passenger seat and his cousin started the ignition. We drove for no more than four minutes before two unmarked police vehicles hard-stopped our car and we were surrounded by a squad of armed police officers. I heard one say: 'We suspect this car's been used as the getaway vehicle in a recent armed robbery.'

We were arrested and taken to a local police station. All of us gave false names. But I didn't know what name Winston had given, he didn't know what name I'd given and neither of us knew the name TC gave. I didn't want the police to find out my identity and initially refused to let them take my fingerprints and DNA. But they came back the following day, manhandled me and took some swabs.

I explained that at the time of the robbery I was at London Paddington station boarding the train to Bath, and suggested they contact the British Transport Police whose closed-circuit TV system would confirm my location and departure time.

Afterwards I remember sitting in my cell thinking, *I've just come out of prison, the police have raided my home as part of a murder investigation, and now I've been arrested for armed robbery. This is not looking good. I'm done for now. I'm looking at 15 to 20 years in prison. I'm never going to see Darius and Dillon grow up. These feds are going to find out who I am and then it's over. Curtains.'*

However, the following morning a custody officer came and escorted me out of the cell. He walked me through to the custody suite, gave me my belongings and said: 'We've seen the footage from the cameras at Paddington station. Your story checks out. You're free to go.'

I couldn't believe it. Our stories corroborated, so TC and Winston were released within an hour. We had to leave Bath immediately. At any moment a fax would be coming through from Scotland Yard confirming my identity and I would undoubtedly be rearrested. We headed to the train station and went straight back to London.

I went to look for my daughter at her flat in Tottenham and made the mistake of bringing Winston with me. Chineka was furious that I'd brought him to her home. She knew of his reputation through her mother's friend Jennifer (a girl I'd briefly dated, who had children with Winston's brother).

Chineka cussed me off: 'Why have you brought him here?' She yelled. 'I can't believe you're going on like this. You've just got out of jail, you're on the run for [an alleged] murder, and now you're rolling with Winston Brown.' Winston, who'd been waiting in the passage, could hear every word and how strongly Chineka was rebuking me. He came into the front room and said: 'Peter, I'm off. I'm going.'

Chineka continued: 'What about Donna, Dillon and Darius Dad? Are you even thinking about them? I can't believe I'm going to lose you. You're going to jail for life. Dad, your priorities are way off and right now I just want you to go. Just get out. I don't want to see you, just go.' And that was the last time I saw Chineka.

I phoned her a few days later and she said: 'Why are you calling me? Dad, you've made yourself clear by your actions, not with your words.' I asked her to explain, and she reminded me that a year earlier she'd moved flats because a guy had been harassing her. I helped her decorate both properties, but had refused to get involved in the dispute. Now, she accused me of failing to support her.

She said: 'You once told me that "your actions are so loud I can hardly hear your words". Well, when a guy was distressing your daughter, what did you do? Nothing. But some junkie called Danny distresses your friend and now you're wanted in connection with a murder. Dad, your actions have spoken.'

I had no way of knowing that would be our last conversation. I'd never known her to be so angry and simply thought she needed time to calm down and that I would speak with her in a few days.

Winston began drinking heavily, which made him very unstable. I think the more the gravity of his situation dawned upon him, the more he drank. He quarrelled constantly and fell out with one of my friends who said to me: 'Peter, you may have to take Winston out because you cannot go to trial with him. He's drinking every day. Just get him drunk and we'll kill him together.'

I was anxious and my emotions were running high. By now I'd concluded that my best option was to surrender, but Winston wasn't ready to capitulate. We argued, and when he eventually realised that I was determined he tried to tell me what to say to the police.

I told him: 'Look, I'm going to surrender. I'm not going to put you in it, but I'm not going to make my position any worse than it already is.'

I surrendered around five weeks after my chance meeting with Winston in Hoxton. Aside from Janice's phone call from my house, the police had no evidence connecting me to Danny's killing so I was released on bail. Winston surrendered a week later and was remanded in custody and charged with murder attempted murder, and grievous bodily harm.

I went home to reconcile with my wife, but she was pissed and in no mood for appeasement. Her aunt and uncle had gone back to Canada, but my mother-in-law stayed behind. Clearly emboldened by her presence, Donna started acting unusually distant.

I asked her mother to leave while I spoke with Donna, but she refused. We argued and I said: 'Look, my wife and I have some matrimonial issues that we're trying to resolve and you being here really doesn't help. This is my house, I bought it, and I'd like you to leave.' Around 20 minutes after she'd gone the police arrived.

After departing, my mother-in-law (seemingly in a fit of rage) had called the police, gave them my address and told them her son-in-law, who was on bail for murder, was threatening her daughter. Donna was upset that I'd asked her mother to leave, but told the police everything was okay and under control. After they left, she blasted me: 'You're meant to be a successful businessman, but you got mixed up in some high-profile fraud.

'When you went to jail, I said "please, let this be a one-off". So what do you do? You come out of jail and make armed police raid our home at seven o'clock in the morning. 'Then you go missing for six weeks and want to come back and tell me you're on bail for murder. I don't know you anymore. You're not the person I married. This really isn't working out. I think we should separate.'

I hadn't seen that coming. I'd upset Donna before, but there was never a hint that she wanted out of the marriage. I was stunned and concluded that she simply needed some space. I booked a flight to Jamaica where I planned to relax, think and clear my head.

During my time in jail, I'd befriended a Jamaican named Kenneth who'd since been deported. He phoned me regularly and kept saying that I should visit him so we could talk business.

In July 2000, I arrived at Norman Manley International Airport in Kingston, and took a two-hour taxi ride to meet Kenneth who lived in the rural parish of Portland. I booked into a hotel. He picked me up, and we went to his house. I met his family, we ate dinner and the two of us talked about our respective situations.

I told him about Donna and the murder investigation and he told me that he'd acquired another passport and was planning to return to the UK to set up a ganja smuggling operation, which he wanted me to finance.

I explained that I didn't know anything about the drugs trade, but he told me not to worry because he had a powerful obeah man who could make UK customs and immigration officials blind to his contraband merchandise. He assured me the same witchdoctor could 'fix' all of my problems and promised to take me to him the following day.

We left a little after six o'clock the next morning and drove for 30 minutes through the lush Blue Mountains. Kenneth's obeah man operated out of a small wooden shack located at the top of a steep hill, deep in Jamaica's longest mountain range. There was a long queue of around 70 to 80 people of all ages snaking from the shack down to the foot of the hill.

Kenneth took me straight to the front of the line and every few minutes I'd catch brief glimpses of this supposedly mystic man as he'd come outside, go into the vegetation behind the shack and return with a handful of herbs and plants.

After about 10 minutes he called Kenneth inside. Two minutes later, Kenneth returned and said: 'Mi talk to 'im and tell 'im seh yuh come from foreign and got to see him now, now, now. No worry mon, 'im wi' look after yuh.' I went into the shack and sat down at a table where the man was reading tarot cards. He looked at me, turned a card and said: 'Ayyyee! Mi nah wan' read yuh. Mi not going any further.'

I said: 'But hang on a minute, you haven't told me anything yet.' He continued: 'No, no, no, yuh a God-blessed yute. God have 'im hand pon your life, mi nuh wan' interfere.' I surmised that a little cash might make him feel more comfortable and peeled off some US$100 notes. Sure enough, he started to read me.

He said: 'You are in business, but you have been in trouble because you have not been paying what's due to the government. Yuh nah pay yuh taxes. And there's something else. Something's brewing at home. Your wife is very, very angry and her mother is inciting the anger.'

I kept listening and started to wonder if Kenneth had told him these things because he was pretty accurate. Then he asked: 'A who yuh a run from; you a run from police?' I told him: 'No,' but he insisted: 'Yes mon, yuh 'av police pon yuh.'

I explained that I was on bail and had to return to the police station for an identification (ID) parade, and if I was picked out I'd be charged with murder. That's when the obeah man told me: 'I will get you something to stop them from picking you out. Don't worry yourself, we a go fix dem business. You are a very blessed man who can make a lot of money, but you have to deal straight with the government. Give unto Caesar what is due unto Caesar. Pay your taxes and give what is due.'

This comment impressed me because I'd previously been reluctant to pay monies to Her Majesty's Revenue and Customs. And one of the main reasons L&F collapsed was because the company's tax bill had grown so large that I simply couldn't afford to pay it.

Until that moment I'd always equated all government systems as the same. So ignoring and outwitting the taxman felt like some form of twisted retribution for the years of ill treatment I'd received as a child in the state's care.

Then the witchdoctor said something that surprised and puzzled me: 'There is an enemy close by who is going to betray you.' I tried to decipher who he was talking about. Winston and Alan were the first names that popped in to my head, but I never considered he might be referring to Kenneth.

As I reflected on my relationship with HMRC, the man left the table and went out into the bush behind his shack. He returned a few minutes later with a small bottle of what looked like thin, red ink. He told me to dip my finger in the ink and use it to draw a crucifix on my chest every morning. I was given a parchment paper with a few lines of text, which he said I should read backwards before reciting the *Lord's Prayer* and *Psalm 23*.

He then handed me a bag of golden stone-coloured dust that looked like sherbet powder, and said: 'When you go to your ID parade, sprinkle this on yourself and your enemy will never see you.'

I was told to remove a ring from my finger. He took the ring into the bush, returned minutes later and said: 'Put your ring back on. Whenever you feel it burning or irritating it means an enemy is nearby and you must leave the spot immediately because you're in danger.'

Kenneth and I left shortly afterwards. I can't recall what else we did that day, but later in the evening we went to a bar where I met a go-go dancer who I brought back to my hotel room. She tried to charge me a ridiculous fee for a blowjob, so I paid what I thought was a reasonable amount of money and asked her to leave. However, 20 minutes later she returned with around five policemen led by a corrupt inspector who threatened to lock me up if I didn't give her more.

I gave her an additional US$300, but in doing so unintentionally showed the inspector there were more notes in my wallet. He said I was buying myself out of jail, took the remaining cash and confiscated my passport. Before leaving the hotel room he demanded that I pay a further US$500 to get the passport back, and promised to return the following day to collect his money.

I still had some UK pounds in my suitcase, but not enough to get me home. And although I knew I was being extorted I couldn't afford to call the inspector's bluff and end up in a Third World prison without either cash or a passport.

I contacted Alan, explained my situation and asked him to send £1,000. He agreed, but warned that I faced a far more acute challenge back home.

'Mate, shit's kicking off,' he said. 'Donna's phoned me and Simon. She found some letters in the garage and found out about your affair with Dionne Short. She's going berserk.'

While I'd been on the run with Winston, I'd given Marcia and Karl George permission to go in the garage at my house and retrieve £20,000 and some important documents I'd stashed away.

Donna had no idea there was anything of value in the garage, so after a visit from Marcia and another from Karl she became curious. She searched and found some of my personal documents, including correspondence between me and Dionne with whom I'd had an intense, four-month affair before going to prison.

She also discovered the lyrics to more than 30 songs I'd written in jail, which focused solely on my dilemma as a married man who loved his wife but was having an affair with another woman who had a boyfriend. I knew the findings would hurt Donna immensely and could be used as additional justification for the separation she'd proposed a week earlier.

The following afternoon after I received the money and got my passport back I spent the rest of the day thinking about my wife and how I was going to save my marriage.

When Kenneth came to visit I told him about the incident with the go-go dancer and the corrupt police inspector, and he said: 'Yuh shoulda pay di girl di right money. Yuh shouldn't disrespect her 'cause dem police could all be her brother, uncle or cousin. Mi hope yuh learn from that.'

When Kenneth heard how quickly I'd gotten the money to get my passport back he returned to talking about smuggling ganja into England, and again asked me to finance his operation. 'All mi need is £5,000 and we nice. Mi wi' sen' shipment a England all day long, all you affi duh is sit back and collect money.'

I reminded Kenneth that I'd only come to Jamaica to see him, clear my head and give Donna time to calm down. He left and I hardly ventured out of my hotel room. After two days I decided to visit Kenneth at his house. When I arrived, his wife claimed her husband had been arrested for possession of two pounds (just under one kilogram) of ganja after being held in a roadblock by the same police inspector who'd extorted money from me.

She seemed to suggest that I was the main reason Kenneth had been arrested, and subtly implied that if I didn't put up the money to bail him she'd tell the police that I'd come to Jamaica to finance a drug deal.

I told her I'd return shortly with some money. But instead went back to my hotel, collected my belongings and headed to the capital city, Kingston. I booked into a hotel near the airport and spent the final two days of my Caribbean adventure thinking about my life, my marriage and the ID parade I was scheduled to take part in the following month.

I returned to London and attempted to patch things up with Donna, but she was absolutely livid. Undoubtedly encouraged by her mother I suspect, she'd drafted a divorce petition and refused to listen to anything I had to say. We argued for two days, mainly about Dionne. On the third morning we fought, I lost my temper and foolishly struck my wife. She went to work and later that day I took Dillon and Darius to the park.

The police had parked their cars around the corner from the house so I didn't notice them when we retuned. As soon as I took my key out of the lock and stepped past the street door Donna grabbed the kids and took them to another room. Two police officers walked out of my kitchen and I was arrested and charged with assault.

They could've taken me to the local police station in Harrow, but instead (just to piss me off I guess) I was taken to Hendon Police Station; the same place where less than two weeks earlier I'd been questioned about the killing of Danny Green by the newly formed Murder Investigation Team.

The police tried to suggest I was dangerous and implied the decision to grant me bail was a mistake. But Alistair came and quickly resolved the situation: 'There's nothing in it, it's just a domestic,' he told them. I was bailed on condition that I could not return home or communicate with Donna, and contact with Darius and Dillon had to be arranged via a third party.

I sent Alan to the house and Donna gave him two holdalls of clothes she'd packed. When he returned I broke down and cried: 'That's it. It's all over now,' I said. Alan put his arm around my shoulder and wiped the tears from my face. I think that was the first time I'd ever seen him demonstrate a human instinct.

On balance, pound for pound, Donna is the best woman I've dated by far. When my mother passed away I saw that my sisters had their families and realised I needed to build my own.

I'd watched how a lot of my friends had cocked up with their partners and decided that I was going to do things differently. I wanted a house, family and for the rest of my children to be with one woman. I asked myself: 'Do you believe in the institution of marriage, and is this woman the one for you?' The answer to both questions was a resounding 'yes'.

Donna's star sign is Leo. She's a lioness, which means you have to know how to stroke her the right way. When you do that you'll have an incredible force on your side. But if you go against the grain and stroke her the wrong way she'll come straight at you, hard and roaring.

Now when we speak I've learned when to say certain things and when to shut up. But I didn't know that back then, and was absolutely devastated by the breakdown of my marriage. And my wife's refusal to let me see my children.

***

I was using some of the paraphernalia the obeah man had given me, and it had started to influence my state of mind. I was incensed, stressed, depressed and had come to the conclusion that Donna was the source of all my problems. I contemplated killing her.

I decided to buy a gun and asked my sister's son Patrick, who was in his late teens, to hook me up with a dealer. He came back the following day saying he'd arranged for us to meet in an empty field in Alperton, northwest London, with a guy named T from a local gang.

T and two others arrived shortly after us, but the pistol they brought looked old and well used. I asked for something newer. We were told to wait for 20 minutes while they went for another firearm.

The ring started to burn my finger, but I'd forgotten the obeah man's warning so was caught completely unaware when two of the gun dealers returned without T, knocked out my nephew and robbed me at gunpoint. They took my car, Rolex watch, money, mobile phone and shoes so I couldn't chase them.

With the benefit of hindsight, I truly believe I witnessed divine intervention that night. God saved me from buying a gun to kill my wife. And God saved me and my nephew from being murdered. There's absolutely no doubt in my mind that had either one of us resisted in any way Parick and I would have been shot and killed.

We managed to get a taxi back to the flat in Hampstead that I rented with Alan. I gave Patrick some money to get another taxi home and began plotting my revenge. At the time, I don't think I was entirely aware that the focus of my anger had shifted from Donna to the robbers.

Aside from a heart-wrenching desire to see my children and reconcile with Chineka, my thoughts were now almost permanently sinful. I was angry, ashamed and disgusted with myself for becoming a gullible victim of crime like the many West End shoppers I'd preyed on in my pickpocketing teenage years. Ironically, the robbers were teenagers and I was 34. I became unreservedly convinced the only response that would heal my battered ego was to retaliate, viciously.

I suspected they thought I was a drug dealer and would probably keep my phone on to see if they could make any money from the calls I received. I attempted to lure them into a trap, and dialled my number. A stern but youthful voice answered the phone: 'Yo, yo, yo.' I disguised my dialect, and using a cockney accent pretended to arrange a drug deal.

'Yeah mate, where's Peter?' I asked. The Voice at the other end replied: 'Peter ain't around y'know, but I'm managing his phone. What do you want?' I said: 'Tell him that I've got the product, but if he wants it he'll have to come and get it.'

The Voice said: 'Yeah, yeah, yeah. How much is it by the way?' I toyed with him: 'You should know that. I've got two keys, and he knows that's 40 big ones. What time shall I phone back tomorrow to arrange the meet?'

I heard the young man trying to contain his excitement as he replied: 'Yeah man, call back the same time tomorrow.' I hung up the phone and smiled thinking, 'gotcha, you little bastard'.

I called my good friend Slinger, who came to visit. When he arrived I asked him to help me get a strap. Slinger stared at me for a long while and said: 'It's all around the hood that you're mixed up in something with Winston, and I'm busy telling people it's got nothing to do with you. But now you're coming to me on some different ting, talkin' bout you want a strap. Yo Peter, what's happened to you?'

I assured Slinger I was just taking care of business and he had nothing to worry about. He looked to the heavens, shook his head and tried to talk me out of the purchase. But after a few days he arranged for another supplier to deliver a MAC-10 machine pistol.

I was aching to exact my revenge on the ballsy, young thugs who'd disrespected me earlier that week. I called my number again hoping the same person would answer. He did, and seemed excited and anxious to meet up: 'How come you ain't phoned?' He asked. 'Are we still doing this deal or what?'

I tried to make the set up appear as genuine as possible and replied: 'Yeah, we're gonna do the deal but I wanna speak to Peter first and make him give me the green light.' I let the guy convince me that he had permission to act on Peter's behalf before agreeing to confirm a time and location later that day.

Alan thought I was nuts. I told him I was serious and arranged to meet them at the South Mimms service station on junction 23 of the M25 motorway in Hertfordshire. My plan was to lure them by parking my car in an area away from the public. Then find somewhere nearby to hideout, and when they approached the car to rob me I'd sneak up and shoot them all.

But the scheme fell through when T recognised my voice. I was giving them directions and they must have had me on speakerphone because midway through the conversation I heard him say: 'Peter, is that you?' I recognised his voice from the field in Alperton and tried to put on my thickest cockney accent: 'Mate, what are you talking about?' I replied. But it was too late. T was on to me: 'Peter, what are you going on with,' he probed. 'Are you trying to set us up?' He ended the call. I tried ringing back, but kept getting voicemail.

***

It was August 2000 and I was becoming increasingly anxious about my appearance at the police ID parade, which was scheduled to take place later that month. Slinger and Alistair both kept trying to calm me down, and Alan was particularly concerned as he knew the guns I'd purchased were hidden somewhere in the flat we shared.

Alan and Delroy said the firearms were likely to cause me more harm than anyone else, and on several occasions both men tried to convince me to sell them. But I refused. Neither man wanted to be around me and Delroy, who I'd told about my trip to the obeah man, was convinced that my actions were being governed by black magic or some otherworldly source.

He said: 'You know what's wrong with you, mate? It's that obeah t'ing you're dealing with. It's sending you mad. Since you've come back from Jamaica it's like you think you're untouchable.'

I tried to convince him he was wrong, but deep down knew that my vibes, temperament and psychology had been altered. Just 18 months earlier I'd been a successful company director struggling to keep one of his many businesses afloat. Now, I was a gangster working with witchcraft. Or to use Delroy's words: 'Peter, you've become an agent of the devil. You're Satan.'

CHAPTER FIFTEEN
Hell
(August - December 2000)

I went to visit Winston who was being held on remand at HMP Pentonville near his home in Hackney. He said if I agreed to share the burden with him and profess to stabbing Keith, he'd admit to killing Danny.

Even though I hadn't committed any such crime, when I went to see him again (this time with his girlfriend Janice) at HMP Belmarsh, Winston repeated the proposal and insisted I'd only receive a two- or three-year prison sentence for wounding his neighbour with a knife.

I explained I couldn't help because if I took the blame for stabbing Keith, under the doctrine of joint enterprise in English law I'd also be held responsible for Danny's murder. Winston became angry and ordered me to leave the visit.

Driving home with Janice I broke down and started to cry. I'm not sure why I chose to speak with her, maybe I just needed to offload. I told her everything about my argument with Chineka, my plan to kill Donna and how I'd been robbed trying to buy a gun in preparation for her murder.

I think Janice was either too shocked or frightened to challenge anything I'd said, but I remember before leaving the car she looked at me, sighed and whispered: 'You really need to get some help or I think something bad's gonna happen.'

The ID parade was just days away, and I spoke regularly with Alistair to prepare myself for another dreaded encounter with the Metropolitan Police. Alistair was very clear: 'If anyone picks you out on this ID parade you will be charged with murder, attempted murder and joint enterprise. And you will be remanded into custody.'

According to Janice, the police's main eyewitnesses were a gay couple who lived on the floor below her and Winston's apartment. It may sound far-fetched, but at the time I was absolutely terrified they'd seen me visit Winston's flat in the hours before the murder and might mistakenly remember me as someone who'd been at the scene of the crime.

Patrick came to one of my meetings with Alistair, who took one look at him and said: 'Your nephew looks just like you. I think we should bring him on the ID parade.' After protesting, I eventually conceded.

On the day, I woke up petrified. I did all the ritualistic chanting the obeah man had instructed me to do and sprinkled a fair amount of magic dust over my head and shoulders to make myself invisible to the eyewitnesses.

It worked. There were six eyewitnesses, including the gay couple, and not one of them picked me out. Ironically, four out of the six identified Patrick as someone who was present at the scene of Danny's murder, even though he'd been nowhere near Hackney.

When the police discovered that Patrick was my nephew they got vexed and ordered another ID parade. But it didn't make any difference. On the morning I was scheduled to reappear at the police station I chanted with greater emotion and doused myself with even more powder. The result was the same. Not a single eyewitness picked me out.

I refused to acknowledge that my newfound good fortune derived from some type of demonic energy and simply believed that the paraphernalia I'd received from the Jamaican witchdoctor gave me awesome, superhuman powers that placed me in a different realm to everybody else.

I confessed to myself that Delroy had been right; I did feel invincible. There was no DNA linking me to the crime scene at Winston's flat. So now I just had to wait for the police to finish their investigation, admit they had no evidence and drop the charges against me.

I relaxed a little and started thinking about getting my life back on track. Inspired by the 30 songs I'd written in prison, I enrolled on to a music business course at City, University of London in Islington.

Then, at around 7.30am on 14th September 2000 I received a phone call that changed my life forever and sent me spiralling into a deep and exasperating depression (even now I'm still perturbed whenever someone calls me that early in the morning).

The Voice on the other end of the line belonged to my sister Chrissie. At first I thought she was going to tell me something dreadful like my nephew had been arrested, stabbed or shot. I was in no way prepared for the words that eventually stumbled out of her mouth.

'Um... It's Chineka,' she said. 'What's wrong with Chineka?' I asked. Chrissie took a deep breath: 'Uhm... She's passed away. She's dead.' I'd heard what my sister said but my brain refused to process the words.

I spewed a string of profanities: 'Fuck off. Sis, don't play a random joke like this on me.' The tone of Chrissie's voice changed: 'No Peter, I'm serious. She committed suicide. You really need to get round to the house.'

A series of nationwide fuel protests in the preceding days made travelling awkward. My Toyota Land Cruiser had no petrol, so Alan's friend Mark lent me his car. I called Donna. We weren't speaking to each other, but when I explained that Chineka had killed herself one month and one day after her 20th birthday she dropped everything and agreed to meet me at Georgina's house in Fulham.

Much of that day is a haze, but I clearly remember speaking to Chineka's best friend Carline Corbin who explained that although Georgina's partner Zeb found my daughter on 14 September, she'd hung herself the day before — exactly three years after her 17-year-old boyfriend Dean had died from leukaemia.

I'd met Dean on several occasions and thought he was a nice guy. He came up to the penthouse a few times and we'd joke and talk about designer labels because we liked fashion and both owned the same pair of Dolce & Gabbana trousers.

He was cool and Chineka, who'd endured a series of bad relationships, really loved him. We all knew that he was going to die one day, but I told Chineka to follow her heart.

Georgina was more cynical and would say: 'Why are you with him? You need to end that relationship because if you don't he's going to break your heart. He's not going be around, he's going to die. Leave him to die.' But Chineka either wouldn't or couldn't.

When Dean eventually passed I don't think Georgina allowed Chineka to grieve and would criticise her for spending hours and hours at his graveside: 'It's just a bag of bones, there's nothing there,' she would say. 'Cut him off and let go.' But Chineka never got over him.

I remembered how 16 years earlier while serving time in HMP Chelmsford I'd woken up one morning to discover that my cellmate had committed suicide. I'd only ever known prisoners in jail to hang themselves. But this wasn't an inmate, this was my first born child. Her lifeless body had been hanging for 12 to 18 hours before Zeb found her.

I went back to Chineka's flat in Tottenham to search for clues to help me understand what could've possibly driven her to take her own life, and in such a brutal manner.

I discovered a pair of letters. One addressed to me, the other to Georgina. My letter wasn't nice. Chineka tore me to pieces; berating my parenting style, and accusing me of being a 'chequebook dad' who put his friends before his daughter.

In her mother's letter she apologised, criticised me and heaped praise on her step-father Zeb, which was the final blow that really wounded me. I believed that I should have been the one to discover Chineka's body, and was jealous of Zeb for the adulation she bestowed upon him.

My daughter's condemnations pained as if hot metal stakes had been poked into my eyes. I was devastated and couldn't understand why she was so disparaging when all I'd ever done was try to get close to her.

For some reason my mind drifted to when I'd taken Carline and Chineka ice-skating for her 17th birthday. I remembered that as we left the rink in Bayswater we got into an altercation with a man who was driving a black taxi. I became furious when he drove past and called the girls 'hoes' and must've ran a quarter of a mile down the road trying to catch him.

In the decade that had passed since Georgina first made me aware that I was a father I'd tried my best to protect Chineka, but was angry with myself for failing to go and see her during the two months prior to her death. I wasn't sure how she would've reacted if I returned to her flat, and didn't know how to deal with the situation.

After consulting with Chrissie I decided not to share the contents of either letter with Georgina, but have always felt bad about depriving her of our daughter's final correspondence.

I had trouble accepting that Chineka had really gone, and even the next day when we went to identify her in the morgue I still believed I could wake up her motionless body lying on the slab in front of me.

Chineka's funeral took place on 30th September 2000. My recollection of the day is disjointed, but I remember the reading of the eulogy felt surreal. After a service, mourners are supposed to follow the body out of the church. But at Chineka's funeral the mourners left first because I was crying so much and wouldn't let go of the casket. I'll always love and appreciate my cousin Carlton for trying to pull me away so the burial could start.

At the graveside a tsunami of tears swept down my face, and as Chineka was being lowered into the hole I developed an overwhelming urge to fling myself on top of her casket. I've always wondered if Dennis read my mind because at that very moment he grabbed me firmly by the shoulder and kept me vertical.

Even though Georgina's family didn't contribute financially towards Chineka's funeral they were adamant that she be buried at Camberwell Old Cemetery in Lewisham, the same spot as her maternal great-grandfather.

Not wanting to upset anybody, I agreed. Only to discover weeks later that even though I'd paid for the funeral and internment I was forbidden from either decorating or placing a headstone on my daughter's grave because I did not own the burial plot.

As a result, anyone can unknowingly walk over Chineka's grave because the only thing that denotes its location is a small patch of grass. I appealed to Georgina several times to let me erect a headstone, but she refused to admit that Chineka had died. I can't be 100% sure, but I think she was angry with herself and feeling guilty. We all were.

I tried everything to resolve that situation, including hiring a private detective to find out who owned the plot of land. But there was nothing I could do and Georgina remained silent.

We exchanged a few words about four months later at the inquest into Chineka's death, but nothing of importance. I tried calling and wrote two letters asking if we could grieve together, but she never responded or answered my calls.

About a week after Chineka's funeral I received a call from Alistair informing me the police had dropped the charges and I was no longer a suspect in their investigation into Danny's killing.

Later that day, Donna and I had another blazing row. Everyone assumed that after the funeral she'd soften up a little and let me come back home. But she was unyielding, and by then had moved her mother and two brothers from Jamaica into our matrimonial home.

I had no income but was paying the mortgage and all the bills for the three-bedroom, semi-detached house that I'd bought three years earlier. And was barred from entering my own home.

In October, around the same time the clocks went back, I began to experience a curious combination of loss, guilt and bitterness. I was cold, despondent, and found myself considering murderous thoughts.

Once again, I erroneously concluded that my wife was the source of all my problems and resolved to cause Donna and her support network maximum inconvenience.

I visited my mother's grave and remembered when I was a teenager she'd tell me stories about her friends and insist that: 'Whatever you do, never buy a house with a woman.' At the time I had no idea what she was talking about, but she'd warn me nevertheless: 'Never you buy a house with a woman because they will call the police and say you beat them, whether it's true or not.

'Then you'll have to leave, and if you want to keep that house you'll have to continue paying the mortgage even if you're not living there. She can move another man into the house and do whatever she wants. But as long as you want that house you'll have to keep paying the mortgage. And even when you're ready to sell, if the woman has children you'll be lucky to get anything because the law is in her favour.'

I remember crying at my mum's graveside and saying: 'You're so right,' because that's effectively what Donna had done; kicked me out of the house and moved her family in so there was no way back.

Weeks earlier I'd fallen out with my flatmate Alan who thought I'd lost the plot. He'd become uneasy and wanted to know why I was still using the supplies the witchdoctor had given me if I was no longer under investigation. He kept asking where I'd hidden the guns. I told him they'd been sold, but he didn't believe me. We argued and I became angry, erratic and irrational. I moved out and went to stay with Delroy.

But after a couple of nights, the same thing happened. I tried to convince him the weapons were no longer in my possession, but he didn't believe me either. We argued and again I became angry, erratic and irrational.

I'd developed a fear of blades when I was 15 years old after being stabbed by Randy Pryce. However, on this particular night when I upset Delroy and he brandished a knife and told me to get out of his house my phobia disappeared.

Instead, the ring started to burn my finger and I felt my supernatural powers kick in. I sprang to my feet, pushed out my chest and dared Delroy to stab me with his kitchen knife. He said: 'You're fucking nuts mate. You need help.' I told him he couldn't throw me out because I had nowhere to go. But he was unwavering: 'That's not my fucking problem. You're mad,' he grunted, before kicking me onto the street.

I spent the next 10 days sleeping in my car. I thought about Chineka's suicide and how Donna had revoked access to my remaining children while playing happy families with her mother and brothers in my house.

Aside from my car, two holdall bags of clothes and a tortured soul, I had nothing. I was bitterly cold, extremely uncomfortable and severely depressed. I wanted Donna to feel the pain I felt. My thoughts became murderous and evil.

Alistair, Alan and I had invested in a franchise of legendary boxing trainer Emmanuel Stewart's Kronk Gym, which we established in Kentish Town. One day when I was returning from the gym having used the showers to freshen up, I met and befriended a woman named Marcia Bonner in nearby Camden Town. We connected on a spiritual level almost instantly and not long after we started talking she told me: 'I can feel your pain,' which made me cry again. I hadn't realised my grief was so palpable.

Marcia invited me to stay with her and her child, and I thankfully agreed. Around the same time, I contacted Donna and requested contact with Darius and Dillon. But she refused and kept saying: 'You're in no fit state to see the boys.'

I'd been instructed by the courts not to enter the family home, so one day when she'd gone to work I phoned the au pair and told her to bring my children outside because I was on my way to see them.

The au pair must have told Donna because just as she brought the boys outside to meet me, Donna's best friend and Dennis's former side-chick Sandra Barrett turned up. She was a songwriter who I used to really like. Usually we had a great rapport, but not on this occasion.

Sandra tried to pull Darius and Dillon away and I remember saying: 'Are you nuts? Just don't get involved with a man and his wife because you'll pay a price if you do.' She called the police who arrived just as I was driving off with my children. The police phoned and I told them to 'piss off'.

When I brought Darius and Dillon home later that evening, the police said Sandra had accused me of abducting them. I asked how someone can abduct their own children and explained that I was grieving the loss of my recently deceased daughter and hadn't seen the boys in many weeks.

Sandra's car mysteriously blew up a few days later. Around the same time, Marcia asked me to leave her home: 'You've done something,' she said. 'I can feel your energy; it's negative and dark. I don't want to know what you've done, but you can't stay here anymore. I've got to think about my child. You have to go.'

Nobody would take me in. Even my sisters were scared to be around me. While I'd never harm my children, with the benefit of hindsight I now understand why Donna was so reluctant to let me spend time alone with them. Alan and Alistair found me a garden flat in Hampstead and paid for my rent. I was sullen and spent most days alone battling to keep my sanity and focus on turning my life around. I cried continuously and only left the flat to buy groceries and attend the two music business courses I'd enrolled in at City, University of London.

I simply couldn't face the outside world and broke down whenever I saw black girls of Chineka's age. My sisters would tell me to come to their houses. They had no way of knowing that I didn't even feel comfortable being around their children. Not while I had a daughter in the grave and two sons I desperately wanted to see, but couldn't. The only person I wanted to be around was Georgina, but she had Zeb who I viewed as an obstacle.

I thought I was going nuts and wondered if my daughter's death was in any way connected to Danny's murder four months earlier. I spoke to my sister Chrissie who convinced me that as a sacrificial payment for visiting the obeah man the devil had taken control of Chineka's mind and driven her to hang herself.

She further claimed that Chineka would not rest in peace and was doomed to suffer in eternal damnation because she'd committed suicide. I doubt Chrissie realised that her comments were driving me to suicide. I was so unstable that anyone could've told me anything and I would've accepted it.

I held myself solely responsible for Chineka's death and believed that if I'd returned to her flat during the eight weeks after my visit with Winston she'd still be alive.

I thought it was wrong that Chineka had been left on her own and wondered if she was with Dean, or perhaps in a better place. I considered taking my own life and thought to myself, *'Chineka did it, and if she can do it to escape the pain so can I.'*

It felt as if I'd been disloyal to my daughter and that I should be with her. I'd failed to protect her when she was alive. Now surely the least I could do was be with her in death?

I thought I deserved to die and believed my career as a successful entrepreneur and businessman had been nothing more than a protracted 'Cinderella experience', which began when I was released from prison in December 1985 and ended when I was sent back in June 1999.

During those 14 years, I'd risen to great heights, but now I'd fallen back into the gutter where I belonged. Mother used to say: 'Every dog knows its four o'clock,' which means that no matter where you go or how far you reach in life, at some point you'll have to return home.

For me, that meant my corporate highlife and get-out-of-jail-free passes had expired, and I was destined to return to the hood, penniless. *'I'm 34 years old,'* I told myself. *'I've had a good run, but now it's time to bow out.'*

I remained steadfastly committed to murdering Donna and was trying to work out how to either kill myself or get the police to kill me after I'd committed the crime. The only problem was, if successful my plan would leave Darius and Dillon as orphans.

I spent many days contemplating these and other acts of wanton self-destruction. I was morally, spiritually, psychologically and emotionally bankrupt, and felt a sickness in my stomach as if my intestines were being ripped out. There's no doubt in my mind that I had become demon-possessed.

Meanwhile, I was attending two music business courses at City, University of London. The first ran for 12 weeks and was led by music lawyer Kienda Hoji and former artist Ade Adefolalu. The second course was led by a Nigerian lecturer named Boomy Tokan, a committed Christian who invited me to visit him at the Portobello Business Centre (PBC) in Ladbroke Grove.

On the first course there were between 15 and 20 attendees who must've thought I was extremely miserable. Slowly I began to introduce myself, and soon made friends with Patrick Lane, Mark Anderson, Marianne Miles and Deborah David, who looked vaguely familiar.

Around the same time, I also made friends with an attractive, dark-skinned lady named Jenny Charles, who attended Boomy's music course. Jenny and I developed a kinship and I dropped her home a couple of times after class.

One November evening we were talking in my car whilst parked outside of her flat in Hackney. Jenny always wrapped herself in elegantly patterned scarves, which she used to disguise ugly scars on her neck.

I knew she liked me so felt comfortable asking where the scars came from. Her answer made me reconsider the revengeful plans I had for Donna. Jenny had fallen in love with a man who began to physically abuse her very badly. One day she almost died when he smashed her face through a window, causing the mutilation to her neck. He received a lengthy prison sentence and eventually committed suicide days before he was due to be released.

When she told me I was instantly outraged and caught myself thinking, 'You hypocrite. What are you planning to do to your own wife, the mother of your children?' In that moment I decided that I would never harm a hair on Donna's head.

Over the next few weeks, Jenny stayed at my flat a couple of times. We slept in the same bed but I never touched her, nor did I tell her anything about Chineka, Donna, my sons or the murder. Although I refused to tell Jenny anything about myself, without knowing it she saved Donna's life.

Furthermore, I rekindled my relationship with my personal assistant Marcia Abbott, and started visiting Boomy at the PBC for weekly one-to-one consultancy sessions.

As part of the final project for Kienda and Ade's course, which culminated a few days before Christmas, each participant was expected to deliver a presentation outlining everything they'd learned during the past three months.

My presentation blew everyone away and when I mentioned that I'd founded and published *Pride* magazine Deborah jumped out of her chair and said: 'That's where I know you from!' We'd never met, but had seen each other's faces before as she'd previously worked for Dyke and Dryden, a British hair care company that advertised in *Pride*.

There's a special place in my heart for Deborah because during some of my darkest days after Chineka's suicide her infectious sense of humour and enthusiasm unknowingly provided a great source of comfort.

I believe Kienda and Ade used their course as a recruitment tool to source and cream off the best and most talented students for their own personal projects. And that's exactly what I did. After my presentation, I told everyone I'd incorporated a new company, the Trinity Music Group (TMG), and encouraged them to come and join my foray into Britain's underground music scene.

As I drove home, I laughed to myself for the first time in a long while. Unconsciously, I'd observed Kienda and Ade's business model, adapted it, and delivered a more polished version, just as I'd done many times before.

I was trying to steer my life in the right direction, but knew that it would take a lot of time, effort and positive energy before my fortunes became more favourable. If I really wanted to be happy and successful again I'd have to abolish all the dark and negative energy I'd invited over the past six months.

My healing process started on 25th December 2000 when I spent most of Christmas Day in bed, curled up in the foetal position bawling my eyes out like a newborn.

I remembered how Alan and Delroy both chastised me when I told them about my trip to the obeah man, and thought back to a few months earlier when Alan and I had been hanging out with a guy called Dave. He was a 40-something, ex-con from the Holloway Road area of north London who suffered from a droopy left eyelid, and had served time in several prison institutions including Feltham.

We used Dave mostly as an errand boy, but he became very concerned when I told him about the paraphernalia the witchdoctor had given me. 'Kiddo,' he said. 'You don't know what you're playing with. You can't come back from that Kiddo, that's Satanic. Do you realise what you've done? You've traded with Satan.'

Delroy had said the same thing and deep down I knew they were right.

When I was sent to prison for fraud in 1999 I became angry and turned my back on God. I blamed God for my extraordinary fall from grace and remember thinking, *'God, I honour and pray to you every day, how come you didn't save me?'*

In prison, I read and liked a book about science and religion that explored the idea of giving God a P45 (the UK tax document workers receive when their employment contracts are terminated).

I stopped praying, started saying that I'd given God a P45 and eventually negotiated a deal with the devil. I felt ashamed, dirty, vile and so disenfranchised that I didn't even feel worthy to call God's name.

I'd previously accepted there was a higher power controlling my mind, but only now did I acknowledge that Satan had a hold of me. The very thing that my mum had warned me not to get involved in, I'd gone and dabbled with: obeah.

I encountered my biggest fear and began to suspect that I was losing the plot. I thought about my brother Aaron, and remembered the horrible outings I'd taken as a child with my mother to see her friend Vivienne at the psychiatric hospital in Shenley.

Around this time, the lyrics to rap duo Outkast's song *Ms Jackson* rang inside my head like a bell. Throughout the autumn of 2000 that song (which explores how breakups are influenced by the relationship a man has with his mother-in-law) was everywhere; reminding me that to get Donna, my family and house back all I had to do was apologise, a trillion times, to my mother-in-law for kicking her out. But I couldn't do it.

I had nowhere to go, no one to talk to, and cried for weeks. Until one day, I turned to God and begged for forgiveness: 'God, I'm so sorry,' I wailed. 'I surrender to you because there's no way I can continue by myself. Please, just take this burden from me. Take this burden so I can move forward.'

CHAPTER SIXTEEN
Scrambled Eggs and a Quick Million
(2001)

During the first few months of 2001 I attempted to piece my broken world back together and began recruiting for Trinity Music Group (TMG).

I spoke with Dennis during the first week of January and asked why he hadn't called during the Christmas period. My lifelong friend was vex because I'd been visiting Andy Roberts (his co-defendant in the kidnapping, false imprisonment and grievous bodily harm court case). Dennis accused me of taking sides and spreading rumours about him.

Although over the next week I helped arrange his sister Violet's funeral and attended his father's funeral 12 months later, Dennis and I never spoke again after that phone call.

Similarly, although Delroy and I remained on good terms we eventually fell out in 2002 after he made an inappropriate comment about Chineka. I thought, *'Enough is enough.'*

I'm sure if you mention my name to Dennis or Delroy they'd cuss my clart. Still, regardless of the fact that I haven't spoken to either man in more than 15 years, I'll always consider them as my brothers.

A few weeks after my last conversation with Dennis, on 28th February 2001 another old friend who I no longer speak with, Winston Brown, was found guilty of murdering Danny Green.

I remembered how 24 years earlier, following a long chase Winston had laughed at me from the other side of a wire fence after he got away and I was arrested by the police. I also thought about how he was unapologetic and didn't give a shit about Danny's death, which alienated us because when he was acting indifferent and showing no empathy, I was grieving for Chineka.

Winston was sentenced to serve no less than 14-and-a-half years in prison. During the first part of his stretch he lost his 20-year-old son in a drive-by shooting. I had lost a 20-year-old daughter through suicide. Danny's children lost their father. We all lost.

A couple of weeks before Winston was found guilty, application forms for American Express and another credit card came through the letter box at the flat where I was staying. In a moment of madness, I filled them out but slightly misrepresented (by some years) the length of time I'd been living at the premises.

Three weeks later I found myself in possession of two brand new credit cards, and decided to take my PA Marcia out shopping for the day. They say 'behind every successful man is a woman', and maybe 90% of the time that woman is his wife. The remaining 10% are most likely PAs, and that's the position Marcia holds in my life. She's my rock.

I met her in 1991, when she was 17 and fresh out of school. She came to *Pride* on work experience, secured a post as the office junior and became such an integral part of the management structure. Faye and I both shared her as our secretary.

I noticed there was some common ground after it transpired that Marcia was from Harlesden, and although I'm almost 10 years older we both knew the same people. I liked her because she was and still is the perfect all-rounder; teachable, reliable, and very friendly.

But more importantly, I also found her to be extremely loyal. There were tough times at *Pride* when we couldn't pay the staff's wages and Marcia took the brunt of that but was always there.

Since I established L&F in 1994, I've incorporated and operated more than a dozen businesses and Marcia's been involved in almost every venture. No matter what happens, I may get rid of all my other staff but I'll always keep her.

As an entrepreneur there are times you'll fall flat on your face. And whenever that's happened to me (which has been a good few times) Marcia's always been there.

She's seen all my trials, tribulations, ups and downs. From gunmen storming into our offices to Chineka's suicide, and my entire relationship with Donna, including the birth of our three kids and the bitter divorce that followed.

I remember when I was getting divorced and everything I touched crumbled. Marcia's father had just died and I was flat broke, in mortgage arrears, and had smashed up my car. Even though I hadn't paid her in months, Marcia gave me £1,500 from the money her father had left behind. I felt bad taking it, but she insisted. I was so grateful, and the faith she showed in me that day is something I'll never forget. To me, that was more significant than a multi-millionaire giving me £1million because he can afford such extravagances.

Not long afterwards, I remember looking out of my bedroom window one morning and watching Marcia drive up to my house, park her car and walk across the road to start work. I was feeling dejected, but as I watched her stroll towards the house I began thinking about how for years she'd been coming to work for me day in, day out. I said to myself, *'You need to pull yourself together. This isn't just about you. Look at Marcia. She's placed all of her hopes and trust in you. You've got to succeed for her.'*

Marcia and I have never been romantically linked, but we've definitely grown together. She's like a younger sister, and I'll always be grateful for her years of devoted service and friendship.

When I linked up with Marcia for the shopping spree in February 2001 she'd been working for me for almost 10 years. I thought it would be a good idea to show my appreciation by taking her to the West End with my newly acquired cards.

We went to Selfridges where I used the credit cards as proof of identification to apply for a store card, which was issued instantly. I caned the shit out of the store card, purchasing bags full of clothes and consumer goods before moving on to Harrods where I did exactly the same thing.

Only this time, Marcia and I were apprehended by the store's security guards who turned us over to the feds. Unfortunately, the police took away my keys, located my car and found all the goods we'd bought that day. Worse still, they raided the flat while Alan was there, and tried to claim that both the cars I owned had been purchased illegally. Marcia and I were arrested, charged with fraud and deception and released on bail. I was furious with myself.

Just eight months earlier I'd been in the exact same situation in Bath: banged up in a police cell, lamenting my future and the possibility of once again losing my freedom. It felt as though every time I made one step forward I'd instigate some self-inflicted calamity that set me back three paces.

Around the same time Marcia and I were scheduled to appear in court, Alan and Alistair asked me to leave the apartment. So I moved into my sister's two-bedroom flat in Harlesden.

I knew if I pleaded guilty I'd be sentenced that day and probably taken into custody, or the magistrate might indict me and send the case to be heard at a Crown Court. I decided to plead not guilty because I knew the case would then be deferred to a Crown Court and I'd have six or seven months of guaranteed liberty to build up my good character. My plan was to gather some references, plead guilty at Crown Court and hope the judge appreciated the mitigating circumstances that led to my indictment.

Marcia pleaded guilty at the magistrates' court and got off with a non-custodial sentence. She warned me against going to Crown Court and suggested that I take my chances with the magistrates. Her argument made sense, but I wasn't prepared to take the risk of being incarcerated immediately. There was too much to lose and I'd come too far to simply go back to jail.

I wanted to push Trinity Music Group (TMG), which was slowly developing, and transmute my run of bad luck into something positive. I continued to attend the Portobello Business Centre (PBC) in Ladbroke Grove for one-on-one sessions with Boomy, who encouraged me to commit my life to Jesus Christ.

While attending a business outreach meeting in Harrow I befriended another Nigerian Christian named Pastor Joseph Jesuloba, and later became a member of his House of Hope church in Euston.

One day during a counselling session, Pastor Joe told me I should call my wife. I explained there was no point as she refused to answer my calls: 'Right now, Donna wouldn't give me the steam off her shit,' I told him.

Nevertheless, he asked for her number and called it. When Donna answered, he said: 'I have Peter here, and I'd like to talk with you.'

Lo and behold, what I'd previously considered unimaginable actually happened. Pastor Joe met and talked to Donna and called me afterwards. He said: 'I spoke with your wife and she gave her life to Christ. I expect to see you both at church on Sunday.'

I was gobsmacked. I couldn't believe what he'd achieved and told him for the first time about Chineka's suicide, the breakdown of my marriage, and how not seeing Darius and Dillon was tearing me apart.

He listened intently and said: 'Give your life to Christ and trust me, Donna will come back to you.' But I told him: 'Nah, nah, nah, you don't understand. She's gone for good.' And then Pastor Joe uttered a phrase I'll never forget and still use to this very day: 'Only God can unscramble a scrambled egg.'

As I drove home, I thought about the depth of this statement and remembered how he'd also said: 'There is no problem that God cannot deal with for you.' I decided to commit my life to Christ, and Donna began attending Pastor Joe's church. We arrived and left in separate cars. She never spoke to me, and although she brought the boys we sat in different sections of the congregation.

However, eventually we grew closer and later that year Donna and I were baptised together at the Kensington Temple London City Church in Notting Hill Gate.

My life was slowly improving and I decided to kick-start my new music business venture by establishing a network of inter-related organisations. These included Trinity Publishing Company, Trinity Record Company, Trinity Management Company and So Damn Tuff Productions - all under the umbrella of the TMG parent company.

I recruited some of the people I'd met on Kienda and Ade's course and set about trying to navigate my way into London's underground music scene. Jenny (the lady who'd unknowingly saved Donna's life) was the first to come on board. Deborah, the most popular member of the class, quickly followed: 'Look,' she said. 'You set up *Pride* so I'm definitely in,' which encouraged Patrick, Mark, Marianne and Michael Adelakun to join us.

I had neither money nor experience and was flying completely by the seat of my pants. Nevertheless, I believed wholeheartedly in TMG and was determined to make the project a success.

I scraped some money together and held an audition in a film studio in Bow, east London, to find talented but unsigned, singers and rappers. We promoted the event well because 300 artists turned up. By the end of the day, we'd signed seven acts: Vula Malinga who later recorded the UK top 10 hit *Oh My Gosh* with Basement Jaxx; Jeanine Jacques who recorded the Dizzee Rascal hit *I Luv U*; Robert Allen aka Shylo Soulstar who lost to Leona Lewis in the finals of *The X Factor* in 2006; gospel trio Mirror Of You; Bolton-based pop singer Chelsea; neo-soul singer Joy Morrison; and a rap duo comprising my nephew Patrick and Slim Dutty.

In April 2001, around the same time I turned 35, I went to see Karl George who told me about Individual Learning Accounts (ILA), an exciting new government project that was popular in Birmingham. As part of a government initiative to improve information and communication technology, every adult in England was entitled to apply for an ILA training grant which cost £300 and aimed to provide people in disenfranchised communities with a computer literacy certification programme.

Delivering the service simply involved sending applicants a compact disc and instructing them how to use it to assess their computer literacy skills. However, before they were allowed to start training, providers had to apply to the Department for Education and Employment (DfEE) for a licence.

Karl introduced me to four of the scheme's operatives who comprised brothers Robert and Andre Smith, Ian Rowe and Gary Mills who'd previously worked for L&F and my utilities company, Utilco Ltd. They were all delivering the service on a small scale, but Karl knew that in a short space of time I could develop a much more profitable and professional operation.

Once we were all in agreement, I applied to the DfEE for the licence and set up a company to provide the service throughout the West Midlands. Ian and the Smith brothers came on board first and when Gary, who worked in Leicester, saw the scale and efficiency of the operation he joined us.

I was hungry, sensed an opportunity to make some serious money, and just went for it. We set up shop in May 2001, and by the time Tony Blair's Labour government was re-elected following a landslide general election victory a month later, the company was already banking £50,000 a week in profit.

The business thrived, and not long before American Airlines Flight 11 and United Airlines Flight 175 crashed into the World Trade Centre on 11th September 2001 I'd established offices in Ladbroke Grove for TMG.

To cut a long story short, the ILA scheme grew rapidly and in the space of six months me, Gary, Ian and the Smith brothers grossed a total of £1.4 million. I took the lion's share of the revenue and split my profits with Karl. I can't remember exactly how much I made, but it was somewhere in the region of £600,000.

My religious and business mentors Boomy and Pastor Joe were amazed. Boomy was in awe of how quickly I'd made the money and Pastor Joe (who'd seen my tithes increase from £5 to £500 a week) said: 'God has blessed you. Everything the enemy took from you in 2000, God has blessed you with it in 2001.'

By autumn, ILA training providers had started receiving a lot of bad publicity. Media reports claimed that in the 14 months since its launch, more than 18,000 people had complained about the scheme which had been hijacked and abused by gangs of door-step conmen.

To help increase sales, I used to purchase mailing lists with the names and details of people who might be interested in signing up for an ILA. I'd persuaded Ian, Rob and Andre to pay around £17,000 each for a mailing list that would have earned us a shitload of cash. But the negative publicity caused the government to shut down the scheme before we had a chance to work the list.

Ian and the Smith brothers went ballistic and turned to me to replace the £50,000 they'd lost. I told them: 'This is business. You knew what you were getting in to. If the scheme hadn't crashed you'd be laughing now.'

Rob understood where I was coming from and we still remain good friends, but his brother and Ian stopped talking to me and the business subsequently collapsed.

A few weeks later, I appeared at Blackfriars Crown Court in Southwark on charges of fraud and deception relating to my unfortunate credit card shopping spree. Having amassed eight months' worth of credibility and good character through my ILA and TMG projects, I was optimistic.

But Judge Deva Pillay refused to believe that I'd gone straight. He said: 'Mr Murray, you are a professional criminal, a thief. You're not going to set this court up. You are a convicted trickster who was recently sentenced to 18 months in prison for fraud.'

Pillay simply would not accept that I'd turned my life around and achieved so much in the music business in such as short space of time. It took references from Pastor Joe, Alistair McIntyre, Karl George and my pregnant wife (who virtually begged the judge not to send me to jail), before he eventually conceded.

'Okay Mr Murray,' he said. 'I'm going to suspend your sentence for six months. But let me tell you something. If you find yourself involved in any criminal activity within that period, you will be going to jail for a very long time.'

***

Before I made any money from the ILAs, I'd been pushing the TMG project on a shoestring budget. I'd conscripted an enthusiastic and youthful team of individuals who'd all bought in to my dream. But progress was slow and we frequently held meetings at the Grosvenor Hotel in Victoria simply because we had no office space and it was an easy location for everyone to get to.

I took the role of business affairs manager, while Deborah was responsible for artists and repertoire; Mark and Marianne handled marketing; Michael, Patrick and Ernest Kwei handled production; and I brought in Marcia as administrator. Jenny was supposed to be dealing with publishing, but had left after a few weeks.

Once I started making money from the ILAs I was able to acquire trendy new offices, provide Deborah with a car and start planning a launch party to showcase the label's acts. We booked the Cargo music venue in Shoreditch, and I gave Deborah and Marianne £2,000 so they could buy new clothes for the acts.

I hired a £700 stretch Hummer limousine and booked rooms for some of the talent at the Holiday Inn hotel on Old Street around the corner from the venue. It was a fabulous night and great promotion for the artists.

We followed up with a record label launch party, which took place at the Emporium nightclub in Soho and was advertised on Choice FM. During one of my brief visits to the radio station I bumped into Neil who'd been my mentor when I first entered black media 10 years earlier.

I told him about TMG and he recalled how he'd encouraged me to sell *Pride* to a black owner because it would enhance my standing and reputation if I were to ever return to the world of media: 'Weh mi did tell you; weh mi did tell yuh?' He said. 'Yuh see how you use *Pride* and bring back everything again? You see how you come back now, stronger and better?'

We hired Galaxy FM DJ Steve Sutherland and Choice FM DJ Jiggs (who failed to turn up) for the party, which was another great piss-up, and set about establishing the TMG brand.

Throughout 2001 I spent £120,000 on TMG and was so extravagant with my expenses that Marianne started calling me P Diddy. My team didn't have a clue that I'd only just acquired the money they were spending, and probably thought I was some eccentric, deep-pocketed millionaire with a passion for music.

Pride was their only reference point, so they had no idea about the hundreds of thousands of pounds I'd made with Champion Results, L&F and the many other businesses I'd established.

TMG recorded and released an eclectic multi-genre album that was packed with quality music but impossible to market because the project was too futuristic and diverse.

I honestly believe we were ahead of our time because the album would've slotted perfectly into the catchall term 'urban music', which the British music industry introduced 12 months later to promote similar hip-hop, r&b and UK garage projects.

***

Donna and I reconciled and in July 2001 (exactly a year after my trip to the obeah man in Jamaica) I took her and the boys on a beautiful holiday to Marbella in Spain. When we returned, Donna suggested I come back home. My mother-in-law and her sons left the family home after discovering that Donna and I had reunited.

I returned, but it just didn't feel the same. I no longer felt like the king of my castle. I suggested we buy a new house and started looking for properties. I found one I liked and went to see it. The next day, I brought Darius aged five, Dillon aged three and Donna, who was four months pregnant, to view the property.

It was a six-bedroom house with three reception rooms and three bathrooms in Hatch End, less than two miles from the family home in Pinner Park. The owners wanted £369,000. I offered £350,000 and they accepted.

I was ready to start making calls to put the house in Pinner Park on the market, but had a niggling concern that would not go away. I spoke with Donna to see if she could help remove it. I asked: 'At any stage in the future, do you plan on entertaining your mother and brothers in the new house?' After a brief moment of contemplation, she replied: 'Yeah, why not? There are six bedrooms, so even after the baby's born there should still be plenty of room.'

The instant Donna uttered those words I said to myself, *'I can't buy this house with you.'* I heard my mother's warning reverberating in the back of my head as if her message was stuck on repeat: 'Never you buy a house with a woman,' she kept saying.

The emotional scars I'd received 12 months earlier following my ejection from the family home had not yet healed, and I remembered how after I'd slept in my car for 10 long, cold nights I'd promised myself that I'd never make the same mistake again.

I prayed for guidance and actually received it in the form of a dream. I was still angry with Donna, her mother and brothers for taking over the house I was paying for. But in my dream, Donna's mum and siblings took their belongings and left.

I interpreted that as a sign from God telling me to reconcile with my pregnant wife and bring her and the children to live with me in the new house. But I was too unforgiving to trust the dream.

Pastor Joe was very upset. He said: 'The church has done all this work to reconcile you and your wife. And God has blessed you and brought you back together. But rather than being a man and reuniting with your wife, you have poked your fingers in God's eyes.

'When you came to me, you said you wanted your wife back. Now you've got that and so much more. But you don't want her, because if you did you'd let her move into the house.'

Eventually, I told Donna how I was feeling: 'I'm sorry, but I can't do this with you,' I confessed. 'I'm still hurting. I'm still in pain, and the memories of living in my car are still very raw. I believe that if there's another issue and we fall out, you'd kick me out and call the police on me. I'm sorry, but I just can't go through that again.'

I got a valuation surveyor to conduct a meticulous examination of the property, and his appraisal reduced the estimated price by £20,000. I told the owners about the assessment, informed them full payment would be made in cash and made a final offer of £330,000 which they accepted.

Including £10,000 for the taxman's stamp duties, the total cost came to £340,000 which I gave to my sister. I then arranged for my solicitor to set up the contracts so the house was purchased in my sister's name with money that came from her account.

Donna was horrified. She couldn't believe I'd changed my mind and was planning to move into the new property alone. She was pissed and I know that decision really hurt and took a long while to get over.

Donna stayed at the house in Pinner Park, and for almost a year I continued paying all bills until she started a new relationship and filed for divorce, which came as a complete shock. I hadn't accounted for the fact that she was still a young woman who would naturally want to get on with her life, either with me or someone else. To be honest, it's that 'someone else' part that caught me off guard. It simply never crossed my mind that she was seeing another man.

It's very sad that we couldn't save our marriage, but I don't regret securing the property in Hatch End for myself because during the divorce, when we were doing the Financial Dispute Resolution and evaluating assets, Donna's lawyer said she wanted 50% of the house's value, and 50% of my pension (which she contributed nothing towards).

Donna had assumed the house in Hatch End would be included in the matrimonial assets, and was stunned to discover the property was exempt because it was never registered in my name. Ironically, if I did own the property I'd probably have had to sell it just to raise the money to give her 50%.

Moreover, during the divorce proceedings I discovered she had remortgaged the family home and removed a substantial amount of equity without my knowledge. I was dumbfounded as I had not consented to any remortgage and screamed foul play.

Secretly, I admired Donna for making such an audacious move. But nevertheless threatened her lawyers saying unless they started to deal with me fairly I'd bring up the unauthorised remortgage during the next court proceedings.

Eventually, we worked out a deal and I estimate that Donna walked away from our 10-year marriage with around £115,000 in equity (including the money from the remortgage).

I got to keep the contentious house in Hatch End and received 25% of the money she'd collected from the remortgage. Additionally, the court declared that once our youngest child leaves full-time education, or if Donna lives with or marries another man, I'm entitled to 25% of the net value of the family home.

With the benefit of hindsight, I should have definitely shown Donna more love. Although, I guess the relationship would've unravelled in the end because we were living separate lives and never really reconciled. But perhaps most importantly, instead of addressing the issue properly and comprehensively I foolishly assumed that we'd eventually work something out.

I finally took possession of the property in Hatch End towards the end of December 2001, and remember on Christmas Eve sitting alone crying my eyes out.

I told myself, *'Bwoy, this time last year you were in Alan and Alistair's Hampstead flat depressed, tormented and demon-possessed. You were crying and saying that you'd done a deal with the devil and wanted to be released.*

'You'd lost your daughter your home, and had become estranged from your wife and kids. Now, exactly 12 months later, you've got your children back, money in the bank and a yard that's twice the size of the one you got kicked out of.'

It felt like I'd been cast in a lengthy Hollywood adventure movie that started when I was released from HMP Weare in Dorset just after Christmas 1999 and ended two Christmases later.

I'd endured a hectic, 24-month-long rollercoaster ride comprising one year of hell and another of recovery. The second year was amazing. I felt awesome and very appreciative; and that was my mentality heading into 2002.

CHAPTER SEVENTEEN
Public Relations and Sharing the Knowledge
(2002 - 2004)

2002 proved to be another pivotal year. TMG started to collapse, however in March (18 months after Chineka's tragic passing) God blessed me with another daughter, Jada.

If I had to sum up the reason for TMG's disintegration in one word, I'd say 'Impatience'. I'd launched the label and the artists, and spent close to £12,000 kitting out a music studio in Bermondsey. But the team wanted more. Patrick, a fellow Christian who was head of production and the team's youngest member, left first. Marianne followed. She didn't agree with the direction I was taking Slim and thought he should stay more 'hardcore'.

Deborah became disappointed and uneasy, which was sad. I think she felt I'd let everybody down because we'd been working for a year and were still waiting for success. I decided to accelerate the process and shut down the operation after Slim told me that Marianne and Mark asked him to leave TMG and join a label they were starting up.

I dropped all the other artists, and over the next year or so spent £60,000 pushing Slim towards chart success. It didn't work, but I learned first-hand exactly how the industry operates.

The music business courses I'd studied taught me the theory of how things like public relations (PR), studio time and radio plugging worked. But now I had practical experience.

Many of the other upstart labels, managers and artists on the scene started asking for assistance because they saw what I was doing with Slim and how my operation was on point. Some of the managers asked me to deal with their artists' lawyers, and many of them needed help writing and negotiating their recording, management and publishing contracts.

Then it occurred to me, 'rather than spending money developing acts and being the record label, publishing and management company, why don't you just supply support services to the urban labels'? I began to work with many new record labels, sharing much of what I'd learned about business, industry, commerce and media over the past 15 years.

Around the same time, Simon told me about his neighbour who was running a wheel-clamping business. He said the man's operation was haphazard, but explained that if set up correctly the business could be profitable. I did some research and created a business model for a wheel-clamping and vehicle removal company, which I took to Rob Smith in Birmingham.

A year earlier when Karl had introduced me to Rob I liked him instantly. He's around six foot two, 16 stone and looks a lot like the rapper Jay Z.

Rob is a fellow Aries who acknowledged early in our relationship that there was much he could learn from me, and was therefore teachable and receptive to my leadership.

In 2001, Karl, Rob and myself were able to purchase second homes from the money we earned from the ILAs. But when the scheme collapsed prematurely, Ian Rowe fell out with Rob and his brother Andre. And Andre stopped talking to Rob because he stayed friends with me.

As a result, I've always tried my best to be there for Rob and we still maintain a close personal and professional relationship. He's a family man who's always been focused on personal development, so we understand each other.

I knew Rob to be a good salesman in the field, but weak operationally. So I suggested he set up the company, but licence the backend of the business to me.

I explained that wheel clamping on private land was unregulated. All he had to do was buy the clamps, find car parks in shopping centres, pubs and on private housing estates and ask the property owners to give him the contract to issue permits and clamp unauthorised vehicles.

I coordinated the back end of the business, which involved taking payments and managing the call and admin centre back in London. I purchased a credit and debit card machine and developed a script for the staff manning the phones, while Rob contracted several guys to help him travel around Birmingham clamping cars and securing new sites.

Drivers who had their cars clamped were given a number to call to make a payment, and once we received the money we'd call Rob and tell him to remove the clamp.

It was a seven-day-a-week operation; Marcia ran the call centre Monday to Friday, Marianne from TMG worked on Saturdays, and my sister Chrissie covered the Sunday shift.

I took a management fee of 25% from the revenue generated, which was good income because our fees were excessive and penal. We charged £125 to de-clamp a car, and if the vehicle was towed away it would cost the owner £475 to get it back.

Rob and his guys made a lot of money at locations around Villa Park (Aston Villa's football stadium), and I remember telling them on many occasions: 'Don't clamp the car, just tow it away.'

However, after a few months I noticed that Marcia and my sister began complaining about the job. They felt bad taking money from some of the people who'd been issued with parking charges. Particularly mothers who told them: 'I was only gone for five minutes. The money I'm giving you now was for this week's shopping. What are my kids gonna eat?'

We discussed whether it was morally right to take money from people in such circumstances. But I overlooked the ethics and said: 'I've got a mortgage to pay and we're running a business. These people chose to ignore the instructions on the parking enforcement signs, so they have to pay the price.' That's how I justified it.

Then one afternoon about nine months after we launched, Rob clamped a car and when the owner returned and saw the clamp he had a heart attack and died. The death was all over the news. I felt terrible about the loss of life, and the situation really affected Rob who decided to sell the company.

As a result, early in 2002 I accepted a part-time appointment as a financial controller for a public relations company, House PR, which specialised in clothing brands, celebrities and sports organisations.

I was offered the post after an ex-neighbour, a young Irish girl named Gillian Farrell, contacted me out of the blue. She'd been working for a major advertising agency, Lowe Howard-Spink, but wanted to launch her own recruitment agency.

I gave her some money, incorporated the company and got her going. Gillian started making sales and doing deals, but one of her clients (House PR) claimed they didn't have the funds to pay. As co-director of the business, I contacted House PR and told them we wanted our money. The company was run by a Portuguese man, Phil Severs, and an East End girl called Tracey, who was married to a City broker.

Neither of them took me seriously, until I turned up at their offices in Hoxton Square. When they saw me come and press for payment they realised the debt wasn't going away and arranged to settle the £6,000 with a series of disbursements.

When they paid the final instalment, Phil said to me: 'Look, we like how you work. We're in a mess, can you sort out our finances?' I agreed. They retained me as a consultant, and a few months later I was hired. I had knowledge of the media and entertainment industries through *Pride* and my recent venture into the urban music scene. But this was my introduction into the fascinating world of PR.

House PR had some nice mainstream clients, including Katie Price aka Jordan; fashion brands Henri Lloyd, Ted Baker, and Ellesse watches; the Football Association and I think they did the celebrity launch for Planet Hollywood restaurant at the Trocadero in the West End.

Phil and Tracey taught me about PR, and I helped restructure their business and hold off creditors including their landlord. They were spending more than they were making, which was obviously affecting the business. But instead of reducing their outgoings they wanted all three of us to sacrifice our salaries for a few months. I refused, we went our separate ways, and House PR folded later that year.

***

Following a recommendation by my Christian mentor and former lecturer Boomy Tokan, I was invited to take a post as a business consultant at the Portobello Business Centre (PBC) in Ladbroke Grove.

My job was to mentor and provide consultancy to the owners of small local businesses. I'd write their marketing plans and executive summaries, and summarise their business plans. I relished the opportunity to get back in touch with the professional business world and was happy to discover that I could work for the organisation in my own time.

The relationship was mutually beneficial because over the next four years I brought in more clients than any other consultant, and only used the PBC's resources to hold meetings and submit business.

During my time there, I supported more than 100 micro and start-up businesses and became the organisation's top consultant, generating a combined income for Marcia and I of around £70,000 a year.

Marcia and I would often joke about the PBC's cheques because whenever cash flow was drying up we could always rely on one to come through the letter box. Moreover, I enjoyed the working environment probably because most of the staff including Boomy, my pastor Joseph Jesuloba and the CEO were all Christians.

***

In spring 2003, I met and befriended Akosua Annobil, a 22-year-old cockney-Ghanaian entertainment journalist who wrote a popular showbiz column, The Gist, in *New Nation* newspaper - a tabloid-style rival to *The Voice*.

Akosua helped to promote Slim by writing about his music, and getting him gigs and personal appearances. I told her she'd be very good at PR and asked how much she'd charge to develop and execute a publicity campaign for my artist.

'Why would someone pay me for that?' she replied. I explained that people got paid for delivering publicity services and shared with her everything I'd learned from my time at House PR. I was encouraged by how Akosua responded and told her to develop and execute a three-month PR campaign for Slim, and invoice me £500 at the end of each month for the service.

The entertainment scene was changing rapidly, and I could see that if I positioned myself correctly many new opportunities would soon become available. It wasn't long before I gathered evidence to support my theory.

In the summer of 2003 I became aware of Channel U, a new music TV station available through the Sky satellite network that had become popular among fans of the underground music scene.

Initially, the station started off in the traditional mould, playing pop and rock videos. But whereas market leader MTV Base only played songs by (mostly American) acts that'd been signed to major record labels, Channel U's brand and programme manager Charlie Beuthin quickly discovered that viewing figures peaked whenever they aired videos by unsigned British acts.

This subtle difference quickly transformed the station into Britain's coolest youth media platform and a pioneering enabler of the emerging grime and dubstep scenes. Channel U had unwittingly removed the many layers of bureaucracy that independent artists previously faced when attempting to get their music videos played on mainstream TV.

Rappers, singers and grime MCs no longer needed approval from senior executives at major record labels to get their video broadcast across the nation at peak times.

The advent of digital video camcorders during the previous decade had reduced filming costs, so anyone with basic recording and editing skills could produce a video and send it to Channel U who had a business model for their product and would play it.

Within three months of launching, it was reported that Channel U had overtaken MTV Base in viewership figures and under Charlie's guidance unknowingly began to reshape the face of contemporary British music.

I spotted an opportunity to generate revenue after realising that although Channel U had huge amounts of street cred, the station ran very few adverts. I rebranded my company from Trinity Music Group to Trinity Media Group (TMG), and contacted the station's offices in Soho to set up a meeting.

I met with Charlie who added Slim's *Blood Puddles* video to the playlist and arranged for me to speak with the company's CEO, Stewart Lund (who was German I think). I asked him to sell me airtime, which I planned to resell to local advertisers who'd want to reach Channel U's audience. He didn't believe it would work, but still entered into a contract to sell me 30 seconds segments of the station's airtime for £5.

Later that year, my IT technician Andrew introduced me to a graphic designer named Las Oke who worked in retail but owned some properties with his business partner, Dwayne Byfield. Las and Dwayne were looking to get into the urban music scene. I told them about the contract I had with Channel U, explained the model and suggested they come into business with me selling ad spots on the fledgling station.

I incorporated a new business called Trinity Media Broking (TMB), divided the company equally three ways, appointing Las and Dwayne as co-directors, and took the position of company secretary.

Additionally, I created a contract where TMB bought 30 seconds of Channel U air-time from TMG for £10. TMB's business model was to repackage the airtime by selling 10 x 30-second slots to advertisers for £300. Dwayne sold the ad-spots and Las created the adverts. They took offices in Harrow, and I left them to get on with it.

The following year, Charlie left Channel U and was replaced by another of the station's executives - a young black guy from east London named Riki Bleau who I clicked with instantly.

Charlie was a cool person; someone I could do business with. But Riki was someone I could *really* talk to. I discovered he was friends with Akosua and began to share with him much of the knowledge I'd revealed to her about PR and the business of media.

Riki had established a video plugging service where he charged around £250 for heavy, peak-time rotation. I advised him to direct his clients to me and offered to deal with them on his behalf, and he agreed.

The same acts Riki charged £250 were paying me £2,500, which I'd split with him. He was blown away, but I simply explained that I understood the value of the service and could convince his clients to do the same. Subsequently, over the course of the following year, Riki and I received more than £50,000 from video plugging.

Around the same time, Akosua observed there was an increasing number of people approaching her for help with their publicity. But she wasn't sure how to convert their enquiries into revenue. During a meeting to discuss strategies for Slim's PR campaign, she asked: 'How can I get some of these people who keep seeking publicity advice to pay me the type of money that you're paying?' I replied: 'That can easily be arranged. All you have to do is refer them to me.'

I explained there was a niche in the marketplace for providing publicity services, and encouraged her to launch a PR company specialising in urban media and music. In the summer of 2004 we incorporated Fire Media UK. I managed the company whilst providing consultancy to Akosua who was responsible for finding clients and delivering the service.

Fire Media's business model was unique because we ran the company on minimum costs, without offices or any other usual expenses. The business was structured like an agency and we employed several young, female media graduates and journalists who were trying to break into the industry and wanted to work with Akosua. They were all retained as self-employed publicists who worked from home and had their expenses paid. Earnings came directly from each client's payments, which the publicist, Akosua and I shared equally.

We offered a relatively expensive but excellent pay-as-you-go service that was very addictive. Clients could easily find themselves spending £5,000 in a couple of months.

At its peak, Fire Media employed eight publicists and managed a roster of around 10 paying clients each month. We all earned a healthy income, and the model was good because we had no overheads.

In the years ahead, Akosua's value continued to rise as she expanded in to broadcasting with her own Saturday morning talk show on Choice FM, *Girls like Us*, and productions for US satellite and cable TV station BET.

One of my highlights during this period was negotiating her £500 a show contract for *Girls like Us* with the station's managing director (MD) Ivor Etienne. Prior to landing the contract, Akosua had spent four years working on the station for free as a correspondent on Angie Le Mar's popular talk show. However, her £500 fee was crazy money for Choice at the time and caused a huge amount of resentment among the other presenters and DJs who were regularly heard complaining '...but she's not even a DJ!'

CHAPTER EIGHTEEN
Channel U Awards and Sciatica
(2004 - 2006)

After Riki introduced me to his friend and business partner Ezra Christian who ran the radio plugging service Fire on the Streets, I became determined to break new ground in the underground music scene.

I thought back to when I'd launched *Pride* 13 years earlier, and remembered how Yvonne Thompson (the PR specialist who launched Britain's first black marketing agency) controlled access to black media through her associations with Choice FM, *The Voice* and the Afro Hair and Beauty Show.

My brain began to race and I considered how a four-way alliance between TMG, Fire Media, Fire on the Streets and Riki at Channel U would be a powerful force to be reckoned with. The idea was to develop a collective gateway that new acts would have to pass through if they were serious about launching their careers.

We offered everything that a small, independent label or production company needed to be successful in the marketplace: press coverage, radio promotion, gig bookings, business management services and, of course, heavy rotation on the country's most popular music TV station. We pooled our resources, leveraged our positions and worked together pitching our services to managers and artists throughout the scene. And it worked for a long time.

I remember concert promoters who wanted to advertise on Channel U would come to TMG to buy ad space and we'd tell them: 'Unless you put some of our clients on the lineup of your show we're not going to sell you any airtime.' Using this method, we got two of the artists we represented to perform as warm-up acts for US rappers The Game and T-Pain when they toured England, which was a big coup. Of course, there were challenges. Fire on the Streets struggled as Ezra found it difficult to persuade DJs at prominent radio stations to play songs that hadn't yet developed a sufficient underground buzz.

During the summer of 2004, my divorce from Donna was made absolute following a contested financial settlement that cost me over £100,000.

Around the same time, Akosua and I came up with an idea to launch a membership-driven, weekly club night that offered a year's free entrance to participants who paid a one-off fee.

I recruited and trained eight young ladies and two guys in club hospitality, and spent a lot of money on branding. We held the night (called Club House) in the West End at the same venue where I'd launched my record label three years earlier, Emporium, which had since been renamed Tantra.

It was a novel but loss-making venture that I had to pull the plug on after three weeks. That event was probably Akosua's first unsuccessful entrepreneurial endeavour and I suspect the failure bruised her pride somewhat. Sadly, I had little choice as the expenses (which included paying for late night taxis for all the staff) had bruised my bank balance.

In those days, the urban music scene was a wonderfully diverse place, and Channel U director Darren Platt (RIP) was one of its most colourful and enigmatic characters.

I first met Darren around six months into my relationship with the station, after he replaced Stewart as the company's CEO. He called me one morning, introduced himself and said: 'Right, Stewart is no longer here but I am. My staff tell me that you're buying our airtime and have influence in various parts of our business, so you need to come and see me.'

When we met he immediately tried to increase the price of the airtime, but after some negotiations I persuaded him that would be a mistake. We talked, went out for a meal and realised that we liked each other.

Darren was a few years older than me, and although we became friends I must admit to sometimes feeling pangs of jealously when I thought about the position he held as gatekeeper for the new wave of mostly black, underground music.

He told me he was worth £5 million. I'm not sure whether I believe him, but he was certainly a millionaire. I remember visiting his home in Essex; a massive, old-fashioned house with a maid and gardener, situated on what he said was 15 acres of land.

I was genuinely gutted when I heard he'd passed away in 2016 because irrespective of the negative things people have said about him, Darren made a massive contribution to the music scene. I've heard people refer to him as a pirate and a parasite, and while that may or may not be true it can't be denied that at a time when mainstream media shunned unsigned local grime and rap acts, Darren provided them with a national platform. In the autumn of 2004, around six months after I met Darren, I attended the Music of Black Origin (MOBO) Awards with Las, Dwayne and a few other people from TMG.

Akosua and Riki were there, and I remember all of us discussing the UK music scene and how MOBO had developed a reputation for ignoring local talent and giving American acts preferential treatment.

During subsequent conversations, Las, Dwayne and I revisited the topic many times. Then in spring 2005, Las said they wanted me to pitch an idea to Darren.

Dwayne said: 'Why don't we put on a music awards show dedicated to British music, an event celebrating the most popular unsigned artists on Channel U?' Las added: 'Forget about all of the different genres and categories, let's keep it generic. The public gets to vote for 30 acts, and then the 15 artists with the most votes perform at the show. So if you're in the top 15, you're a Channel U Award winner.'

I didn't get it: 'How can everyone be a winner?' I asked. 'It's a unique idea, but sounds a bit daft to me. I don't think it'll work.' But Las and Dwayne continued to push because they knew if they couldn't convince me the idea would never reach Darren.

Eventually they persuaded me. We put a proposal together, and I went to see Darren. He was the type of person who wanted to control and own whatever idea you gave him, so pretty early into the conversation I had to tell him: 'You can't control this Darren, we won't let you.' He replied: 'But you're selling my brand.'

Before the discussion became heated I told him I had to leave for another meeting and would resume the conversation upon my return. I left Channel U's offices off City Road and drove across Southwark Bridge to Choice FM on Borough High Street.

There, I spoke with the station's MD Ivor, and told him that TMG was producing an awards ceremony with Channel U. I asked if he wanted to bring Choice on board as a media partner with equal prominence to Channel U, and he agreed.

I flew back to Darren and told him: 'Hey, if you don't want to do this then Choice FM will. We can take exactly the same model and call it the Choice FM Awards,' which absolutely riled him. He became insecure, completely flipped and agreed to give us an exclusive deal.

I wrote the contract, but Darren refused to sign it. He never said: 'I'm not signing,' but always had an excuse whenever I put the contract under his nose, which was a good few times. I didn't worry though. I knew he was just as invested in the project as we were. We booked the Shepherd's Bush Empire in west London and set about developing, coordinating and marketing the show. At the time, concert hall events featuring grime and UK rap acts were rare because urban music fans had a reputation for carrying guns and knives.

We knew security would be one of our biggest challenges as less than a year earlier an innocent passerby had been maimed during a gunfight in which 18 shots had been fired outside the Urban Music Awards at the Barbican in the City.

However, I became starkly aware of this issue towards the end of summer 2005 when Darren, Ivor and the venue manager all told me they'd received calls from the police who 'were apparently not happy' the event was being staged. I spoke with the police and was basically told that I wouldn't be allowed to hold the event unless I paid them to coordinate the security, which I calculated would absorb all of our profits.

I decided to speak with Bethan, a white community activist from Harlesden who I'd met in 2002 while promoting Slim Dutty. At the time, she'd been working on an anti-violence campaign, *Not Another Drop*, alongside the police and the London Borough of Brent.

I was introduced to her and the borough's police commander, and they asked me to get Slim to support their campaign, which I did in return for £5,000 towards the production cost of his next music video. They paid the money, we supported the campaign and both parties earned some valuable press coverage from the collaboration.

I decided to call in the favour, and explained the situation to Bethan. 'You've got to help me,' I told her. 'The police can't do this. Remember when you guys came to me looking for an ambassador? You've got to help me out.'

She contacted Brent's former borough police commander, who'd since been promoted to a senior figure at Scotland Yard. He said: 'Leave it with me and I'll see what I can do.' He called a couple of days later to say: 'Yeah, you can do it.'

But as the event drew closer, he told me there was intelligence that gang members were planning to come to the event to fire gunshots: 'It's not going to be pretty,' he said. 'There will be armed police stationed both inside and outside of the venue.' I considered what he said then realised I was in no position to object, so replied: 'Do what you want, but the show must go on.'

We were asked to provide the names, addresses and dates of birth of everyone who'd be going onstage, a move I later realised was a precursor to the Metropolitan Police's dreaded 696 risk assessment, which promoters and venue owners had to complete prior to hosting any music event.

In addition to demanding the personal details of the DJs, artists and other performers, Form 696 (which was formally introduced around the same time as our event) also requested information about the target audience and genres of music that would be played.

Critics claim the form was used specifically to target black music events, but the police have always denied this allegation.

After we collected all the data and forwarded the information to the police, they tried to tell us that several acts would not be allowed to perform. I took note of the request, but told them: 'It's impossible to change the lineup at this late stage, and nine times out of 10 these artists are going to have criminal convictions anyway.'

Following an extended period of diplomacy with the police, I was eventually told: 'Okay fine, you can go ahead as long as you continue to cooperate with us.'

To help brand the event, TMG engaged graphic design twins Marc and Richard Denton, while Akosua coordinated a PR strategy, edited the commemorative magazine we published and produced the awards ceremony alongside her then-partner Orantes Moore.

From a list of 30 acts that were promoted on Channel U and Choice FM, viewers and listeners were encouraged to vote for their favourites by calling a premium rate number, which was a great money-spinner for the broadcasters who earned revenue from each call.

Choice were happy because they received national TV visibility for the first time, and Darren was pleased because his brand had led an eight-week marketing campaign that hadn't cost him anything.

Still, neither Choice nor Channel U earned a penny from any other source because all the revenue went straight into TMG's coffers. It was us who secured the marketing deals, including the contract with lead sponsor Vauxhall Motors. And when the sold-out event ended, we collected the gate receipts.

Channel U's Best of British Awards ceremony took place on Saturday 15th October 2005 and will be remembered as one of the first large-scale events to acknowledge Britain's new generation of pop musicians. It was a roadblock, literally.

Armed police were stationed at the venue's entrance and inside the foyer, and outside they coned off the road so vehicles could neither slow down nor stop anywhere on Shepherd's Bush Green.

Performers on the night included rapper and singer Estelle, who went on to win a Grammy Award, Bhangra and r&b singer Jay Sean who later became the first British urban act to top the US *Billboard* Hot 100 chart, as well as Lethal Bizzle, Roll Deep, Akala, Blak Twang, LOC, Sway, Mitchell Brothers, Nathan, Choong Family and SLK.

Ironically, although the show was successful and trouble-free, one of the rappers the police asked us to drop from the lineup, Carl 'Crazy Titch' Dobson, delivered a memorable and show-stealing performance, but was arrested for murder three weeks later and subsequently sentenced to 30 years in prison.

***

Since rebranding myself as a provider of PR and business management services to the urban music scene, I'd developed a diverse network of young media professionals and increased my annual income to around £100,000. I closed 2005 feeling content and took the children on holiday to Disney World, Florida. Life was good and I looked forward to the New Year with all the anticipation of a child waiting to open presents on Christmas Day.

Early in 2006, Darren and Ivor both expressed a desire to be involved in another awards ceremony but that never materialised because of an irreconcilable breakdown in Las and Dwayne's relationship.

They fell out over a property deal that had nothing to do with TMB, but our business suffered nonetheless. I was unable to heal the rift, and eventually Las forced me to choose between them: 'It's either me or Dwayne,' he said, which I thought was unfair because he introduced me to Dwayne. But on that basis, I had to show him my loyalty.

I didn't want to lose both, but knew that's exactly what would happen if I didn't make a choice. I asked myself: 'Who would you prefer to lose? Probably Dwayne,' that's how I reasoned it. Naturally, Dwayne took exception to this and hasn't spoken to me since.

The demise of TMB severely ruptured my relationship with Channel U because I was no longer purchasing airtime and had therefore lost all my bargaining power.

I searched for new opportunities, but as my 40th birthday approached found myself losing confidence and questioning my ability to bounce back, which was strange and uncharacteristic.

I attempted to get back on my feet and persuaded Darren to give TMG a TV programme; a dancehall music chart show called *Turn It Up* hosted by BBC 1Xtra presenter Robbo Ranx, who I'd employed years earlier as a *Pride* advertising sales executive.

At the time, I was dating a girl from Birmingham who I'd met towards the end of 2005. To celebrate my birthday, she took me to a castle in the Scottish Highlands but we fell out and during an argument she called me 'a narcissist'. I'd never heard the term before so picked up a dictionary, and was horrified to discover its meaning.

When we returned to London she gave me head on my doorstep, then got up and said: 'Right, I'm off. You won't be seeing me again.' And I never did, which completely threw me.

I entered into a mild state of depression and refused to go to bed alone for almost six months, preferring instead to fall asleep on my sofa. The consequences of this new nocturnal routine would prove to be devastating.

One weekend early in June 2006 I went to see Mary J Blige perform at Wembley Arena. On the Monday morning I travelled to Covent Garden for a meeting that Fire Media's new business manager, Shakira Henry, had arranged with a potential client who wanted to set up an online recruitment company.

We met and I agreed to work on the project. But while travelling unda di eart' on the way home I felt a sharp pain in my leg. I couldn't sit down properly, and by the time the train reached Harrow & Wealdstone station I couldn't move at all.

The guards had to carry me off the train, lay me down on the platform and call an ambulance. I was admitted to hospital, dosed with painkillers and diagnosed as suffering from sciatica, which had been caused by discs in my lower back rubbing against the sciatic nerve (running from the bum down to the foot).

I concluded I must have damaged my back sleeping on the sofa. The pain I felt was excruciating and unlike anything I'd ever experienced. I was immobilised, housebound for 10 long weeks, including four weeks in bed. I phoned a girl who worked at Choice FM that I'd been seeing. She came to visit, but we fell out. She told me to 'piss off' and accused me of being 'too full of myself'.

I tried my luck elsewhere with a neighbour who was a newly qualified teacher and about 10 years younger than me. We'd been speaking on the phone, but she was taking her time to get to know me. I turned to her, but she was busy and couldn't give me any attention. I pressured her to take my calls, but she refused and I never saw her again.

In an attempt to generate revenue, I was still working on my laptop and taking calls. But my disability, coupled with knock backs from three consecutive women led me to feel weak, vulnerable and exposed.

During the day I'd hold meetings in my living room with Fire Media publicists and the girl who was launching the recruitment website. But my nights were spent screaming and yelling in pain.

Both Akosua and Riki had gone off to explore new prospects and I was still disappointed over the demise of TMG, but pretending as though the dissolution of my relationship with Channel U wasn't really an issue.

I received the odd piece of work to either negotiate or write a music contract, and the PBC allowed me to submit business here and there. But my income plummeted nevertheless.

For the first time in my adult life, I was both incapacitated and unable to kick-start my career. I was getting more frustrated with each passing day. I had no girlfriend. My relationship with Donna was at best estranged, and the word 'repossession' had started to appear in the monthly correspondence I received from my mortgage provider.

Thankfully, I was able to pull through with the support of friends such as Marcia, Raymond (who was living with me at the time) and Rob Smith, who arranged for his sister-in-law to travel from Battersea to bring me cooked food. I was down but not out, and began hunting for new ideas, prospects and enterprises to get me back on my feet in 2007.

CHAPTER NINETEEN
ACPA, Bamboula and Hong Kong
(2007 - 2008)

In the autumn of 2006, the young woman I met earlier in the year who wanted to launch an online recruitment agency gave me a fantastic idea.

We were discussing the news that Prime Minister Tony Blair was about to acknowledge Britain's role in the kidnap, torture and trafficking of tens of millions of people from west and central Africa to Europe and the Americas between 1562 and 1807.

When he released his statement of regret in *New Nation* newspaper, four months before the 200th anniversary of the abolition of the slave trade in March 2007, I thought, '*How can I capitalise on this?*'

I mapped out a proposal to celebrate and acknowledge the occasion by hosting the African Caribbean Peoples' Awards (ACPA) ceremony to pay tribute to the numerous, but often forgotten, black pioneers, heroes and sheroes who helped to shape Britain over the past two centuries.

When my ex-wife Donna sold the family home in Pinner Park I received £30,000, which I divided equally among my three children and deposited into their respective savings accounts.

I was convinced the event would be a roaring success and decided to use the money to fund the event and simultaneously launch an online recruitment website, ACPA Jobs.

I paid a deposit of £10,000 to secure the Grosvenor Hotel in Mayfair, and spent a further £5,000 on office space and salaries for Marcia and former TMB employee Kris Andon-Smith who I had recruited to work with me on ACPA.

Akosua and Orantes spent their days coordinating the production schedule and executing a PR strategy that included securing letters of support from the Prime Minister and the leaders of the UK's two main opposition parties.

My days started in the office at 8.00am when I would pitch and seek sponsorship from corporations such as HSBC, Barclays and Tesco. I knew decision-makers in large companies are usually in their office an hour before their PAs start work. So if you make your calls early, chances are you'll get to pitch the person directly because nobody's there to screen the calls.

This method proved successful and I got through to CEOs, financial directors and managing directors with astonishing ease. They just weren't buying what I was selling.

Surprisingly, Labour MP David Lammy, who was then Minister for Culture at the Department of Culture, Media and Sport, proved to be one of ACPA's biggest supporters, organising a donation of £12,000 from his agency.

After spending more than four months pitching, I'd attracted less than £20,000; nowhere near the amount that was needed. The Grosvenor Hotel wanted the second instalment of their payment and I simply wasn't prepared to commit another £10,000.

So in April 2007, around the time of my 41st birthday, I abandoned the project. Six months earlier, I'd hyped up the event to Choice FM's MD Ivor who was very receptive following our success with the Channel U Awards. Now, I had to announce that ACPA had been scrapped and ask Ivor to pull the adverts he'd been running on the station for the past week. He was pissed and tried to force me to keep promoting the event. But I refused: 'Ivor, I'm not doing it. I don't have enough money.'

I received a call from someone at David Lammy's office. They'd heard the event had been cancelled and wanted their money back, but I told them: 'Come on, that went on overheads.'

To be honest, I remember very little from that period because I was still suffering from something akin to a midlife crisis, the after-effects of sciatica and mild depression, which deepened as I ran out of money.

I set up a meeting with a budding, young media mogul named Leonard Foster who, alongside his girlfriend Annika Allen, produced an annual beauty pageant and urban news, entertainment and lifestyle publication *Flavour Magazine*. Their brand had potential and I planned to make some money just as I'd done with Channel U three years earlier. I met the couple and told them I could remodel their business and make us all a lot of cash.

Leonard rejected my plan, which pissed me off. I think he felt threatened by my presence, whereas Annika probably would've gone for the idea but couldn't because her loyalties were with him.

Soon after, I decided to cancel *Turn It Up* (the weekly dancehall show I'd been producing for Channel U). Although Robbo was getting national visibility and the TV station enjoyed a rise in viewing figures, I wasn't earning anything from it.

As a result, I fell out with the show's cameraman and editor Mikey Green who was owed £3,000. I told him: 'Look mate, when you invest in a business and it flops you accept whatever you've lost and move on. You don't cry about it.

'I don't have your money because it went into the business and that business went down the pan. That's how it goes sometimes. You can't come to me looking for money, you knew the risk.'

I remember having a similar argument around the same time with Orantes's friend Ike Okosa, who was owed around £6,000 for building the ACPA Jobs website. Neither Mikey nor Ike were satisfied with my explanation and I slipped further into depression as I tortured myself for spending my children's savings.

I guess Mikey must've told one of the staff at Channel U to let him know whenever I showed up at the office because one day when I went to speak with Darren he arrived shortly afterwards with two very big dudes. Mikey started going on about his money, but I was in no mood to entertain his foolishness. Before getting into my car and driving off I looked directly into his eyes, and did the same to each of his friends: 'Mate, whatever you may think I'm not a dickhead. So if you want to press some buttons, go ahead. But the consequences are yours,' I told them.

To keep myself busy, I used the knowledge I'd amassed during the previous six years to write an e-book, *Secret Guide to Success in the Music Industry* which I completed and published online in the autumn of 2007.

By then, I'd been dating Angela Banks for over a year. We met during the 2006 MOBO Awards after being introduced by a mutual friend. I don't think she realised, but I was probably depressed throughout the entirety of our three-year relationship. If Angela and I met now, things would be completely different because back then she was more of a crutch for me. At that time, I had no prosperity whatsoever. Nothing I attempted was fruitful. But Angela was there for me, especially when my relationship with my son Dillon became strained.

Between 2006 and 2014, there were three occasions where I attempted to discipline Dillon and the police got involved. The first happened when he was removed from my home after complaining to social services who told me not to contact Darius or Jada.

Dillon was placed in foster care for a couple of days before moving to my sister's house and then returning to live with his mother. It took a while before I eventually got to see him. Then in 2007, he complained to social services again and the cycle repeated. It was a stressful time and Angela provided genuine support.

I'd been totally rocked by ACPA's collapse and couldn't find a way to replenish my children's savings. Everything I touched crumbled and I remained acutely depressed. I remortgaged my house and used the money to take the kids on an inspirational three-week holiday to Ghana. I also travelled with Angela to Budapest in Hungary where I received dental treatment.

Around the same time I published *Secret Guide to Success in the Music Industry,* Lawrence Fearon asked me to help him manage Bamboula, a restaurant in Brixton that he'd purchased with his wife Marlene.

I could no longer afford to pay Marcia. She was the only person who knew how broke I was and quickly found employment with Marks & Spencer. When Lawrence approached me I thought, *'Peter, you've been given another opportunity to do something, make good use of it.'*

If I'm honest, the whole experience of having to get on a train every morning and work long hours for a pittance was humbling, and whenever people asked what I was doing I'd jazz it up and say: 'I'm taking time out and helping a friend.'

I leaned heavily on Angela during this period and remember being totally skint; taking food from the restaurant for her, me and her daughter then riding on a Victoria Line train from Brixton to their home in Tottenham Hale. It was difficult because they lived in a one-bedroom flat, so I rarely stayed longer than one night.

In 2008, my financial situation worsened and I missed several mortgage payments. Angela lent me her last £1,500, and when the internet was disconnected at my house I was forced to stay with her for three weeks.

Almost a year after ACPA I was still on my face and fuming at how quickly I'd squandered my children's money. I felt like shit and questioned whether I still had the ability to transform imperfect business models into profitable operations. Maybe I'd never again generate sums large enough to replace the £30,000 I'd lost.

Lawrence said he wasn't in a position to pay me, so I earned money based on the improvements I made to the business. I always had love for the Fearon family, particularly Lawrence and his wife who'd been together for 30 years.

In the past, I'd put them on the front cover of *Pride* when we ran a special feature on successful, married couples. So I was happy to help out with the restaurant and sink my teeth into something commercial. I had no catering or restaurant experience, and although it was a steep learning curve I quickly discovered two significant problems: the business was losing £8,000 a month and not a single member of the Jamaica-born staff delivered a suitable level of customer service.

It was a tough task, but I plugged the leaks and had Bamboula breaking even within six months. Lawrence and I made plans to develop a chain of restaurants, but that plan was abandoned when he refused to give me 50% of the business. He asked: 'If I take 50% and give the other 50% to you, what happens to Marlene?'

I remembered how Zimbabwean entrepreneur Alfred had taught me never to purchase less than a 50% stake in any venture, and tried to explain to Lawrence that he and his wife would share their percentage. They rejected my offer and we parted on good terms as I simply couldn't afford to continue working on the project.

Watching the international news on TV I saw how the European Union was attempting to extend the four-year-old travel ban and asset freeze they'd imposed on the President of Zimbabwe Robert Mugabe, and observed as Britain and the US tried to introduce an arms embargo.

I saw an opportunity to capitalise on Fire Media's core strengths as a professional but grassroots marketing organisation. I contacted the Embassy of Zimbabwe and pitched them about delivering PR and media services for Mugabe's government.

I attended a meeting at their embassy on the Strand and delivered a presentation to two members of staff. They agreed to pay £30,000 for the development and delivery of a bespoke PR campaign but had to get the project sanctioned in Zimbabwe, which they said would take a couple of weeks.

I met with Akosua and Orantes and told them about the meeting. 'Look, we've done the local urban thing. Now it's time to globalise and do some international PR with an African government,' I said.

However, Akosua (who was busy working on TV productions for BET) rejected the idea, which left me feeling frustrated, broke and completely dejected. I called Simon and arranged to go out for dinner with him the following week. During the meal, I told him: 'Mate, I'm totally skint and need some money.' Simon didn't like my approach and replied: 'Peter, you don't just come to me and ask for money like that.' I said: 'Yes I do, and I am. I need some money.'

Simon was clearly offended. 'You're coming to me with a begging bowl,' he sneered. I replied: 'Yes, I'm bringing a begging bowl to you because you're my friend. And for that reason, you're going to put some money in it.' After dinner he gave me £500, which we both knew was chickenfeed. He called a few days later, saying: 'You should be back in sales, mate. You were the sales guru, a god of sales. That's where you should be.'

I'd heard him, but didn't entertain the idea as I hadn't worked in that industry for almost 20 years and was unlikely to return anytime soon.

After his real estate venture Simon had returned to sales, and in 1994 launched Ink - a company that grew to become the world's largest publisher of inflight magazines. Ironically, his introduction to magazine publishing came through sharing office space with me at *Pride*.

Back then, I spent my days training and coordinating advertising staff. Now, Simon was in a similar but much bigger role, managing local and international sales teams for around 40 publications. A few days later, he called again: 'My business has an office in Hong Kong, but we can't get it to function right. I've put a few people in there but so far no one's been able to get the office profitable,' he said.

'The entire workforce is made up of Chinese citizens who were born in Hong Kong and they're used to doing things a certain way. What we need is for someone to go there and introduce Western-style practices. Do you want to go to Hong Kong for me?' I told him to piss off, but Simon was persistent: 'Why are you saying no?' He asked. 'You're just being proud. You need the money.'

Over the course of two weeks he persuaded me to take the job. Simon knew me well; I was both proud and broke. It was a great offer, but I was reluctant to commit and reminded my friend that I hadn't worked for someone else since Larry fired me from the Moore Group 20 years earlier.

'No one is going to be your boss,' he assured. 'You can do your own thing. You won't even be on the pay-as-you-earn tax system, so you can work through Trinity Media.'

I pointed out: 'If I take this job I can't let anybody know that I'm working for you.' Simon paused, then asked. 'Why not?' I replied, 'Because you're my pal. I'm not working for you, I'm working with you.'

A hint of frustration crept into Simon's voice: 'Pete, you really need to get that stuff out of your head. If it makes you feel better don't tell anyone that you're working with me. Say you got an offer through a recruitment company. Say whatever you like, I really don't give a shit.' And whenever anyone asked what I was doing with myself that's exactly what I said: 'I've been headhunted to take a job in Hong Kong.'

I went to Ink's offices in Shoreditch and spent a few days familiarising myself with the company's products and titles. Simon agreed to pay me £10,000 a month for three months and said that if I liked the project I could extend my stay for another three months.

We flew to Hong Kong for a few days and I was introduced to the MD of the office, Steven Wong and his team of about 20 staff. Simon told me: 'Pete, this office is losing money big time. I need you to turn it around.' We returned to England and I spent the next two weeks preparing for my big move to East Asia.

Moving to Hong Kong was probably the best thing I could've done at that time. A change of environment helped to lift my spirits and I began to consider the opportunities that lay ahead in the Orient.

Steven Wong was nervous and thought I'd come to Hong Kong to take his job. It took a good few days to convince him and his staff that I was nothing more than an external consultant who'd been brought in to provide support, coaching and mentorship.

Initially, around half of the staff were open to new methods while the others remained indifferent. Eventually I got everybody on board, and within three weeks things started to improve.

I resided in a fashionable £2,000-a-month studio apartment in one of the world's most expensive residential areas, Causeway Bay. But spent most of my time in the office less than a mile away.

Hong Kong was a great experience, but I didn't know anyone there and missed my children terribly. I spent weekends travelling the region; starting with a trip to Lantau (Hong Kong's biggest island), followed by excursions to Lamma and Ma Wan, both beautiful locations.

I journeyed to Malaysia and spent a weekend at a health club in Shenzhen, China, where I slept with four women in one night. Additionally, I visited Taiwan with Steven and returned to China where he introduced me to the world's most populous city, Shanghai.

I adapted to the Hong Kongese lifestyle, starting learning Cantonese, and noticed that whenever I went to restaurants the locals were always fascinated that I knew how to use chopsticks. They'd never look at me directly but I could feel them staring.

Although the Chinese may classify Europeans as one or two notches above Africans, there's no real difference between how they treat blacks and whites. Either way, you're an outsider simply because you're not Chinese. That's probably why I never experienced any hardcore racism there.

I lived well and life was good. In the evenings after work, I'd have some dinner and go to either a nightclub where they played mostly hip-hop and r&b, or a karaoke bar, which is their equivalent to a British pub. If I was lucky, I might pick up a girl and take her back to the apartment. Chinese women would speak to me but not in public, so the majority of girls I dated were from Malaysia and the Philippines.

I travelled to Macau, a former Portuguese colony that had become a territory of China and the world's gambling capital. Macau is like a bigger version of Las Vegas, generating around US$2 billion each month from the mostly wealthy Asian tourists. The sums of money circulating on the island were truly mind-blowing. I thought about my trip to Ghana the year before and wondered if the business model for a resort city dedicated to gambling could be replicated in West Africa.

When I returned from Macau I received a phone call from Simon who asked me to fly to Singapore to meet Tommy Wilkins, a former British army officer who was running Ink's office there. After two months in Hong Kong I'd settled comfortably into my role and sales in the office were picking up, so I was looking forward to the meeting. I met with Tommy and spent the day getting to know him. He asked a lot of questions and was trying to get into my head to find out about my sales principals and philosophies, management style and how I built up teams.

Angela arrived about a month later. It was her birthday and she'd come to spend some time with me. However, I quickly discovered that I was no longer attracted to my girlfriend and what should have been a romantic seven-day reunion turned into a week-long nightmare.

I felt no desire to ignite the sexual side of our relationship and while that may sound extremely detached, the simple truth is that I'd acclimatised to the svelte and skeletal frame of Asian women, and found Angela to be over-voluptuous.

As a result, I woke up one morning to find her on top of me attempting to have sex and felt violated. 'Get off,' I shouted, still half asleep. Naturally, she became embarrassed and started to cry.

'I can't believe how horrible you're being,' she said. 'I've come all this way to see you and you're acting as if you don't care.' I felt bad and tried to make it up by taking her on a trip to Thailand. We didn't have sex because she was on her period. So, cruelly, I played away. I don't think she knew, but was nevertheless upset.

When we returned to Hong Kong, she said: 'This has been a holiday from hell, and you're a total bastard.' I remained indifferent and vowed to reconcile with her when I returned to the UK.

***

Simon flew in to see me. 'I've got a plan,' he said, to which I replied: 'What is it?' He avoided the question, but was very complimentary 'You're doing fantastic job by the way, and I want you to continue working with Ink.' I told him I missed my children, and he insisted: 'Go home, spend some time with the kids, and speak to Donna about sending them to an international school here in Hong Kong. I hear they're really nice.'

I laughed and asked if he'd be willing to fund that. 'Yeah, sure,' he said. 'But as part of the big plan that I'm about to share with you. Tommy really likes you and wants to work with you.'

My suspicions were aroused, but I told him to continue. 'Tommy thinks we should set up offices in Canada and Australia and wants you and him to do it together. He's an Aries like you, so I think that union should work pretty well.'

I suspected Simon was trying to tell me that his new plan involved Tommy working as my supervisor. I told him: 'Simon, Aries are leaders who have a problem with authority - especially their employers. I think I know where you're heading with this and the answer is no, I will not work for Tommy.'

Simon was smooth: 'Peter, you're thinking about this in the wrong way again. You really need to get your head right. You guys will earn colossal amounts of money and you can travel all over the South Pacific at your own convenience.'

I considered all the travelling I'd done, money I'd made and luxury hotels that I'd stayed in over the past four months. It really was a nice lifestyle. 'Okay. Let me think about it,' I said.

Simon left, and Tommy and I convened for another meeting. Quite early in the conversation it became evident that Tommy was going to deal with me as an underling rather than an equal partner. I explained that I had no problem collaborating, but would not be his subordinate.

The following morning, Tommy returned to Singapore and Simon called from the London office. He asked: 'What's the matter with you?' I replied: 'I told you I'm not working for him.' Simon insisted: 'I keep telling you, you're not working for him, you're...'

I interrupted before he could finish his sentence: 'Yes, I would be working for him. And that's not going to happen because I am not and will never be Tommy's boy.'

The truth is, Tommy had some good practices but I didn't agree with all of them and he wasn't the type of person who'd allow you to choose and discard the parts you disliked. I tried telling this to Simon who had the cheek to say: 'Friends and business are like oil and water.' This upset me even more. Still, during the first week of December I began planning how to collaborate with Tommy without functioning as his minion.

I decided to fly to the UK later that month and spend time with my children before returning to Honk Kong in January to start working on Tommy's grand development plan.

However, a few days later Tommy flew back to Hong Kong. He came to my office and said: 'We can't work together.' I thought, *You tosser, I don't want to work with you.'* But told him: 'Fair enough, I don't have any issues with that. You can go back to Singapore and I'll stay here.'

I'm sure a trace of a smile flashed across Tommy's face as he said: 'Well actually, I'm taking over Hong Kong now and because we can't work together you don't need to stay anymore. You can go home.'

Words cannot describe how angry I was with Simon. I thought, *'Mate, you're a bloody bastard. You brought me to Hong Kong to do a job, which I've done. And now because you've hired Tommy you're planning to enter into the Canadian and Australian territories? That's not your plan, that's Tommy's plan; he's a bloody ex-army expansionist.'*

Tommy liked my sales philosophy and wanted to enter new markets using me as his boy or (to use Surjit Shah's term) prostitute, while he pulled the strings from Singapore. And Simon probably bought into this.

It could've worked. All Simon had to do was explain to Tommy there's no way I was ever going to be his assistant. Instead, he flew in a girl from London to replace me and I returned home just in time for Christmas. I love Simon dearly, but was so pissed off it took almost two years before we spoke again.

CHAPTER TWENTY
New Business and Back to Africa
(2009 - 2011)

Although I'd earned £40,000 during my four months in Hong Kong, I spent it all living lavishly and returned to London penniless. In February 2009 I attended a hearing at Watford County Court and managed to secure a suspended possession order to temporarily ward off my mortgage provider.

It felt as though I'd slipped into a huge, dark abyss and couldn't stop myself free-falling. I had neither a plan nor a new scheme to work on and was completely broke. My depression returned.

The following month, I received a call from Channel U's CEO Darren who was having problems with the station. He'd hired an insolvency practitioner (IP) to put the company into liquidation and wanted to engage in a pre-pack administration where Channel U's assets would be sold on to another business.

He knew I'd previously run an insolvency company and started asking questions. After I'd advised him, Darren (who eventually closed down the business and relaunched as Channel AKA) said: 'Wow, you really know your stuff.'

I explained that I hadn't practised insolvency for 12 years and asked him to throw some work my way. He paused momentarily and suggested I consider returning to the insolvency industry: 'Peter, do you know how much money I'm paying this IP? It's obscene. Why don't you get back in the game?'

I told him I never return to an industry I'd previously worked in, and explained that L&F's sole service was to help businesses retrieve unpaid debts from the directors of closed-down companies.

Darren said: 'Nah, nah, nah. You wanna help people like me; company directors who've run into trouble. You've got experience helping out creditors. Now you should bring that experience over to the other side and help business owners with debts.'

It didn't take long to realise everything Darren had said made perfect sense. As someone who'd developed a profitable business tracking down the directors of failed companies, I knew a lot of information that would be valuable to directors who wanted to lose their companies without opening themselves up to recrimination.

After speaking with several friends and advisors who all encouraged me to go for it, I returned to Darren. 'There could be some mileage in what you're saying,' I said. To which he replied: 'Well, why don't we set up a business together?'

Darren promised to fund the project and gave me a company to use, Alexander-Poultney. I asked where the double-barrelled surname came from and he said: 'It's just a made up name to make the company sound and look typically British and blue-blooded.'

He explained that Channel U's former CEO Stewart was making 'shitloads' of money running a similar business. So I visited Stewart's website and got my designer Marc to develop a comparable but more user-friendly version.

My old business instincts kicked in and I could sense a money-making opportunity. Darren was amazed that I'd developed a business plan so quickly and was able to launch the operation on a shoestring budget. He suggested we use pay-per-click marketing as our primary tool for attracting customers. But when I asked for funds to pay for the online advertising he suddenly became guarded.

Speaking softly, he said: 'Peter, you don't actually need me for anything other than the money. How do I know you're not going to set up and then go off and do your own thing? What do I know about insolvency?'

Darren was a savvy operator. His instincts told him that he wasn't needed and would undoubtedly get manoeuvred out of the venture. He avoided giving me any money, but nonetheless agreed to a deal where the profits would be split 50-50.

I was grateful to him for inspiring me to launch the business, but saw no reason why he should get half of the profits just because he'd promised to cover the marketing expenses. I decided to look for alternative investors and came across two unlikely candidates.

The first offer came during a conversation with a good friend, Shiryn Dodhy, who I met through TMG back in 2002 when we'd worked together on a music project. I was telling Shiryn, now a blue chip marketing executive, about my situation and she stopped me midway and said: 'Peter, how much do you want? I've got £10,000 in savings, it's all I have.'

I was stunned and asked why she felt comfortable giving me such a large amount of money. 'Because you're my friend and I trust and believe that you'll make it happen,' she replied. 'Take £5,000 and if you need the rest, let me know.' Her response made me stop and check myself because I wouldn't have given her my last £10,000. I declined, but thanked Shiryn and told her that I'd come back for the money should I need it, acknowledging to myself that her gesture had cemented our friendship for life.

Former TMB employee Kris introduced me to a short, stocky, entrepreneurial Ghanaian-British guy named Teck who offered to lend me some cash, but something told me not to so I turned down the loan.

Meanwhile, I created online adverts for Alexander-Poultney and set up an alternative company, Legal & Recoveries (L&R).

Darren never gave me a penny but spent around £750 on pay-per-click marketing, which generated our first set of enquiries from business owners who'd phone the number advertised and leave a message. I'd call them back and switch the business over to L&R: 'Hi, this is Peter Murray from Alexander-Poultney. I got your message and think I can help you. But the issue you have would be better served by my other company, Legal & Recoveries...'

The calls kept coming, and after about three weeks on 29th April 2009 I made the first sale. The company was a hair salon, Close Cuts based in Notting Hill Gate, which sold extensions costing between £700 and £1,000, mainly to Russian glamour models.

I didn't have an office and had to conduct my first meetings at the salon. They paid £2,000 including value added tax (VAT) for me to show them a cost-effective way to dissolve their company, leave their debts behind and set up a new business.

A month later, a company director from Science Bloomers paid £1,265 for a similar service. Business was picking up, but my conscience was killing me about Darren whose calls I'd stopped returning.

I got my former ILA associate and wheel-clamping partner Rob Smith to create some online adverts for L&R, invested in a Google Ads pay-per-click campaign to promote the new business, and stopped accepting calls for Alexander-Poultney as I didn't want to be indebted to Darren for any more than the £1,620 I already owed him.

Things really kicked off on 9th June when Home Showroom paid £2,300 and two English guys who were the directors of Scotland-based company A&M Contractors paid £5,750.

For several weeks, I'd been speaking to them about their company, which had a tremendous amount of debt, and they decided to fly to London to see me. When the men arrived at my newly rented offices in Marylebone and realised I was black they were mortified and couldn't look me in the face. One of them later confessed that he feared he was going to be robbed, and they only relaxed after the other man caught a glimpse of my Audemars Piguet wristwatch and struck up a conversation about luxury timepieces. Despite their initial concerns and my utter bemusement, both men left feeling a lot less stressed than when they arrived.

In addition to Darren and Rob, friends such as Marcia, Karl George, Orantes Moore and commercial lawyer Bob Jackson also provided support and encouragement during the early days of L&R.

I first met Orantes back in 2004 when he and Akosua worked as journalists for *New Nation* newspaper. She spoke highly of her partner, but I was in no rush to meet him as some guys get insecure when another man is working with their missus.

I read some of his articles and quickly formed an opinion of him as simply a writer of black news and reggae articles. However, after working with him on the Channel U Awards, ACPA and L&R projects, my opinion began to change.

One of my first big L&R cases really stressed me out because an IP spread false and misleading information to some of my clients. In response, I asked Orantes to write an article outlining the facts and paid for it to be distributed via *Overground Online*, the e-newsletter and website he'd launched with Akosua two years earlier.

Within hours of the story's publication the IP threatened to sue for defamation. I asked Orantes to remove the article from the website, but he refused. 'Peter, there's nothing defamatory or inaccurate in the story. Tell them to go ahead and sue. Trust me, they'll never win that case,' he said.

I was concerned about my reputation and didn't want to become involved in any legal proceedings within the first 12 months of launching my new business. I became annoyed and wondered if he was trying to set me up or pay me back for some past indiscretion he believed I'd committed. 'Look Orantes, I'm paying you for this service. Either change the article or remove it,' I said. But he wouldn't concede.

Still, I had nothing to worry about. Three days later, the IP capitulated and withdrew his threat of legal action. That incident swept aside all previous uncertainties, and my level of respect for Orantes skyrocketed because he'd pushed me outside of my comfort zone.

His blogs for L&R's website were also impressive; something akin to the types of articles you'd expect to find in the *Financial Times*. They were so perfect that I suspected he'd copied them and requested that he start providing posts on specific topics that I knew he couldn't plagiarise. But it didn't matter. He continued to deliver stories with all the nuances, terminologies, style and flow of an expert who'd been writing about insolvency for years.

And that's when I realised that despite my initial misconceptions, Orantes is a first-class media practitioner who, like myself, has many different sides to his character.

***

By the time I launched L&R in 2009 I'd started going to church again following a brief hiatus that stems back to my divorce proceedings when the court asked me to show my earnings and explain my expenses.

Pastor Joe's church refused to provide a financial statement confirming receipt of £15,000 I'd donated because it was wrong for the Church to come between a man and his wife. 'That's not God's way,' I was told. I was upset, so Pastor Joe 'temporarily' signposted me to the Harrow International Christian Centre (HICC), which I attended for about a year but did not enjoy.

While in Hong Kong I tithed to the House of Divinity and Devotion (HDD), a Pentecostal church in North West London that my friend Diane Paris attended. When I returned to London, Diane said: 'My pastor wants to meet you. She keeps asking, "what type of man tithes to a church he's never been to?"

I visited the HDD, met her pastor Hyacinth Jones, and eventually became heavily involved in the church. Between 2009 and 2013 I helped incorporate the organisation into a registered charity, put all the policies in place and tithed £50,000.

Towards the end of 2011 after I'd been appointed as the financial controller and a trustee on the church's executive board, Pastor Hyacinth came to me in tears. She was a businesswoman with two nurseries but her partners, a Sikh husband and wife couple, were trying to force her out of the company.

She asked me for help but the couple were being represented by a West End law firm who were no pushovers. I told Pastor Hyacinth: 'This isn't for me,' and encouraged her to hire lawyers. But she continued to seek my advice and eventually I took her on board as an L&R client.

Our relationship experienced some problems when she brought a Ugandan pastor into the church and wanted to put him on a salary with expenses. I told her: 'Not while I'm here you won't,' which she didn't appreciate. I disliked the man and had a very unpleasant dream about him. I told everyone about the dream and how I felt, but nobody listened. The church was engulfed and really taken in by this man who I called a false prophet. Eventually he was exposed as a fraudster, and on the day everyone found out I walked to the front of the church and gave the congregation a piece of my mind.

I received apologies from Pastor Hyacinth and some of the others who'd ridiculed me, and my estimation in the church soared. Meanwhile, Pastor Hyacinth's business partners were threatening litigation and their law firm was refusing to deal with me because I wasn't a lawyer.

Both parties entered into mediation, and although I was way out of my depth I managed to swing things in our favour and force the couple out of the business, leaving Pastor Hyacinth and her husband as the company's sole directors and equity owners. She was ecstatic, paid me £10,000, and told anyone who'd listen that I saved her business. I was the golden boy who could do no wrong.

Things stayed like that for a while, until a 23-year-old member of the congregation who I'd secretly been dating suggested we go public with our relationship. When I refused and ended the liaison she was devastated and told Pastor Hyacinth, who asked me to leave the church.

I still love and respect pastors Hyacinth and Joe. But now take the view that church is something contrived by clergymen, who are just as fallible as anyone else.

I've seen the machinery that operates behind churches and think that although it's a nice place to worship and praise among likeminded people, I no longer want to be involved in any part of church life. For me, church is no longer a building or place; it's in my heart.

***

During the summer of 2009, I began thinking back to my time in Hong Kong when I spent a weekend in Macau (the gambling capital of the world) and thought, *'If Asia has this place, Europe has Monte Carlo and America has Las Vegas, a resort city in West Africa could do well.'*

I'd read about Sun City, a luxury resort and casino in the North West Province of South Africa that was built in the late 1970s by local entrepreneur and accountant Sol Kerzner.

I considered that a new development in the right location would generate huge wealth and employment and concluded that Ghana was the perfect setting. Within six months of launching L&R I'd generated enough funds to kick-start the project and began contacting the Ministry of Tourism in Ghana to pitch my proposal. I'd developed a skeletal plan which involved the acquisition of 1,000 acres of coastal land to construct three large resorts: one for young people aged 18 to 30, another for couples and a third for gamblers.

My aim was to engage with and create employment for local communities who would benefit from the new school, hospital and fire and police stations that would be established alongside the hotels and condominiums.

In September 2009 I flew to Ghana's capital Accra, and met with then Minster for Tourism Juliana Azumah-Mensah, along with the government ministers for transport and defence.

They were receptive to my idea and we discussed establishing the resort on the south coast of Ghana's Western Region in Shama and arranging for me to acquire a 999-year lease on the military airbase in nearby Sekondi-Takoradi, which I planned to redevelop into an international airport.

Over the next 12 months I returned to Ghana around 10 times, meeting with chiefs and the local district chief executive Emelia Arthur who explained that petrol companies such as Texaco and Royal Dutch Shell had descended upon an area close to Shama after explorers discovered a field containing three billion barrels of crude oil in 2007.

Arthur liked my proposal and suggested the area I wanted could be zoned off for 'economic development'. But only if I let her claim responsibility for the project.

I agreed because I didn't care who got the credit, as long as the scheme was officially endorsed by the government. I struck a deal with the chiefs in Shama who agreed to sell 1,000 acres of land at a rate of US$1,000-per-acre, or US$1 million in total.

My intention was to increase the land's value by selling it on at a rate of £10,000-per-acre, making an instant profit of £9.4 million. The plan was to lease four-acre parcels to investors for £40,000 over a period of 10 years In return, they'd be given a debenture guaranteeing that I'd pay eight per cent interest (£3,200) on their money annually for 10 years. Effectively, the investors would be giving me a mortgage against the land which I'd continue to own, unless I failed to pay the interest, or return their £40,000 at the end of the 10-year period.

Once I'd found investors for the land, developers would come in to build out and find a tenant (usually a hotel chain) to take on a 25-year lease. That way, everyone's happy because the developer makes money leasing the space to hotels and casinos that pay rent and attract high-spending customers.

It was a similar situation with the airport. Once I'd acquired the lease, I planned to rent the land to a developer who'd build and construct the facility, and bring in a company to run it.

The chiefs started pressuring me to do the deal, but Arthur wasn't ready and threatened to sink the project if I went ahead without her. 'Don't buy the land until I give you the green light,' she said. 'If you do, you'll just have to come back to me for planning permission and I won't give it to you.'

I refused to be side-tracked and decided to employ a new strategy that might encourage the Ghanaian government to approve my proposal more swiftly. I wondered whether they'd hurry up if they thought I was going to relocate the project.

Subsequently, in October 2009 I flew to Sierra Leone to speak with government ministers about launching the scheme in their country. At the airport, I befriended a Sierra Leonean lady named Doris Sesay who worked for the United Nations (UN). During the flight she gave me a summary of how the country worked and said I should contact her if I needed help.

After spending a day in Sierra Leone I quickly realised that finding 1,000 acres of suitable coastal land was nigh impossible, as the country is so small.

Nonetheless, I used the opportunity to network and make contacts. I returned two months later and held meetings with the country's then Development Minister for Trade and Industry, Mickail Turay, and ambassador-at-large and permanent secretary in the Ministry of Mining Resources and Political Affairs, Uman Wurie.

We spoke about commerce and development and I told them about the charity I'd just launched, the PJM Trust. They made me a Sierra Leonean citizen and gave me a passport, which made me feel like a real African.

Later that week, someone suggested I visit Kono District — the centre of Sierra Leone's diamond mining industry. The next day, I left the capital city Freetown and set off on the five-hour drive in a UN jeep supplied by Doris. I paid for and travelled with an entourage including a Special Forces policeman, a driver and Mary - an ex-diamond trader who saw me as some sort of opportunity to re-establish herself.

For four days we stayed in a village in Kono where I met local chiefs and miners and purchased uncut rough diamonds. However, I was forced to leave prematurely after discovering that two children had been killed as part of a sacrificial ritual. On the third night, I was awoken by the erratic screams of a young child followed by the ritualistic chanting of adult voices. I stayed awake and heard the same thing again about an hour later. This time, I clearly heard the screams of a young boy, aged between five and eight.

At breakfast the following morning everyone was quiet. I told them what I'd heard and that it had disturbed me. I asked if anyone knew why the children were screaming and they all dropped their heads as if ashamed. I kept asking and wouldn't let it go until eventually the policeman broke free and told me what happened. I was outraged, decided I wanted to leave, and started telling everyone to get ready because we were going back to Freetown.

He pulled me aside again and said: 'You can't just come into our village and insult our customs. That's rude, and we take exception to that. You must remember that you have to get back to the capital and you don't know anyone there.

'And the people you're travelling with, let's be honest, you don't know them. So don't insult their culture because they can abandon you at any time, and what will you do then? Whatever money you have in that pouch of yours won't be able to help you.'

I returned hastily to London, drafted a contract outlining the sale of the land from the chiefs in Ghana to myself for a sum of US$1 million, and sent it off. Around eight weeks later I flew to Ghana for a trade show hosted by a non-government organisation. Everyone who had anything to do with tourism was there and I remember people kept looking at me strangely, but I didn't stop to consider why.

The following day while travelling in Accra I bumped into a government official I'd become familiar with during my numerous trips over the past year. He looked perplexed, exchanged salutations and then sheepishly asked: 'When did you get out of jail?'

His question puzzled me. I asked: 'What are you talking about?' My driver, who'd been listening to the conversation, looked uncomfortable. I asked him and my chaperone from the Ministry of Tourism if they knew what the man was talking about. Slowly they explained that a few months earlier, Arthur had complained to Ghana's President John Atta Mills and accused me of bribing the police in Shama to terrorise local residents so they would leave the land.

Apparently, she told Mills there was no point asking the police in the region to either investigate or arrest me because I'd corrupted them all. Subsequently, the President had sent officers from the army's national security and paramilitary wing, the Border Guard Unit, to hunt for and detain me. After searching the faces of both men and discovering they were genuinely surprised to see me driving around seemingly untroubled by my status as a wanted man, I jumped on the first plane home and never returned to Ghana.

In truth, although I could see commercial opportunities in Africa I just wasn't ready to make use of them. Ghana was great, but I preferred Sierra Leone. The ritual killings were frightening, but I don't believe such issues are exclusive to rural villages in Africa.

Between 1991 and 2002 Sierra Leoneans were engaged in a bloody civil war, which left 50,000 people dead and caused neighbours to turn against each other. Now, they have to live together.

They are a very dignified people who conceal their sense of loss well. But the pain in their hearts is palpable. I nevertheless found the people warm and the government receptive to entrepreneurial investment.

I absolutely love Africa, even more than the Caribbean because it's bigger and has more to offer. So far, Ethiopia eclipses all the other black states I've visited, solely because of its rich culture.

***

After my escapades in West Africa I focused more on family, and in 2010 took the children to Hammamet in Tunisia and on a Mediterranean cruise to Italy, Greece and Israel a year later. I'm proud to say that all three of my kids can jump on and off a plane without assistance because they're so used to travelling. We had fun and it was great watching them broaden their horizons and learn about the world.

That period was about sharing with my children an experience I never had with my mother or siblings. For me, it's important that I ensure their lifestyle exceeds the one I had growing up.

I've told them to make sure the lifestyle they give their children supersedes the one I gave them because it took a long time for me to leave London, let alone England. I don't want my children to go through life with the same localised mentality I had for many years.

CHAPTER TWENTY-ONE
Goodbye Georgina, PJM50 and the Benefits of Sowing
(2012 - 2016)

Georgina never liked Chineka's best friend Carline Corbin. In my opinion, Georgina's family were like snobs of Stonebridge who'd moved to Fulham and thought Chineka was too good for people like Carline who still lived in Brent. Carline was Chineka's best friend, but was always kept on the outside.

Still, I knew how close they were so even after Chineka's passing I maintained contact. In the mid-'90s when Donna and I had the penthouse in Harrow on the Hill, we'd go out partying and leave Chineka and Carline to look after Darius. They had some great times together at my home. Carline is a friend and like a daughter to me now - she's my only connection to Chineka.

In February 2012, a few weeks after Gary Dobson and David Norris were sentenced to life in prison for the racist murder of Stephen Lawrence 19 years earlier, Carline came to see me. She said: 'I've been told that under no circumstances are you to find out... But Georgina has cancer, and they think it's serious. Please don't go to her house, and please don't tell anyone that I told you. If I hear any more information I'll keep you up to speed.'

Georgina and I hadn't had a proper conversation since before Chineka's death 11 years earlier. I desperately wanted to speak with her and considered going to her house. Months later, Carline called to confirm that Georgina had cervical cancer. I told her: 'I'm sorry, but I've got to go and see her.'

I sent Georgina a text message explaining that I was visiting Chineka's burial spot and would stop by afterwards to speak with her about putting a headstone on the grave. When I arrived at Georgina's house a few hours later a woman answered the door and said: 'No, she can't see you.' A few months later, I heard Georgina was in a hospice.

I begged Carline to help me get in touch with her: 'Please, please, please... I just need to see her. She can't go without me seeing her.' But Carline was adamant that I refrain from making contact.

***

Throughout the previous year, I'd been working with an L&R client named Katherine Kelly who owned an Aston Martin sports car and paid me to pursue a man who owed her money and also drove an Aston Martin.

Working on that case probably reignited my interest in luxury motor vehicles because it felt like they were members of a prestigious club that I didn't have access to. When I eventually caught up with Katherine's debtor I tried to convince him to give up his car as partial payment, but he refused.

I made some enquires and discovered that a four-year-old, gunmetal grey Aston Martin V8 Vantage would set me back around £80,000.

Initially, I baulked at the idea of spending such a large amount on a pre-owned vehicle. But business was booming, and when I thought about Georgina lying on her deathbed I said to myself *'life is short'*, and bought the car.

About a week later, on Sunday 12th August, I remember spending the afternoon with my new girlfriend, Denise Young. As we watched the events from the final day of the London 2012 Olympic Games I said: 'I never acknowledge the date of Chineka's passing, but today would've been my daughter's 32nd birthday.'

Less than an hour later, I received a text message from Carline saying: 'Georgina's passed away.' I was furious. Of all the days she could possibly draw her last breath, why did it have to be on 12th August? Now I can never celebrate Chineka's birthday properly because whenever I try I'm forced to remember the anniversary of Georgina's death. It feels like she's robbed me. My firstborn's birthday used to fill me with joy, but now thinking about 12th August fills me with dread and sorrow.

I remember that night in the early '90s when Georgina and I were in my mews house in Hampstead and she was drunk, crying and accusing me of destroying her life. How did I do that? We were kids, we had sex and we had Chineka. What did I know at 13 years old?

I do feel really bad knowing the lives of her and my daughter were cut short, while I'm still here living the life of Riley. Although I never loved Georgina, I know I'm not to blame for the way her life turned out.

It sounds perverse, but sometimes I feel like I don't deserve to be here and think to myself, *'You're supposed to be the head of the family. If you were a man, you'd be with Georgina and Chineka.'* I wouldn't join them voluntarily, but there is a feeling pulling me towards my daughter and her mother.

Yes I have another family, but my first family missed out on an incredible amount, and that's what really haunts me and tears me up. I don't feel it's right that mother and daughter are gone. It's like the story is incomplete and the book only closes after I join them. I guess Jada, Dillon and Darius are the justification for me not joining them. But the relationship I have with my kids is something completely different because they're alive and still have their mum.

I've never previously verbalised or shared this pain or part of my life, and if you were to tell me: 'You've only got seven days to live'. I'd reply: 'Bring it on,' because I'm looking forward to reuniting with Chineka, Georgina and my mum.

Similarly, I feel terrible about the lack of attention I've given to Aaron over the past 30 years. At the time of writing, my brother is 53 years old and has been diagnosed with mental illness since the age of 17. It hasn't been easy. Those years were turbulent, and for most of them I rejected him. I don't think I can forgive myself for that because it was selfish, foolish and narrow-minded, and I kept it up for so long.

He's made it through the worst now, but there are moments when he slips back and starts calling people's names from 30 years ago as if we were still in that time zone. Whenever we talk it's always about that era, even though many generations have come and gone since then. It's a real shame to see my brother like that.

We spent quality time together recently (during the time I was writing this book), which was nice. He reminded me of a soldier who'd fallen on the battlefield. My problem with that is, I feel like I left him wounded in action while I went down the pub for a drink and never returned.

Despite his mental illness, Aaron's actually doing really well and probably lives a better life than a lot of the man dem. He's independent, well looked after, doesn't struggle for money, has clothes on his back and does whatever he likes to keep himself occupied.

I can sometimes be intolerant, indifferent and cut our conversations short, but Aaron is still my hero because he's still here, standing strong after everything he's been through, including suffering from the thing I fear most.

***

Since L&R's formation in 2009, the company has developed into a boutique, business rescue enterprise representing more than 750 local and international (mostly Russian and Southeast Asian) creditors, debtors, individuals and organisations.

Of all the businesses I've launched, L&R is the longest-running and by far the most successful. On average, each customer spends £2,500 and around 10% pay 10 times that amount (£25,000). In the five years leading up to 2017, the income generated by L&R afforded me the opportunity to travel extensively with family and friends, and spend around £1 million on cars.

I've always been passionate about driving, but my penchant for luxury motor vehicles began after I purchased the Aston Martin. Three months later, I found a car dealer in Cardiff, Wales, who was willing to accept £80,000 and my Audi Q7 S-line in exchange for a brand new Range Rover Sport with an exclusive Revere body kit.

Later that year, I purchased a brand new BMW 120i for £28,000, holidayed with Denise in Belgium, Austria and Hungary and took a Caribbean cruise to the islands of Barbados, St Lucia, St Kitts, St Thomas and Puerto Rico.

In 2013, I bought a car for Marcia who I directed to a car dealership website where she chose the specifications, colours and extras she wanted. Her Audi A3 was delivered the following summer at a cost of £30,000.

2015 proved to be another good year. In February, I upgraded my Aston Martin for a £110,000, white V8 Vantage Sport and eight weeks later spent £50,000 on a brand new, white Mercedes-AMG A45. In October, following a trip to the Frankfurt Motor Show in Germany, I forked out £150,000 for a Lamborghini Gallardo Spyder, and later that month traded up my Range Rover for a brand new model.

This time, I asked the supplier to rip out the seats and ship the £75,000 vehicle from the factory straight to Hertfordshire-based Revere specialists R-Tec Auto Design who, for an additional £35,000, refashioned the interior and installed a cocaine white body kit.

The car was delivered in December, around the same time I bought something for my ex-wife who was always talking about upgrading her vehicle. 'Are you joking?' she said. 'Are you going to take it back from me at any time in the future?'

I told her: 'No, it's yours.' And later that month she took possession of a £45,000 convertible BMW 4 Series. Neither Donna nor Marcia pays road tax, insurance or maintenance. All they have to do is put petrol in and drive.

Understandably, Donna was cautious. She asked: 'Why are you doing this?' And I told her: 'Once upon a time you were my wife, and you will always be the mother of our children. I can't look at them and not think of or include you because we created them together.

'I didn't do that on my own, so I've got to recognise your contribution. I failed miserably in regards to our marriage, your future and our family. So I'll do whatever I can to appease and help you. I don't want to succeed alone. I want you to be happy, even if that's in another relationship.

'This is atonement because I shattered your dreams. We were supposed to be together for life. I made vows to you and contravened them. I fell short and as a result there's a broken family here, which I take responsibility for.'

Probably the most startling contradiction in my life is that although I've enjoyed chasing women, the breakdown of my marriage is one of my biggest regrets. I don't think Donna really knows how much I love her or how truly sorry I am for falling out with her mother.

But the sad truth is, I didn't marry for love. I married because I thought it was the right thing to do. But I never attempted to amend my polygamous lifestyle so it was never going to last. For this reason, Donna has a permanent place in my life and any new woman must acknowledge they will never come before her.

In 2016 I made this clear to my partner at the time, a lady from Cricklewood who was 14 years my junior, when I hosted a series of local and international events to celebrate my 50th birthday under the theme 'PJM50'.

The festivities kicked off in January with a dinner party attended by 40 family members at a Greek restaurant near my home in Hatch End and the following month, I took Donna and the kids on holiday to Morocco.

I remember at the time my partner asking why she hadn't been invited on the trip, and I said: 'This is how it is. It's a family holiday, and that's my family.'

In March, I brought in Akosua to coordinate the remaining events and held a reception, dinner and entertainment party for 300 guests at the Royal Garden Kensington Hotel. A month later, we put on a reception, dinner and evening of gospel worship for 150 guests at the Hilton London Kensington Hotel.

In May, I paid 50% of the costs for 10 couples to travel to Grenada for a seafood and Champagne holiday, which was followed by a week-long cruise of the Greek islands with Darius and his partner, my three nephews, their partners and my Cape Verdean love interest at the time.

Again, I paid 50% of the costs for what turned out to be a beautiful experience, island-hopping in the Mediterranean sunshine on a 52-foot-long, £1 million yacht.

By the time I hosted the seventh and final event, a seafood BBQ for 100 young people at my home, I'd spent £100,000 celebrating my 50th birthday.

And would you believe that when I started PJM50 in January 2016, I had no budget or cash set aside for the project? Perhaps not, but it's absolutely true. The vast majority of that money (£80,000) was generated in the same year.

I used exactly the same method to acquire my most prized material possession, a £250,000 Lamborghini Huracán Spyder, which I took home 12 days after my 51st birthday in April 2017.

When I ordered the car six months earlier I didn't have a clue how I was going to pay for it. I had £100,000 from the sale of the Gallardo and £60,000 from the tail end of 2016. But the remaining £90,000 came from L&R's profits between January and March 2017.

If I'm honest, I didn't even notice when I reached my target because as soon as the money came in I threw it straight to Britain's leading luxury car dealership, HR Owen. I didn't want to feel, hold or take possession of that money. I was simply the conduit through which it passed.

I get a tremendous buzz from my L&R work, especially when I look around and see the evidence of my success and consider what I've achieved despite not having any formal education. Sometimes, when I'm battling trained solicitors with first degrees who work for big law firms I remember where I'm coming from and pinch myself. It's a great thing to know that you're succeeding, and it's even more beautiful when you succeed for a client. That's the greatest feeling ever.

I think one of the main reasons I find myself in such a stable position at this stage in my life is because I've never been unemployed or registered for any state benefits, and for more than 40 years I've consistently focused on working hard.

L&R is the culmination of all my illegitimate and legal graft, and the knowledge I've gained from those experiences has equipped me to deal with the law firms I'm in contention with daily because you have to be savvy and know when to negotiate, when to hold back and when to fire shots. And perhaps more importantly, you need to know when to extend a helping hand to someone who is in distress but can't afford your services.

Giving back can be very rewarding, and is something I try to do because throughout my career doors have been opened and people have given me opportunities - even after I'd messed up.

I remember those things and try to give similar breaks to the generation coming behind me. I like the idea of transferring the baton, which is what I tried to do in my commercial life with several people, in particular Akosua Annobil, Las Oke, Dwayne Byfield and Riki Bleau who went on to launch the avant garde music management and publishing company, which found international chart success with producer Naughty Boy and singers Sam Smith and Emeli Sandé.

It's funny though because sometimes I find myself blessing strangers more than my own family, which can be uncomfortable. When I used to attend church, mainly between 2000 and 2013, I'd always listen keenly to the pastor's sermon then seek out people who were struggling and bless them with £20, £50 or sometimes £100 because I remember what it's like growing up in a poor family.

Accordingly, since launching in 2009 the PJM Trust has engaged in a series of charitable projects in Ghana and Sierra Leone. These include the sponsorship of two church schools and an orphanage, the financing of a child protection initiative and separate campaigns in rural areas to support rice farmers and establish a running water pipe.

One day, I hope to return to Africa to do some political and philanthropic work. But in 2010, I remodelled the Trust to focus on individuals, charities and voluntary organisations that support vulnerable people in the UK.

Between 2012 and 2017, the PJM Trust distributed £50,000 to various groups in northwest London, including £40,000 to the Brent Family Support Project, which provides services such as counselling, hospital and prison visits, and basic maths and English courses.

An additional £8,000 was disbursed to the Reform Foundation, an organisation run by David Frederick, a guy I grew up with from the ends who was in and out of jail and dependent on class A drugs. Eventually, he turned his life around and set up a community interest company to help vulnerable prisoners who are about to leave jail. I no longer tithe into or attend a particular church, and consider PJM Trust to be my church because that's how I give back.

When it comes to making money, on several occasions I've been described as a hunter rather than a gatherer. And while that may be true, it's probably more accurate to say that I have faith in my ability to hunt and catch prey everyday.

People who are less confident about their future prospects will gather and store up for a rainy day, but I'm not like that. I take more risks than the average person and live in the moment. I'm not necessarily smarter than the next man, I just try to work harder and be better prepared.

This book is about sharing all the blessings, knowledge and teachings I've acquired because it's important for people to understand that it's not about where you come from, it's about where you want to be. Achieving your objective isn't going to be easy. But whatever your goal is, take it seriously, like nothing else matters. You have to eat, sleep, breathe, visualise, talk, walk, and live it. The more you can do that, the more you'll understand and become it, because you are it.

Learn and understand everything about the numbers, averages and percentages of your project. When you do this in a consistent, dedicated, intensive and focused manner, you start making your own L.U.C.K (labouring under consistent knowledge).

And most importantly, don't give up. The thing few people understand about success is that it doesn't come at the beginning. The whole idea is that you have to make it past the halfway line. Most people give up before they get to that point, and that's why they never reach anywhere. It's impossible for you to reach halfway without getting hit by perceived obstacles and disasters.

To help gauge how far you've reached, try to remember that unless you've gone through some pain, setbacks, tears and changes you're nowhere near the halfway line. If you really you want to survive and succeed, you must work hard over a long period of time.

One of my favourite Bible verses, *Genesis* 3:19, explains this perfectly, *'By the sweat of your brow will you have food to eat until you return to the ground from which you were made.'*

Sow in the first half, and when you're sowing that's all you do. And keep sowing until it's time to reap your harvest, which may take a day, one month or 10 years.

You reap what you sow, which is why you must be mindful of the seeds you plant. And that includes your thoughts, because the ideas you entertain will find their physical manifestations.

There is of course a link between the amount of sowing you do and the length of time it takes for your harvest to come. That's just science, natural, divine, karmic, spiritual and universal law.

If you look hard enough, you'll see examples of this everywhere, at work, in your relationships or just in your own thinking.

There's a direct relationship between what you sow and what you reap, just as sure as night follows day. Which means if you really want to reap, you'd better start sowing today.

EPILOGUE

Before concluding, I'd like to expand on the subject of self-improvement which I briefly touched on in the last chapter. Although *'you reap what you sow'* is a saying I've heard all my life and firmly believe in, I only began to understand what it meant after reading personal and mental development books by authors such as W. Clement Stone, Napoleon Hill, Tom Hopkins and Anthony Robbins. While these books weren't academic tomes, they proved to be more valuable than my formal education. I learned a lot from them during my early 20s; most importantly that you cannot get anything in life without first putting in the graft — you've got to pay your dues.

Additionally, I found I could relate to the topics these authors covered because they were the same things my mother talked about and that I'd read in the Bible, just fashioned in a different way.

On the road to success you have the journey and the destination. I've really enjoyed the journey and my biggest aid during the early days was Napoleon Hill's *Think and Grow Rich.*

Keith O'Rourke, one of my employers at the financial services company Kors Associates, gave me that book in 1986. But it took a second reading three years later for me to really understand it properly.

At the time, I'd just been sacked from the Moore Group and was in the process of setting up Champion Results with my cousin. After he abandoned me, I sought a support structure and dipped into the book for guidance. That's when it became my bible. *Think and Grow Rich* was hugely instrumental in my development and overall success.

I became so imbibed by its ethos that when I started making huge amounts of money through Champion Results and property deals I didn't even realise, because I was too involved in what I was doing to stop, look up and take a breath.

I worked with everything I learned from that book because it made sense to me, and over the years I've discovered that if these lessons and instructions are understood, followed and applied correctly, they will not fail you.

PJ Murray

ACKNOWLEDGEMENTS

In closing, I'd like to acknowledge and thank my friends Raymond Fearon, Simon Leslie, Karl George, Marcia Abbott, Carline Corbin, Deborah David and Shiryn Dodhy. No words can describe how much I appreciate the love and support you've given me over the years.

Similarly, I'd like to pay tribute to Akosua Annobil who reintroduced me to black media, an industry I love but eschewed for 10 years following the sale of *Pride* in 1993. Meeting Akosua a decade later inspired me to remodel Trinity Music Group (TMG) into a business specialising in media services.

The truth is, my alliance with Akosua and her previous company Fire Media made it possible for TMG to exist and become influential in a very competitive marketplace. I'm certain our relationship was as beneficial back then as it is today. Akosua is a true friend of the highest calibre.

Likewise, even though we no longer speak I still have maximum love and respect for my brothers Dennis White, Delroy MacIntosh, Winston Brown and Alan Goldberg.

Additionally, I'd like to say sorry to Angela Banks for how I treated her in Hong Kong, and Georgina's mother who banned me from attending her daughter's funeral and probably blames me for how Georgina's life turned out.

The girl I robbed in 1983, Jackie Green, also deserves a sincere apology. I spent many years angry at her for sending me to jail. But in retrospect she was a blessing in disguise who helped launch my career, and for that I will forever be grateful.

When I think of Jackie, I'm reminded of the Biblical story of Joseph and his coat of many colours. Even though his brothers sold him into bondage, Joseph forgave them and, according to *Genesis 50:20*, the next time they met he said: *'You intended to harm me, but God intended it for good, to accomplish what is now being done; the saving of many lives.'*

If Jackie hadn't sent me to jail, there's no doubt that I would've developed into a hardened criminal. I sincerely believe she was sent to take me off the road for my own good, so that my energies could be redirected. During the jail sentence I received for committing that robbery I learned discipline and perseverance; became a fanatical reader and matured into an adult. When I look back, I have to thank Jackie for helping to change my life.

GLOSSARY

A
AFFI = have to
AV = have

B
BAD BWOY = bad boy
BAL'ED = bald head
BANGED UP = imprisoned
BEASTS = police
BEEF = conflict
BIRD = prison time
BREDDA = brother (not necessarily a blood relative)
BREDRIN = brethren, close friend
BRUK = to brake or injure
BUN = to burn
BUN AND CHEESE = a stolen chequebook and bank-issued cheque guarantee card
BULL = police
BUS' = to burst or bust

C
CLART = arse or ass
CROCS = crocodile skin shoes
CUSSING = to curse or use foul language
CYANN = can't

D
DAT = that
DI = the
DONG = down
DROPPING STICKS = pickpocketing
DUBPLATE = a promotional copy of a vinyl record, usually featuring an exclusive version of a new or unreleased reggae song
DUS = to sprint at top speed, usually away from a crime scene

E
ENDS = area

F
FEDS = police
FLAT OUT = destitute
FLEX = to socialise with
FLOSSING = showing off
FIRM = gang, clique or crew
FRAM = from
FRET = worry
FRONT LINE = an area on All Saints Road in Ladbroke Grove, west London, which from the 1960s to the late 1990s doubled as a trendy celebrity hangout and nucleus of socialisation, entertainment, gambling, illegal drugs and prostitution for the local West Indian community.

G
GANJA = marijuana
GARMS = clothes
GETI = get it
GOVERNOR = the operational manager at a prison
GRASS = to speak to or cooperate with a police officer, prison guard or an agent of the Crown Prosecution Service
'GREE = agree
GYAL = girl
GYALIST = a man who is popular with women

H
HARD STOP = a controversial driving manoeuvre armed police officers use to intercept a suspect's vehicle without any prior notice or warning.
HEAD = oral sex

I
INNIT= isn't that right, don't you agree?

M
MAN DEM = guys

N
NAH = no
NEVER-NEVER = a hire purchase arrangement that allows consumers to acquire products simply by paying an initial instalment and agreeing to clear the remaining debt over a number of months with smaller,

regular payments.
NICKED = to be arrested and or convicted
NUTT'N = nothing

# O
OBEAH = witchcraft or voodoo practised by people from the Caribbean and Africa
OLD-SKOOL OG = old-school original gangster, a well-respected man with a significant criminal past

# P
PAR = to spar or socialise with
PARDNER = a popular and longstanding saving method originally utilised by poor Jamaicans who pool their finances by contributing a fixed amount of money (a hand) over a specified period. At a pre-agreed time, each participant withdraws their accumulated sum (a draw) from the pool.
PON = upon
PRE = a 7-inch vinyl record sold mostly to sound systems, DJs and radio broadcasters before (pre) general release to the public.

# R
ROADMAN = street hustler, petty thief, low-level criminal, rude boy, wide boy, bad bwoy
ROLLER = Rolls-Royce motorcar
RUM AND BLACK = rum and blackcurrant juice

# S
SCREWS = prison guards
SEH = say
SHOT = to sell
SHUBEEN = after-hours black music venues that were popular in the 1960s, 1970s and 1980s, but so small that patrons literally had to be 'shoved-in' to gain entry.
SKANK = to con, trick or swindle
SPUNK = to waste
STEP = to move or leave, usually by invitation
STICKSMAN = a pickpocket
STRAP = firearm
STRETCH = custodial sentence

T
TIEF = a thief, or to thieve
TING = thing

U
UNDA DI EART' = the London Underground metro system
UNU = you (when talking to two or more people)

W
WEH = where

Y
YARD = home
YUTE = youth
YUH = you or your